THE MANAGEMENT OF SMALL TOURISM AND HOSPITALITY FIRMS

Edited by Rhodri Thomas

CASSELL

London and New York

Cassell
Wellington House
125 Strand
London WC2R 0BB

370 Lexington Avenue
New York
NY 10017-6550

www.cassell.co.uk

First published 1998

British Library Cataloguing-in-Publication Data
A catalogue record for this book is available from the British Library.

ISBN 0 304 70196 3 (HB)
    0 304 70197 1 (PB)

Typeset by York House Typographic Ltd, London
Printed and bound in Great Britain by Redwood Books, Trowbridge, Wiltshire

THE MANAGEMENT OF SMALL TOURISM AND HOSPITALITY FIRMS

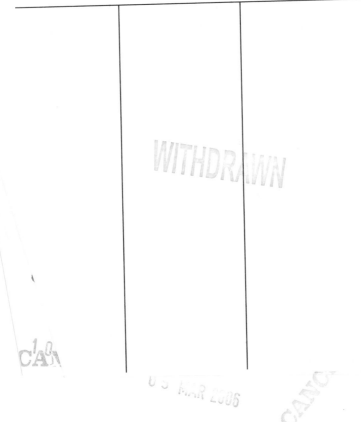

CONTENTS

CONTRIBUTORS

Graham Beaver is Professor of Business Development, Small and Medium Enterprise Unit, Nottingham Business School, Nottingham Trent University.

Andrew Boer is Senior Lecturer in Small Business Management, School of Service Industries, Bournemouth University.

Ivor Church is Senior Lecturer in Quality Management, Centre for the Study of Small Tourism and Hospitality Firms, School of Tourism and Hospitality Management, Leeds Metropolitan University.

Peter Dewhurst is Senior Lecturer in Tourism Management, Centre for the Study of Small Tourism and Hospitality Firms, School of Tourism and Hospitality Management, Leeds Metropolitan University.

Martin Friel is Lecturer in International Tourism, School of Business, University of Buckingham. He was, until recently, at the Centre for the Study of Small Tourism and Hospitality Firms, Leeds Metropolitan University.

Helen Horobin is Senior Lecturer in Tourism and Marketing, Centre for the Study of Small Tourism and Hospitality Firms, School of Tourism and Hospitality Management, Leeds Metropolitan University.

Helene Howie is Lecturer in Accounting and Finance, School of Management and Consumer Studies, University of Dundee.

Stephanie Jameson is Senior Lecturer in Human Resource Management, Centre for the Study of Small Tourism and Hospitality Firms, School of Tourism and Hospitality Management, Leeds Metropolitan University.

Conrad Lashley is Professor of Hospitality Retailing, School of Tourism and Hospitality Management and a member of the Centre for the Study of Small Tourism and Hospitality Firms, Leeds Metropolitan University.

Guy Lincoln is Senior Lecturer in Hospitality Operations Management, Centre for the Study of Small Tourism and Hospitality Firms, School of Tourism and Hospitality Management, Leeds Metropolitan University.

John Margerison is Senior Lecturer in Financial Management, Centre for the Study of Small Tourism and Hospitality Firms, School of Tourism and Hospitality Management, Leeds Metropolitan University.

Alistair Mutch is Senior Lecturer in Information Systems, Department of Finance and Business Information Systems, Nottingham Trent University.

Jim Simpson is Lecturer in Accounting and Finance, School of Management and Consumer Studies, University of Dundee.

Jim Stewart is Reader in Human Resource Development, Nottingham Business School, Nottingham Trent University.

Stephen Taylor is Lecturer in Hotel and Hospitality Management, The Scottish Hotel School, University of Strathclyde.

Rhodri Thomas is Research Manager, Centre for the Study of Small Tourism and Hospitality Firms, School of Tourism and Hospitality Management, Leeds Metropolitan University.

Michele Webster is Visiting Research Fellow, Centre for the Study of Small Tourism and Hospitality Firms, School of Tourism and Hospitality Management, Leeds Metropolitan University.

PREFACE

This book is the product of numerous conversations with colleagues up and down the country who bemoan the fact that, until now, there has been no single point of reference for those interested in issues associated with the management of small tourism and hospitality firms. There are two major factors which have fuelled a sense of frustration. The first is that although there is an established body of high-quality small business literature, much of this is general or focuses upon sectors other than those examined in this book. This is an important omission because there is, by now, widespread recognition that sectoral peculiarities play an important part in explaining the behaviour and development of small businesses. Crudely, few would expect that, say, discussion relating to quality management in high-technology manufacturing firms would be replicated exactly for small travel agents or hotels. There will be common facets, but there is now sufficient empirical evidence to expect significant differences.

The second motivation for producing the book is to challenge the notion that small tourism and hospitality firms are merely miniaturized versions of larger enterprises; a perception which is often implicit in sector specific management texts. This observation is not new, but its implications are important, because it means that the literature which deals with, for example, marketing strategies – even when industry-specific – may be largely irrelevant to small operators. Thus, although the development of such strategies may be an important determinant of business performance, an alternative conceptualization is required when applied to small firms.

The above, coupled with the common observation that the tourism and hospitality industries are characterized by small firms, suggests that a book such as this is long overdue. Moreover, the growing interest in small business research and the increasing popularity of small business modules on undergraduate and postgraduate programmes have added impetus to the project.

The aims of the book are to examine key issues affecting the development of small tourism and hospitality firms and to assess the utility of various managerial techniques for small firms in these sectors. The book is organized to reflect these aims. Thus, the first chapter of Part I reviews the debates about entrepreneurship and the characteristics of small business owners. This is followed by an examination of business failure, an important though often neglected topic of inquiry. The remaining two chapters in

Part I consider, in turn, the current system of financing small businesses (from banks to venture capitalists) and the role of the state in promoting small business development.

The second part of the book explores topics relating more directly to the management of small tourism and hospitality firms. The chapters deal with business planning, marketing, quality management, management development, employment relations, information technology and strategies for growth. Each of these attempts to summarize current debates and to evaluate them in the light of available empirical evidence.

The book is written for a wide readership: researchers, students on final year undergraduate or postgraduate tourism and hospitality management programmes, small business advisers and policy-makers in agencies charged with creating the conditions conducive to the development of small tourism and hospitality firms. Critics will no doubt point to the book's shortcomings. While I have no desire to make their task easier, it is appropriate to note that its limitations are recognized; of necessity, many chapters draw on a body of research which is not always as highly developed as would be desirable. The book should not, therefore, be seen as the final word. Although many observations can be made with a degree of assurance, in other areas the conclusions are inevitably tentative. If the book is judged to have merit, it will perhaps – above all – be for its consolidation of existing knowledge, which should act as a solid foundation for future study.

Finally, I should like to express my gratitude to the contributors, all of whom were enthusiastic and responded positively to editorial suggestions. Unfortunately, the project took longer to come to fruition than planned, and I am particularly grateful to those who were patient as they kept to deadlines which others did not meet. I should also like to thank colleagues at Leeds: Vicky Harris and David Parsons for their professional support and Lynn McVeagh, Jacquie White, Carol Benedict and Berni Little for providing an administrative service of such high quality.

Rhodri Thomas
Centre for the Study of Small Tourism and Hospitality Firms
Leeds Metropolitan University

ONE

An introduction to the study of small tourism and hospitality firms

Rhodri Thomas

INTRODUCTION

The purpose of this chapter is to explore issues which are relevant to the more detailed study of small business management in the tourism and hospitality industries discussed later in the book. It begins by considering how small firms might be defined and why such enterprises might be worthy of study separately from large firms. There then follows an examination of the appropriateness of treating small *tourism and hospitality* firms as a distinct analytical category. Even if the outcome of that discussion is somewhat predictable (had it been considered inappropriate, this book would not have been produced!), it is not undertaken perfunctorily. As is argued in more detail below, if greater understanding of small businesses is to be achieved, it is important for researchers to recognize the importance of sectoral specificities. The chapter then briefly surveys statistics relating to the incidence of small businesses in the tourism and hospitality industries. In doing so, the intention is to alert readers to the limitations of widely cited statistics rather than to offer a definitive profile of small firms in these industries. Finally, by reviewing the various chapters contained in this volume, a summary of the current state of knowledge relating to the management of small tourism and hospitality firms is provided.

DEFINING SMALL FIRMS

Discussions about how to define small firms often begin with reference to the Committee of Inquiry Report on Small Firms (Bolton Report), which was published in 1971. This is not surprising because not only was it critical in establishing the importance of smaller enterprises in the minds of officials and academics, but its deliberations on this question remain pertinent to some extent in the 1990s.

The Bolton Committee adopted several definitions of a small firm. It argued that a small business was one which had a relatively small market share (it could not, therefore, influence market prices – it was a 'price taker' – or to any significant extent affect the level of supply), was managed in a personalized way by its owners and was independent from external control. To this the Committee added a series of statistical definitions for use in different sectors. For some, such as manufacturing, a threshold number of employees (200) was used, whereas for retailing a turnover figure was adopted (Stanworth and Gray, 1991). In the case of the hospitality industry, the definition focused on the independence of the operation (Pickering *et al.*, 1971). The rationale for the multiplicity of definitions was that they might be used for different purposes – for example, a statistical definition would enable international comparisons to be made – and it was recognised that 'smallness' varied between sectors.

During the period since the publication of the Bolton Report, several commentators have noted its shortcomings. Stanworth and Gray (1991), for example, point out that statistical analysis is hampered by the use of varying definitions. Further, any definition which uses a financial indicator inevitably requires periodic adjustment in order to take account of inflation (Burns, 1996). To these, Storey (1994) adds two further problems of accepting the Bolton approach to defining small businesses. First, he notes the incompatibility of a definition which emphasizes the personalized nature of management while *simultaneously* using statistical bands relating to numbers of employees. He argues that there is sufficient research showing that firms employing up to 200 people would inevitably require that business decisions be taken by individuals who were not owners. Second, in challenging the influence which the notion of perfect competition (where small firms are price takers) had on the deliberations of the Bolton Committee, he argues that many small firms operate in niche markets where premium prices can be charged. At an anecdotal level, it would not be difficult to identify small tourism or hospitality businesses which would support his case.

Despite the passing of more than 25 years since the publication of the Bolton Report, there is not, to borrow Storey's (1994, p. 8) words, 'a single, uniformly acceptable, definition of a small firm'. This is illustrated clearly by reference to the 16 studies undertaken during the late 1980s and early 1990s which together formed the UK's largest ever small business research project (funded by the Economic and Social Research Council). The definitions used for those projects included: fewer than ten employees, fewer than 100 employees, fewer than 200 employees, 1 to 500 employees, a grounded definition, users of informal venture capital (Storey, 1994, pp. xvi–xvii). What emerges from a full review of the small business literature is a panoply of definitions which are justified by their users on the basis of their value to particular projects.

Studies of small businesses in the tourism and hospitality industries reflect a similar liberal usage of the term 'small firms' to that found in the general small business literature. Table 1.1 illustrates this by highlighting the range of definitions used by contributors to a special issue of the *International Journal of Contemporary Management* which was dedicated to small business management. At this stage, then, there is no greater congruence among the definitions used for sector specific studies than elsewhere.

In order to meet the perceived imperative of facilitating comparison between sectors and member states, the European Commission recently adopted a common definition of small and medium-sized enterprises (SMEs) which emphasizes numbers of employees as follows: 'micro' or 'very small enterprises' employ fewer than ten people; 'small enterprises' employ between 10 and 49 people, 'medium-sized enterprises' employ more than 50 but fewer than 250 (Thomas, 1996, p. 131). Since it is more discriminating than their previous definition (which had an upper limit of fewer than 500 employees)

Table 1.1 A selection of definitions used in the study of small tourism and hospitality businesses

Author	*Definition*
Hales *et al.*	Fewer than 50 employees
Radiven and Lucas	Fewer than 25 employees
Horobin and Long	Focus on micro enterprises (fewer than 10 employees)
Ozer	Bed and breakfast accommodation units
Ball	Independent single unit businesses
Ingram	Independent. Distinction between guesthouses and bed and breakfasts made on the basis of number of rooms

Source: Definitions taken from articles in an issue of the *International Journal of Contemporary Hospitality Management* (Vol. 8, No. 5, 1996) which was dedicated to small firms.

and will be used for all EU programmes (in the past, definitions of SMEs varied according to programmes), this definition will undoubtedly gain currency. It is now used, for example, by the Department of Trade and Industry (DTI) for its statistical bulletin on SMEs in the UK economy (see DTI, 1997).

Some commentators have been critical of statistical definitions of small enterprises. For example, Burrows and Curran (1989) suggest that the implication of adopting what are ultimately arbitrary (employment) size bands is that too much homogeneity is ascribed to the 'small business sector'. Although their arguments are explored in a little more detail below, the essence of their case is that cross-sectoral comparisons may not be realistic. For research to be meaningful, they promote the use of more *grounded* definitions of size, whereby sector-specific definitions are induced as a result of qualitative research in each industry. It is interesting that the research with which one of those authors was involved on small firms in the service sector – which included free houses, wine bars and restaurants – resulted in much smaller employment size categories (and emphasized independence) compared with the European Commission's definition cited above (Curran *et al.*, 1993). Peacock (1993) has also attempted to construct a grounded definition of small hotels and restaurants. Although geographically limited to London, his work is useful for both its findings and in its description of the problems encountered in undertaking such a task. It is perhaps disappointing that few, if any, commentators have developed his work or utilized his findings.[1]

In the light of the discussion above, contributors to this book have been flexible in their interpretation of the term 'small firm' so as not to exclude discussion of important pieces of research. Further, the chapters which follow are predicated on two important premises. The first is that there are robust reasons for treating small businesses as a separate analytical category from large businesses. Second, it is appropriate to examine small *tourism and hospitality* firms as a distinct category from small businesses in general. It is to these issues that attention is now turned.

THE CASE FOR A SEPARATE STUDY OF SMALL TOURISM AND HOSPITALITY FIRMS

Storey (1994), in his highly regarded review of small business research, suggests that there are key differences between small and large firms. He argues, for example, that the notion of uncertainty differs between the two categories. His proposition is that smaller firms are likely to face greater uncertainty in terms of the market but will display more internal consistency in terms of their actions and motivations. Since small business owners determine their own objectives – which are often to seek a certain level of income or lifestyle – the emphasis on control, which is central to large organizations, is absent. This results in greater internal uncertainty within larger enterprises.

Storey (1994) also argues that small and large firms differ in their approach to innovation. Although small firms are unlikely to invest in research, it is suggested that they are more likely to respond to niche markets. Peacock (1993) provides an interesting polemic on the innovatory capacity of small hospitality firms, which supports Storey's position.

The third difference highlighted by Storey (1994) is the increased likelihood of change in small businesses. Here he is referring to the significant alterations to management organization and structure if small firms grow (though it should be noted that the majority do not).

Others have also drawn attention to significant differences between small and large enterprises. For example, Burns (1996) points out that the financial constraints imposed upon small businesses implies that their strategic options are circumscribed by the availability of capital. Further, Dewhurst and Burns (1993) note that small firms will operate in a distinct manner as a result of their not having specialist managers for the various functional activities of the firm. On the basis of the above, then, it is appropriate to examine the management of small firms in a manner which recognizes their distinctiveness.

Although the case for an analysis of small firms has been made, the justification for studying small *tourism and hospitality* firms remains to be explored. In a seminal review of conceptual issues associated with small business research in the service sector, Burrows and Curran (1989) argue that there are serious methodological dangers of ignoring sectoral contexts: 'Obviously size (however operationalised) *does* influence the internal and external relations of an economic unit, but other factors such as economic sector ... are likely to be just as crucial in determining whatever it is that is being investigated' (Burrows and Curran, 1989, p. 530).

In another paper, they advocate sectoral specificity by demonstrating that within size bands, the differences between sectors are likely to be important influences on the phenomenon being studied. To paraphrase, it is unlikely that a corner shop which employs one full-time and some part-time employees will share the same outlook, encounter similar difficulties and engage with the economy in the same manner as an owner-manager of a high tech electronics firm employing ten well-qualified people or a farmer with two employees supplemented by occasional casual labour (Curran and Burrows, 1989, p. 6).

The above, coupled with the now well-rehearsed arguments that services management and service industries are better understood if their distinctiveness from manufacturing is recognized (see, for example, Voss *et al.*, 1988) further strengthens the case for an assessment of small tourism and hospitality firms which is separate from the study of small firms in general. While it might be argued that focusing on services would be insightful, the position adopted here is that the danger of ignoring differences between, say, a small firm of solicitors and a small hotel may lead to a misunderstanding of the dynamics of such enterprises. There are, after all, established accounts of the factors which influence the demand for and supply of tourism and hospitality products (see, for example, Cooper *et al.*, 1993) which are not transferable to all other services. This is not to suggest, of course, that the non-sector specific literature makes no contribution to understanding these industries, merely that they need to be considered with caution. Moreover, neither is it being suggested that small tourism and hospitality firms are homogeneous (see Chapter 2). However, there are sufficient grounds for examining such organizations as a separate analytical category from both small firms in general and other, larger, tourism and hospitality firms.

ESTIMATING THE NUMBER OF SMALL TOURISM AND HOSPITALITY FIRMS IN THE UK

Perhaps not surprisingly, the difficulties encountered when attempting to define small firms are mirrored when seeking to estimate their number. It is curious that despite the importance attached to the promotion of small businesses by successive governments (Chapter 5), until recently little effort had been made by officials to gauge accurately their incidence in the economy. As will be discussed below, the situation has been slightly ameliorated as a result of developments in the DTI. Prior to consideration of these, it is instructive to compare two prominent sector-specific publications – one from the Department of National Heritage (DNH, 1996), the other published by the Hospitality Training Foundation (HtF, 1996) – which may appear confusing, or even contradictory, to casual observers.

In commenting on the fragmentation of the tourism industry, the DNH (1996, p. 16) notes that 'it is largely made up of small firms. [For example] 81% of hotels and 94% of restaurants and bars have fewer than 25 employees.' The HtF (1996, p. 4), however, focuses upon a broader sectoral category, namely 'small commercial establishments' (restaurants, pubs/bars, hotels, contract catering, clubs, guesthouses and take-aways which employ between one and ten staff).[2] Although both sets of figures confirm an impression of fragmentation, the manner in which the information is presented (with differences in both sectors and size bands) makes comparison impossible.[3]

There are at least two preconditions which need to be satisfied before we can reach sensible judgements as to the utility of quoted statistics. First, it is important to pay careful attention to the terminology used. In the example above, the DNH uses the term 'small firm', whereas the HtF discusses 'establishments'. In an analysis of small business management, this distinction is important, for the dynamics of establishments (or units) of a large chain are likely to be quite different from those of independent owner-managed enterprises. Second, the source of data must be noted and any inherent limitations recognised. In the case of the HtF (1996) study, for example, the principal source of data is the 1991 Census of Employment. On that basis, they estimate that small establishments (one to ten employees) in the hospitality industry comprise 87 per cent of the total stock. Despite their numerical preponderance, they suggest that this category accounts for 36 per cent of employment, which rises to 64 per cent when added to those establishments employing fewer than 25 people. Thus, the remaining 36 per cent of hospitality workers are employed by those so-called large establishments (i.e. employing more than 25 staff). Although undoubtedly useful in other contexts, data from the Census of Employment has limitations for those with an interest in small *enterprises*. The Census covers Pay as You Earn (PAYE) schemes, which do not correspond precisely to firms or establishments. This is because PAYE schemes may cover employees in many locations, or there may be more than one scheme at a single site (e.g. separate schemes for monthly and weekly paid staff). Additionally, since the self-employed who do not employ others and those businesses who only employ people who are not subject to PAYE are excluded, the figures underestimate the numbers of small businesses[4] (Bannock and Daly 1994, p. 45).

Morrison (forthcoming) reinforces this note of caution when she argues that there are several reasons why available statistics are partial in their coverage: lack of universally accepted definitions; many small businesses operate below the threshold at which they would be required to register for Value Added Tax (VAT); many accommodation units are not registered because they have too few rooms; and some small firms operate in the informal economy.

The DTI's relatively new *Statistical Bulletin* series goes some way towards overcoming the weaknesses of using single sources of information such as the Census of Employment or VAT statistics. Their approach is to supplement the Inter-Departmental Business Register (IDBR) with estimates made of those businesses which are too small to be registered.[5] The resulting statistics cannot be considered exact, but they currently represent the most robust data on which to construct a profile of small firms. Although the DTI produces statistics for a range of tourism and hospitality sectors, for convenience only the hotels and restaurants data are referred to here. Obviously, considering these data alone will not provide a complete description of the structure of the tourism and hospitality industries. However, it will serve the aim of this part of the chapter, which is to illustrate the point that some sources of statistical information are more appropriate than others when attempting to establish how many small tourism and hospitality enterprises there are in the UK.

Table 1.2 Hotels and restaurants: number of businesses, employment and turnover by size (1996)

Size (no. of employees)	Number			Per cent		
	Businesses	Employment (000s)	Turnover (£ million excluding VAT)	Businesses	Employment	Turnover
0	41,999	57	1,154	28.2	3.9	2.5
1–4	64,705	221	6,725	43.5	15.1	14.7
5–9	23,692	185	4,887	15.9	12.6	10.7
10–19	12,187	175	4,112	8.2	11.9	9.0
20–49	4,546	137	3,285	3.1	9.3	7.2
50–99	997	68	2,474	0.7	4.7	5.4
100–199	418	57	1,654	0.3	3.8	3.6
200–249	67	15	400	–	1.0	0.9
250–499	129	43	1,550	0.1	2.9	3.4
500+	126	511	19,547	0.1	34.8	42.7
All	148,866	1,469	45,788	100.0	100.0	100.0

Source: DTI (1997, p. 11).

According to the DTI's third, and most recent, *Statistical Bulletin* (DTI, 1997), there are some 150,000 hotel and restaurant businesses in the UK. Of these, almost 99 per cent employ fewer than 50 people. Further, as Table 1.2 indicates, very small (or micro) enterprises predominate, accounting for over 85 per cent of firms in these sectors.

Those companies which employ in excess of 500 people are, however, disproportionately significant in terms of employment generation and turnover. Whereas this category accounts for only 0.1 per cent of all hotel and restaurant businesses, it is responsible for creating 35 per cent of employment and 43 per cent of total sectoral turnover. Nevertheless, over 50 per cent of those working in hotels and restaurants are employed by enterprises with fewer than 50 staff. Small businesses within this category also account for almost half of total turnover.

Although the figures above highlight the importance of small tourism and hospitality firms, they offer no insight into current trends. In the absence of long-term comprehensive and reliable statistics, tracking change is, of course, problematic. Nevertheless, the case is frequently made – from as early as Pickering *et al.* (1971) to, more latterly, Litteljohn (1993) and Mogendorff (1996) – that key sectors of the tourism and hospitality industries are becoming more concentrated. Moreover, it is suggested by some, notably Slattery (1994), that structural shifts in the UK economy have precipitated this development, at least as far as the hotel sector is concerned.

To some extent, the evidence – represented by the growth of multiples, especially in the fast-food and accommodation sectors over recent decades – is incontrovertible. However, the *extent* to which multiples have taken market share and will *continue* to grow at the expense of smaller operators is more questionable. The theoretical constructs which inform explanations and predictions of future changes are underdeveloped. Further, the measurements of concentration which are sometimes used to support propositions have been challenged for their crudeness (Hughes, 1993).

There is also a suggestion that the standardization inherent in chain operations stifles innovation (Peacock, 1993). As a consequence, dynamic small firms might continue to thrive, even in prime locations. Given the low barriers to entry, and the highly segmented nature of demand (Morrison, 1996), such an argument is not implausible. Certainly, recent survey evidence (Thomas *et al.*, 1997) – which included a broad range of small tourism and hospitality firms – found that the majority of almost all the 1400 firms sampled had experienced stability or growth in revenues, profits and employment during the 12 months prior to questioning and were optimistic about the future. In addition, comparison between the second and third DTI statistical bulletins (DTI 1996, 1997) suggests that in the case of hotels and restaurants, the proportion of employment and turnover accounted for by small firms has remained relatively constant (see Table 1.3).[6] Clearly, this is an issue which requires careful monitoring in the years ahead.

Table 1.3 Small firms (< 50 employees) as a proportion of total sectoral employment, turnover and number of businesses: hotels and restaurants, 1995–96

	1995	*1996*
Employment (%)	57	53
Turnover (%)	45	44
Number of businesses (%)	99	99

Source: DTI (1996, 1997).

THE MANAGEMENT OF SMALL TOURISM AND HOSPITALITY FIRMS

Some guides to small business management – notably those aimed at the practitioner market – provide a checklist of actions for those seeking to create a thriving enterprise. Typically, they begin with lessons on planning and strategy development and invariably promote the benefits of marketing and training. Such publications frequently contain a blend of simplicity and clarity which, when combined with an intuitively sensible set of ideas, may be appealing for those with an interest in small business management. Too often, however, the texts are informed by little more than the (limited) experiences of the author(s). As interesting as these may be, such approaches are insufficiently rigorous to provide an understanding of the various factors influencing the success (however defined) or failure of small firms.

The chapters in this book adopt a *critical* perspective in relation to the various issues they address. Chapter 6, for example, does not begin from the premise that business planning is essential, but instead considers carefully the research which has been conducted on that topic (and is some respects finds it wanting). Other contributors approach their subject matter in a similar manner. The remainder of this chapter offers a summary of their work.

Chapter 2, by Dewhurst and Horobin, reviews those studies which have attempted to understand the impact of the differing characteristics of owners and the notion of entrepreneurship. In doing so, they comment upon the perspectives brought by a range of disciplines, notably economics, psychology and sociology. Their observations suggest that some studies have faltered precisely because of the constraints imposed by their disciplinary boundaries. They are critical, for example, that in the case of some psychological studies, the enthusiasm of researchers to identify entrepreneurial personality traits has resulted in insufficient attention being paid to wider factors, such as the environment within which business owners operate. As a result, they argue for greater inter- and multidisciplinary approaches to the study of small business ownership.

Drawing on available sector-specific material, which is supplemented by previously unpublished research of their own, Dewhurst and Horobin then summarize what is currently understood about the characteristics of those owning small tourism and hospitality firms. First, they point to the importance of recognizing the heterogeneity of motivations for ownership. Thus, the financial imperative implied by some economists is questioned as a range of empirical studies have demonstrated the predominance of business owners who are driven by non-financial motivations. Indeed, the extent of such 'lifestyle' motivations has led some commentators to argue that small business ownership in the tourism and hospitality industries should often be viewed not in terms of production but rather as forms of consumption (Williams *et al.*, 1989). Second, Dewhurst and Horobin draw attention to the very small scale of a high proportion of small businesses in these industries. This has important implications for the study of such enterprises, for their management will be highly personalized. The third defining characteristic which is emphasized relates to the high incidence of personal sources of capital that are used by small tourism and hospitality firms (an issue explored in more detail in Chapter 4). This, they argue, implies that most small business owners are likely to have little knowledge of business planning (which would be required by funding agencies external to the enterprise).

In the final part of their chapter, Dewhurst and Horobin propose a new 'grounded taxonomy of small business owner-managers' and a 'model of entrepreneurial tendencies'. The value of their contribution is that it recognizes the peculiarities of small businesses in the tourism and hospitality industries, and is sufficiently flexible to accommodate the dynamic nature of ownership behaviour.

The remaining three chapters of Part I examine factors which are likely to have a bearing on small business development. Chapter 3 provides a sector-specific assessment of small business failure. Boer begins by explaining the difficulties associated with defining an apparently unambiguous concept. For example, if official statistics are examined in order to identify trends in business failure, it is important to recognize that discontinuance of an enterprise may be caused by failure, but equally may be accounted for by retirement. As has been discussed earlier in terms of the incidence of small firms, official statistics have severe limitations in this context. Despite these, Boer is able to offer a statistical overview of small tourism and hospitality firm failure in the UK over recent years. Perhaps the most notable feature of this part of his chapter is the generally high business failure rate among tourism and hospitality firms. His analysis suggests that this is the case almost regardless of the prevailing economic climate.

Boer notes that the reasons for small business failure are complex and is critical of those who have concentrated their research on one aspect of this issue. In reality, he argues, it is helpful to examine the causes of small business failure under two broad headings: those which are endogenous (internal), e.g. poor management; and those which are exogenous (external to the firm), e.g. the economic environment. If the former is predominant, responsibility may generally be ascribed to the owner-manager of the enterprise, whereas public sector agencies – notably the government – have a role to play in terms of the latter.

Broadly, Boer is sympathetic to those studies which emphasize the following as primary causes of small business failure: undercapitalization, poor operational management, high gearing, poor senior management and a weak local economy. He presents a persuasive case for why these issues are likely to be important variables in any explanation of small business failure in the tourism and hospitality industries.

The issue of financing small firms, discussed briefly above, is examined in more detail by Taylor, Simpson and Howie in Chapter 4. Their starting point is to consider theory relating to the capital structure and financing decisions of businesses. The main outcome of that discussion is that there appears to be no optimum capital structure for small tourism and hospitality firms. Their contribution then focuses upon both supply side (the availability of capital) and demand factors which influence the financing of small firms. In terms of the former, they note that banks – the main lenders to small firms – face two problems: project selection and moral hazard (the difficulty of monitoring projects which they have funded). To overcome these, the requirement for collateral is now almost routinely required. However, there is a danger that this results in some otherwise viable projects being rejected. How such projects might be identified is, of course, problematic. It is interesting, for example, that there is evidence of significant variations in bank managers' perceptions of viability (Deakins and Hussain, 1993). Taylor *et al.* advocate banks becoming more closely involved with those small businesses to which they have made debt finance available as a means of improving monitoring. However, as they acknowledge, this aspiration must be set against the reluctance by many small firms to relinquish any form of control (which, in turn, influences the potential level of demand for funding).

In reviewing the sources of finance available to small tourism and hospitality firms, Taylor *et al.* examine the role of banks, venture capitalists and the state. Drawing on their own research, they tentatively suggest that small tourism and hospitality firms are treated less favourably by banks than those in other sectors. Further, it seems that these industries are relatively untouched by funding from venture capitalists and, it is argued, this is likely to remain the case in the future. The role of the state, by contrast, has been important in recent years. Their research findings point to high usage of the Small Firms Loan Guarantee Scheme by small firms in the tourism and hospitality industries. It is of some concern, therefore, that catering firms were recently excluded from the initiative.

Thomas pursues a wider perspective on the role of the state in influencing the development of small tourism and hospitality firms. In Chapter 5, he summarizes small business policies under four headings: measures to create a favourable business environment, financing small businesses (not discussed in detail), the provision of business information and support, and management training and development. Although each heading invariably incorporates numerous initiatives, Thomas's approach is to concentrate attention on the major aspects of policy. For example, he offers detailed assessment of official claims that small tourism and hospitality firms face an unreasonable regulatory burden, which, the government claims, needs to be addressed in order to improve the business environment. The outcome of his analysis is that, despite an apparent party political consensus, there is little evidence to suggest that small firms face a regulatory regime which stifles enterprise. Further, the value of intuitively attractive policies relating to information provision, business advice and management development is questioned. Although evidence which supports the government's approach is identified, there are conflicting research findings.

Chapter 5 also explores the role of the European Union (EU) in supporting small business development. From the review of initiatives which is provided, it is clear that there are many similarities between the UK and EU approaches. In addition to these areas of commonality, however, are programmes which aim to encourage the Europeanization of small firms (i.e. cooperation or partnership between firms in different member states). At this stage, participation rates among tourism and hospitality firms are low. It is not yet clear whether this is because the programmes offer more benefits to manufacturing firms (a case not yet proven) or simply that the promotional methods used do not pay particular attention to those in the tourism and hospitality industries. The chapter concludes by arguing that although efforts by the state to promote small business development have increased significantly during the 1980s and 1990s, evaluation of their effectiveness is partial. Further sector-specific studies need to be undertaken so that appropriate policies may be devised to support the development of small tourism and hospitality firms.

In Part II, contributors focus on issues relating more directly to the management of small tourism and hospitality firms. Margerison begins by examining what is one of the most widely advocated aspects of small business management, namely business planning. His contribution (Chapter 6) explains in some detail what are generally considered to be the key components of good business plans. In providing an outline of the planning process, he emphasizes both financial considerations – such as cash flow and profit forecasting – and the non-financial, such as matters relating to employment, product or service development and marketing. In order to illustrate the principles of this process, he provides an example of how it has been operationalized by a small restaurant business. The descriptive case study is useful, as it draws attention to the informal as well as the formal process of planning, which is sometimes neglected in comparable publications.

Arguably, the key element of Margerison's contribution is its critical evaluation of any connections between business planning and small business success. The potentially ambiguous notion of 'success' is used merely to enable the author to be inclusive in his review of available research. In practice, most of the studies referred to relate to the search for an articulation between business planning and small business growth. Perhaps the two most important aspects of the review are its demonstration of the complexity of establishing causality between business planning and growth and its revelation that relatively little robust research has been undertaken in this area. The latter is disappointing, given the importance currently attached to the topic by banks and a wide range of private and public sector advisory agencies. The somewhat inevitable conclusion of the chapter is that although business planning appears to play a role in the 'success' of small businesses, it is not possible at this stage to be confident of its importance *vis-à-vis* other variables.

The role of marketing in small business management is examined in Chapter 7. Friel begins his discussion by reinforcing the differences between small and large enterprises outlined earlier in this chapter, but with specific reference to marketing. This is instructive, for it establishes the inappropriateness of assuming that marketing techniques developed in the context of large enterprises may be replicated to good effect in small firms. In addition, it is persuasively argued that sector specificity has a bearing on the suitability of particular approaches for small firms in the tourism and hospitality industries.

The marketing issues discussed are wide-ranging, including product formulation, pricing, research and planning. Whereas previous studies are carefully reviewed, perhaps the most interesting insights are those which emerge from a research project with which the author was involved (Thomas *et al.*, 1997). That study, based on a survey of almost 1400 small tourism and hospitality firms, enables Friel to document current practice and to examine its implications on a sub-sectoral basis. For example, when considering promotional methods used by small tourism and hospitality firms, he is able to differentiate between those activities commonly undertaken by, say, visitor attractions and those of restaurants or cafes. That there are sometimes significant variations highlights the need to avoid ascribing too much homogeneity to small businesses in the industries examined.

To some extent, Friel's work challenges some common perceptions relating to marketing activities in small tourism and hospitality firms. Although he is cautious – as a result of the limited research on which he is able to draw – he suggests that the majority of small businesses in these industries undertake some kind of research into customer needs and formulate a marketing plan, even if only on a short-term basis. Moreover, a variety of promotional methods are used, and there is some evidence of market-oriented pricing, even though the 'cost-plus' approach remains most dominant. His impression, therefore, is that there is greater dynamism in terms of marketing among small tourism and hospitality firms than is generally considered to be the case.

In recent years, there has been an explosion of interest in quality management. The debates surrounding the most appropriate means of ensuring and enhancing the quality of products or services are examined in the context of small tourism and hospitality firms in Chapter 8. Church and Lincoln begin by arguing that if the issue of quality management is addressed by small firms, they might expect to gain advantages over their competitors which should result in a more secure financial future.

A central tenet of Church and Lincoln's chapter is the rejection of retrospective methods of quality control. They argue that such approaches, with their emphasis on comparing outputs with a given standard, are both expensive and highly intrusive in the context of services. As a result, they promote preventative systems of quality control. Their proposition is that if the various stages of the process of production and/or service delivery are controlled, little, if any, testing of the final product or service is required. Against this background, they examine the potential of two methods: hazard analysis critical control points (HACCP) and failure modes and effects analysis (FMEA). Both are seen as potentially valuable, but two limitations are recognized by the authors. First, there has so far been little systematic evaluation of these systems in small tourism and hospitality firms. Consequently, their strengths and weaknesses in such environments remain to be tested. The second is that the approaches are partial: they do not necessarily produce the holistic approach to quality management which many commentators now advocate.

In order to overcome the second of these limitations, Church and Lincoln review a range of alternatives: Investors in People (IiP), benchmarking, BS EN ISO 9000, total quality management (TQM) and quality costing. They see potential merit in both IiP and quality costing. Notwithstanding possible marketing advantages, they display more ambivalence towards the remainder: unless small firms have already established preventative quality control mechanisms, benchmarking, BS EN ISO 9000 and TQM, they argue, are not likely to be as effective as their proponents would claim.

One of the incidental themes considered by several contributors is the possibility that owner-managers may develop skills which enable them to become more effective. This issue is taken up in Chapter 9 by Beaver, Lashley and Stewart. Their chapter starts by exploring the nature of management in small tourism and hospitality enterprises and examining the reason for the perceived lack of importance attached to the development of managerial skills among the owner-managers in these industries.

As far as the former is concerned, the authors emphasize several distinguishing features of the management process. They argue that it is largely adaptive; instead of attempting to predict events, as is the case with larger organizations, they adapt to the changing demands of the business environment. As well as being highly personalized, the management process is closely controlled, and any organizational structure which may exist often emerges to reflect the interests of key role players. These factors, it is argued, coupled with a range of motivations for business ownership and a common lack of appreciation of the competencies required, conflate to produce numerous owner-managers who do not recognize the importance of management development. The consequence of this is a diminution of competitiveness.

The remainder of the chapter is concerned with developing suitable management development programmes for small tourism and hospitality firms with aspirations for growth. Although a range of possible approaches are examined, it is suggested that a key feature of the process should involve self-development or self-managed development. This implies that programmes of management development for small tourism and hospitality firms need not be overly formal or particularly resource intensive in order to achieve their goals.

The focus on owner-managers is extended in Chapter 10 to include their relations with employees. In order to understand employment relations in small tourism and hospitality firms, Jameson argues, it is first necessary to appreciate the differences in the types of jobs and the characteristics of employees between large and small firms and between manufacturing and services. Among other things, her examination of labour market issues considers the participation of women and ethnic minorities, and the incidence of part-time, casual and temporary employment. This is followed by an assessment to two themes: harmony and conflict, and levels of formality. In terms of the former, Jameson explores the extent to which small tourism and hospitality firms may be characterized as harmonious or paternalistic environments with limited industrial conflict, or whether the portrayal of such enterprises as exploitive 'sweatshops' with 'poor' employment relations is more appropriate. Although hampered by the lack of sector-specific research, she tentatively argues that research in comparable services (and the initial findings of her own ongoing project) suggests that the former is a more appropriate assessment.

One of the key distinguishing features of employment relations in small enterprises is the level of informality. This is not surprising given the scale of operations and the resultant close contact between owner-managers and their employees. Its implications are important, however, because it may result in a lower incidence of those things associated with formality – for example, contracts of employment – and in less developed procedures of consultation.

The penultimate chapter of Part II (Chapter 11) explains the possible uses and potential value of information technology (IT) for small tourism and hospitality firms.

It argues that smaller enterprises can gain significant benefits from IT. However, Mutch suggests that there needs to be a clear distinction between the information requirements of organizations and their technology needs. In too many cases, the technology used is inappropriate and reorganization of manual systems in the light of an enhanced awareness of information needs may well prove to be more productive.

Nevertheless, in some cases IT may play a significant role in supporting business development. In addition to a review of the relevant literature, Mutch uses the findings of his own research in the tourism industry to illustrate his case. It is clear from his analysis that the growth of one case study company examined – Country Holidays – can at least be partially attributed to its careful management of information needs and the appropriate use of technology. However, as the chapter makes clear, while the case study may illustrate potential benefits, such effective use of IT currently remains relatively isolated among small tourism and hospitality firms. This has implications for a range of agencies which have an interest in promoting the development of small tourism and hospitality firms.

The final chapter, provided by Webster, considers the role that strategic management plays in the growth of small tourism and hospitality firms. Her focus of attention is, therefore, on the minority of businesses which have aspirations to grow and those which have actually grown since their inception.

Webster takes Storey's (1994) position as her starting point. Thus, she argues that small firms appear to grow when three influences on growth overlap: a particular blend of ownership characteristics and the start-up resources available, the features of the firm itself and the strategic decisions taken by the business. To that extent, she argues that although strategic decisions are important for growth, they are unlikely to be effective if they are taken in a context where other factors which are necessary for growth are absent.

CONCLUSIONS

This chapter has sought to serve as an introduction to the study of small firms in the tourism and hospitality industries. In doing so, it has explored the varying usage of the term 'small firm' and the difficulties associated with measuring the numbers of such firms in the economy. Despite these barriers to precision, there is sufficient information which highlights the numerical domination of smaller enterprises in these industries. The extent to which small firms will flourish in the future or contract in the face of competition from larger enterprises remains to be seen. Regardless of the assertions of some commentators, there is at this stage insufficient understanding of the structural dynamics of the tourism and hospitality industries to reach a judgement on that issue.

There are three recurring themes in the contributions reviewed in this chapter. The first is that there is a strong case for the separate study of small firms in the tourism and hospitality industries. The various authors reinforce the case made at the outset by illustrating how the topics they deal with might be misunderstood if the focus of attention were on small firms in general. Notwithstanding this observation, the second common feature of the chapters which follow is their acceptance that there is a need to recognize the heterogeneity of the enterprises within particular sectors. For example, many small firms are characterized by owner-manager motivations which relate more to lifestyle considerations, whereas others have more overt commercial objectives. Clearly, a failure to appreciate the importance of these differences (and others) will serve only to obfuscate rather than illuminate developments. Finally, all contributors emphasize the inadequate research base which currently exists in this field of study. It is to be hoped that their efforts in establishing the 'groundwork' will act as a solid foundation on which to further our understanding of small tourism and hospitality firms.

NOTES

1. Peacock suggests that the distinction between small, medium and large enterprises is unhelpful in the context of hotels and restaurants. Instead, he argues that there is greater utility in using a small/large dichotomy. Although levels of turnover are considered, Peacock ends up with a definition – based on the perceptions of practitioners – which centres on numbers of employees; his suggestion is that small restaurants employ up to 30 employees, whereas small hotels employ up to 80 people.
2. There is some degree of ambiguity in the HtF's figures, to the extent that the commentary defines small establishments as employing *fewer* than ten people, whereas a figure suggests that the category *includes* those with ten employees (see HtF, 1996, p. 4).
3. Commercially produced reports also present varying estimates of the number of small tourism and hospitality firms in the UK – see, for example, MSI (1991), Key Note (1993), Wedgwood Markham (1994). It should be recognized that although many market research reports appear to be authoritative in their declarations on this matter, the impression of precision and reliability which pervades such documents is usually overstated. For a more comprehensive review of the various estimates relating to numbers of small firms in the hotel industry, see Morrison (forthcoming).
4. The HtF uses 'establishments' throughout its report and does not, therefore, claim to provide a profile of the industry based on enterprises. It is not surprising, however, that some commentators have interpreted the figures in such a manner.
5. The IDBR records all businesses registered for VAT and those operating PAYE schemes, and is careful to avoid duplication. The main source of employment data is the Annual Employment Survey. For details of how estimates of unregistered businesses are constructed see DTI (1996, pp. 4–6).
6. Table 1.3 is interesting but its value is limited; no trends can be inferred from the data. Unfortunately, because the method of estimation changed after the first *Statistical Bulletin*, it is not appropriate to include the figures for 1994 (Dale and Kerr, 1995).

REFERENCES

Bannock, G. and Daly, M. (1994) *Small Business Statistics*. London: Paul Chapman Publishing/Small Business Research Trust.

Burns, P. (1996) 'Introduction: the significance of small firms', in Burns, P. and Dewhurst, J. (eds) *Small Business and Entrepreneurship*, 2nd edn. Basingstoke: Macmillan.

Burrows, R. and Curran, J. (1989) 'Sociological research on service sector small businesses: some conceptual considerations', *Work, Employment and Society*, **3(4)**, 527–39.

Cooper, C., Fletcher, J., Gilbert, D. and Wanhill, S. (1993) *Tourism: Principles and Practice*. London: Pitman.

Curran, J. and Burrows, R. (1989) 'Shifting the focus: problems and approaches to studying the small enterprise in the services sector', Twelfth National Small Firms Policy and Research Conference, Greenwich, November.

Curran, J., Kitching, J., Abbot, B. and Mills, V. (1993) *Employment and Employment Relations in the Small Service Sector Enterprise – A Report*. Kingston-upon-Thames: ESRC Centre for Research on Small Service Sector Enterprises, Kingston University.

Dale, I. and Kerr, J. (1995) 'Small and medium-sized enterprises: their numbers and importance to employment', *Labour Market Trends*, December, 461–6.

Deakins, D. and Hussain, G. (1993) 'Overcoming the adverse selection problem: evidence and policy implications from a study of bank managers on the importance of different criteria used in making a lending decision', in Chittenden, F., Robertson, M. and Watkins, D. (eds) *Small Firms: Recession and Recovery*. London: Paul Chapman Publishing, 177–87.

Department of National Heritage (DNH) (1996) *Tourism: Competing with the Best 3 – People Working in Tourism and Hospitality*. London: DNH.

Department of Trade and Industry (DTI) (1996) *Statistical Bulletin: Small and Medium-sized Enterprise (SME) Statistics for the UK, 1994*. Sheffield: DTI.

DTI (1997) *Statistical Bulletin: Small and Medium-sized Enterprise (SME) Statistics for the United Kingdom, 1996*. Sheffield: DTI.

Dewhurst, J. and Burns, P. (1993) *Small Business Management*, 3rd edn. Basingstoke: Macmillan.

Hospitality Training Foundation (HtF) (1996) *Research Report 1996: Catering and Hospitality Industry – Key Facts and Figures*. London: HtF.

Hughes, H. (1993) 'The structural theory of business demand: a comment', *International Journal of Hospitality Management*, **12(4)**, 309–11.

International Association of Hotel Management Schools (IAHMS) (1996) *Issues Relating to Small Businesses in the Hospitality and Tourism Industries*. Proceedings of the Spring Symposium, Centre for the Study of Small Tourism and Hospitality Firms, Leeds Metropolitan University.

Key Note (1993) *Fast Food and Home Delivery Outlets*. Hampton: Key Note Publications.

Litteljohn, D. (1993) 'Western Europe', in Jones, P. and Pizam, A. (eds) *The International Hospitality Industry*. London: Pitman, 3–24.

Mogendorff, D. (1996) 'The European hospitality industry', in Thomas, R. (ed.) *The Hospitality Industry, Tourism and Europe: Perspectives on Policies*. London: Cassell, pp. 35–45.

Morrison, A. (1996) 'Guest houses and small hotels', in Jones, P. (ed.) *Introduction to Hospitality Operations*. London: Cassell, pp 73–85.

Morrison, A. (forthcoming) 'Small firm statistics: a hotel sector focus', *Service Industries Journal*.

MSI (1991) *Hotels: UK*. London: Marketing Strategies for Industry (UK) Ltd.

Peacock, M. (1993) 'A question of size', *International Journal of Contemporary Hospitality Management*, **5(4)**, 29–32.

Pickering, J.F., Greenwood, J.A. and Hunt, D. (1971) *The Small Firm in the Hotel and Catering Industry (Committee of Inquiry on Small Firms: Research Report 14)*. London HMSO.

Slattery, P. (1994) 'The structural theory of business demand: a reply to Hughes', *International Journal of Hospitality Management*, **13(2)**, 173–6.

Stanworth, J. and Gray, C. (eds) (1991) *Bolton 20 Years on: The Small Firm in the 1990s*. London: Paul Chapman Publishing.

Storey, D.J. (1994) *Understanding the Small Business Sector*. London: Routledge.

Thomas, R. (1996) 'Enterprise policy', in Thomas, R. (ed) *The Hospitality Industry, Tourism and Europe: Perspectives on Policies*. London: Cassell, 117–34.

Thomas, R., Friel, M., Jameson, S. and Parsons, D. (1997) *The National Survey of Small Tourism and Hospitality Firms: Annual Report 1996–97*. Leeds: Centre for the Study of Small Tourism and Hospitality Firms, Leeds Metropolitan University.

Voss, C., Armistead, C., Johnston, B. and Morris, B. (1988) *Operations Management in the Service Industries and Public Sector*. Chichester: John Wiley and Sons.

Wedgwood Markham (1994) *Hotels and Guest Houses*. London: Wedgwood Markham Associates Ltd.

Williams, A.M., Shaw, G. and Greenwood, J. (1989) 'From tourist to tourism entrepreneur, from consumption to production: evidence from Cornwall, England', *Environment and Planning A*, **21**, 1639–53.

Part I

Understanding Small Business Development

TWO

Small business owners

Peter Dewhurst and Helen Horobin

INTRODUCTION

The individuals who establish new businesses have, since the turn of the twentieth century, fascinated political scientists, sociologists, anthropologists, historians and psychologists. A second and related focal point emerged following the publication of Schumaker's (1973) seminal work *Small Is Beautiful*, with attention being focused on small firms and their growing importance to the economic health of nations. More recently, the emphasis has shifted to the creation, role and nature of small firms (Burns, 1989).

Yet, despite the close academic consideration of small businesses, there has been little scrutiny of those operating within the tourism and hospitality industries. This failing, which has recently been highlighted by Shaw and Williams (1997), has begun to be addressed by, among others, Stallinbrass (1980), Brown (1987), Williams *et al.* (1989), Danvers and Thomas (1995) and Thomas *et al.* (1997). However, while there has been a recent increase in the amount of material appertaining to small tourism and hospitality firms, it has failed to keep pace with the burgeoning growth in the generic body of work. The result is a gap between a generally advanced level of insight into small firms *per se* and a rather more limited insight into small tourism and hospitality firms.

This lack of detailed understanding of small tourism and hospitality firms is disappointing, not least because the tourism and hospitality industries have begun to be recognized as being of tremendous significance, at both national and global levels. As noted by Davis (1991, p. 3),

> Tourism is one of England's largest and most important industries. It makes a major contribution to the national economy, provides thousands of jobs, spends billions of pounds with manufacturing industries and supports communities throughout the country.

Van Harssel (1994, p. 1) notes:

> Tourism is the largest industry in the world today in terms of economic activity and as a generator of employment. One out of every twelve workers world-wide works in the tourism and hospitality industry.

The failure to study tourism and hospitality small businesses adequately is further compounded by the fact that the industries are dominated by such firms, as has been discussed in Chapter 1. The purpose of this chapter is, therefore, to utilize the contemporary body of knowledge of small firms as the basis for a more incisive study of such businesses operating within the tourism and hospitality industries.

It can be argued that a structured understanding of any functioning environment relies upon a clear and rigorous classification of the elements which combine to form that environment. Yet, unfortunately, there is no existing broadly accepted classification which can be directly applied to those small businesses that are currently operating within the tourism and hospitality industries. Instead, there are numerous competing small business oriented classifications which are of varying degrees of relevance to tourism and hospitality firms. This chapter will endeavour to profile and evaluate the various generic classifications, before proceeding to offer a new tourism- and hospitality-specific insight. This new insight will incorporate the outline of a procedure for assessing the entrepreneurial tendencies of small business owner-managers. The chapter will explore the policy implications of the proffered insight prior to concluding with suggestions for future research programmes.

CHARACTERISTICS OF OWNERSHIP: A LITERATURE REVIEW

The student or researcher approaching the small firms literature for the first time now has a vast array of textbooks, research reports, academic journals and other sources to consult regarding the characteristics of the small firm owner-manager. The vast majority of this body of knowledge can be described as stemming from three disciplines: economics, psychology and sociology.

An economic perspective

For those viewing small firms from an economic perspective, the primary interest has been the pursuit of an understanding of the impact of entrepreneurial behaviour upon an economy. The first study from this perspective is often attributed to Cantillon (Stanworth and Gray, 1991), who, as early as 1755, identified the entrepreneur as someone who confidently pursues profitable exchanges even when faced with uncertain market conditions. Cantillon is also credited with being the first to suggest that an entrepreneur can be characterized as both a risk taker and an innovator, and it is these 'themes' that have been hotly debated by economists ever since (see, for example, Knight, 1921; Schumpeter, 1934; McClelland, 1961; Casson, 1982; Carland *et al.*, 1984). While several schools of thought have emerged over time, the common factor among all has been the pursuit of an understanding of the entrepreneur as an instrument of macroeconomic change (Hornaday, 1990). Most recently, the so-called 'enterprise culture' fostered in the UK during the 1980s was underpinned by the assumption that free market economies send 'signals about economic opportunities to those individuals alert enough to observe them and with the will to act upon them' and 'are, by definition, entrepreneurial economies' (Goss, 1991).

Reviewing the development of the economists' work, it is clear that while many have used the term entrepreneur to refer to any business owner or founder, the focus of much of the work in this area has shifted to consider those characteristics which typify entrepreneurial acts (Stanworth and Gray, 1991). In other words, there has been an increasing tendency to separate the 'entrepreneur', particularly the 'successful' entrepreneur, from the 'small business owner'. In this, the entrepreneurial characteristics have been identified as including innovation, with the entrepreneur being recognized as an agent for change (Schumpeter, 1934), having the willingness to take risks (Knight, 1921) and the ability to make confident, judgmental decisions (Casson, 1982). Indeed, there is now some consensus that there is a distinct set of behaviours that characterize entrepreneurial acts (Stanworth and Gray, 1991) and an agreement that such characteristics are rare. One key issue is whether all small business owners may occasionally behave entrepreneurially, or whether only a minority might be termed 'entrepreneurs'. If, as Drucker (1985) has argued, the latter is more precise, the utility of the work in this area to those seeking an understanding the small business community as a whole is questionable. Perhaps more critically, the fact that many of these characteristics can only be identified with certainty in retrospect raises questions as to the value of this identification for those seeking to assist small firm development.

A psychological perspective

Turning to the work of psychologists, the majority of studies rooted in this discipline have concentrated on trying to identify the personality traits of the entrepreneur. Once again, the focus is firmly on the separation of the 'entrepreneur' from the 'small business owner'. Stanworth and Gray (1991) provide a critical review of the key studies that have purported to identify entrepreneurial 'traits', which effectively summarizes the literature in this area and identifies the following traits as being those most commonly discussed: need for achievement (McClelland, 1961), risk-taking propensity (Brockhaus, 1980), locus of control (Brockhaus, 1982; Caird, 1990) independence (Collins and Moore, 1970) and innovation/creativity (Kanter, 1983). However, there has been robust and sustained criticism of attempts to identify personality traits as characteristic of entrepreneurs (see, for example, Hampson, 1982; Chell and Haworth, 1988, 1990; Chell et al., 1991). These criticisms range over a variety of issues including the need to identify constellations of personality characteristics rather than individual traits, methodological difficulties inherent in the identification of personality characteristics and the conflicting findings of different studies. As noted by Stanworth and Gray (1991, p. 158): 'This list of difficulties is now long and formidable; and it might be argued that this is sufficient reason to abandon the trait approach.'

The most damning criticism of this approach challenges the assumption that entrepreneurial behaviour is a function of an individual's personality, rather than a response to the environment or context in which the business is operating (Goss, 1991). This, in turn, leads to the inevitable conclusion that the trait approach can at best offer only a partial analysis of behaviour (Chell, 1985).

A sociological perspective

Work in the sociological field has focused upon attempts to differentiate between different types of business owner, in order to create typologies which allocate business owner-managers to differently named and described categories. These sociological studies have as their principal focus the social relationship which lie at the heart of small business organization and which allow for a greater tolerance of diversity among small firms (Goss, 1991). This approach has been described by Chell *et al.* (1991) as an attractive first step in research and by Woo *et al.* (1988) as highly useful in capturing frequently occurring combinations of characteristics, thereby reducing the number of profiles from potentially infinite to a manageable few. Therefore, as Woo *et al.* (1988) suggest, the typology approach aims to contribute to a more sophisticated description of entrepreneurs and their behaviour.

The contributions of Collins *et al.* (1964) and Smith (1967) represent the origins of work in this area, and were concerned with distinguishing between different types of business owner in pursuit of the entrepreneur, and then further dividing the entrepreneurial 'type' to achieve three types, labelled craftsman entrepreneur, opportunistic entrepreneur and business hierarch. At this stage, however, the business heirarchs were not a third category of small business owner, but salaried managers used primarily to distinguish the characteristics of the entrepreneur. Once again, the focus was on understanding the entrepreneur rather than on attempting to categorize all types of business owner. This has been followed by numerous further attempts to build small firm owner typologies: included among such studies are those of Stanworth and Curran (1982), Dunkelberg and Cooper (1982), Goffee and Scase (1983) and Stevenson and Sahlman (1986). When these are compared it becomes clear, as noted by Hornaday (1990, p. 27), that these 'theorists and researchers are chasing three types of business owner'. It also becomes clear that the key determinant of many of these types is the business owner's motives or intentions, the factors regarded by many as critical to an incisive understanding of the performance of small firms (Stanworth and Curran, 1982; Bird, 1988; Carland *et al.* 1988; Katz and Gartner, 1988; Goss, 1991). The three types of small business owner can be summarized as 'craft' owners, who pursue personal satisfaction and are therefore motivated to do work they want to do; 'promoters', who seek personal wealth and/or financial return; and 'professional managers', who seek to build a successful organization which they can manage (Hornaday, 1990).

Sociologically focused attempts to categorize the small firm community have also been subject to criticism. Earlier two-fold typologies were criticized as being too simplistic, while those that have indicated the existence of at least three types have revealed somewhat contradictory findings or have not been tested. More fundamentally, the typologies have been dismissed by some, including Chell *et al.* (1991), for not having been developed in line with the theory of categorization.

In summary, the contribution of the economists appears to indicate the existence of a distinctive set of characteristic behaviours, which serve to determine entrepreneurial acts and which provide some useful insight into the effect of the entrepreneur on the economy. However, not all business owners are entrepreneurs. Furthermore, as some economists have indicated, a psychological examination of the nature of entrepreneurship is also necessary if a more rounded understanding is to be achieved (Chell *et al.*, 1991). The work of psychologists has resulted in some agreement as to a constellation of personality traits which might characterize entrepreneurs and enable the identification of the 'entrepreneurial personality'. The focus is again on the entrepreneur, and it is acknowledged by many that links to the context in which the business is operating are necessary if a full analysis of their behaviour is to emerge. Finally, the small business owner typologies drawn up primarily by sociologists, while inherently appealing and considered useful by some, have been fundamentally challenged on methodological grounds. A by-product of this 'grail-like search for the entrepreneurial personality' (Goss, 1991, p. 48) by researchers from all disciplines 'has been confusion, as writers have either used the concept in a vague and unspecified manner ... or have constructed definitions of an extremely restricted nature' (Goss, 1991, p. 47).

One means of overcoming the deficiencies of the different classificatory regimes has been proffered by Stanworth and Gray (1991), who suggest an amalgamation of the sociological and psychological approaches. Just such a socio-psychological approach has been utilized by Chell *et al.* (1991), who have attempted to link a set of personality traits with different types of business owner. The resulting classification makes clear use of the principles of categorization. It also uses measures of business performance and an assessment of the firm's stage of development, in order to establish links to the context in which the business is operating. However, this work again seeks to separate the 'entrepreneur' from the 'small business owner'. More importantly, the methodological difficulties experienced in applying the classificatory framework to a sample of small tourism firms have been shown to be both fundamental and wide-ranging (see Danvers and Thomas, 1995).

It can be argued, based on the preceding discussion, that there is considerable value in Hornaday's (1990) belief that it is time to leave the search for the entrepreneur and 'focus on the legitimate problem of the effects of owner intentions and capabilities on the performance of small firms'. After all, as noted by Goss (1991), if Drucker's (1985) 'rigorous conditions for the identification of entrepreneurial behaviour' are applied, 'few UK small business owners would merit the title of entrepreneur' (Goss, 1991, p. 47). This leads to an acceptance of Goss's pragmatic conclusion that it is preferable to use the term entrepreneur in its loosest form, with specific types of entrepreneurial activity being identified as and when appropriate.

A tourism and hospitality perspective

It has already been established that 'tourism research has largely bypassed the study of entrepreneurial activity' (Shaw and Williams, 1997, p. 118). This is especially disappointing given the substantial attention directed over many years to the impact of tourism in general economic terms. Indeed, as Harper (1984) notes, the literature is remarkably uninformative on the influence of small and medium-sized tourism businesses in economic development. Thus, 'little is known about the economic behavioural characteristics of entrepreneurs within tourism economies or, more importantly, the impact of these entrepreneurs on economic development' (Shaw and Williams, 1990, p. 71).

Tourism and hospitality firms have also received scant attention within the general area of small firms research. This neglect is conspicuous and has been described by Shaw and Williams (1990, p. 74) as 'in marked contrast to studies in other economic sectors, especially manufacturing'. The literature is particularly silent in respect of the characteristics of those who own and operate such firms (Williams *et al.*, 1989). However, those few studies which have focused on the owners of small tourism and hospitality firms, do provide some valuable insights. First, they have succeeded in identifying a variety of business motivations among small tourism and hospitality firm owner-managers. Yet what has emerged is the importance of non-economic motives. The work of both Stallinbrass (1980) and Brown (1987) with small firm owners, in Scarborough and Bournemouth respectively, identified that many had non-economic motives for entering the business, and this finding was replicated in the study of small firms in Cornwall conducted by Shaw *et al.* (1987). Respondents in the Cornish study were as likely to name non-economic reasons for leaving previous jobs, such as 'to come to Cornwall' and 'semi-retirement', as they were economic ones, such as 'the attraction of more money' or the 'desire to enhance careers' (Williams *et al.*, 1989, p. 1648). This study particularly emphasized the locational benefits sought by small firm owners when establishing businesses in Cornwall, and concluded that, for some business owners, 'tourism entrepreneurship can be seen as a form of consumption rather than production' (Williams *et al.*, 1989, p. 1650).

More recently, the work of one of the authors (see Danvers and Thomas, 1995; Horobin (née Danvers) and Long, 1996) and the survey conducted by Thomas *et al.* (1997) add weight to these assertions. Horobin and Long (1996) report on a small-scale study of small tourism firms in North Yorkshire which has identified business owners as being twice as likely to give non-economic reasons for being in business as economic ones. Similarly, Thomas *et al.*'s (1997) survey of over 1300 small tourism businesses in four UK Tourist Board areas revealed that almost 80 per cent of respondents described their motivation for owning their own business in non-economic terms. Thus, it is recognized that, for many small business owner-managers, the pursuit of growth and business expansion is not a priority (Storey, 1994), and evidence from the tourism and hospitality industries appears to indicate that a significant percentage of entrepreneurs are driven as much by social as by economic motives (Williams *et al.*, 1989).

A related issue to emerge from the research conducted to date is the very small scale of these enterprises. The survey conducted by Williams *et al.* (1989) identified almost one-half of tourism businesses in Cornwall as having no full-time employees except the owner, and a further 10 per cent as having only one full-time employee. Danvers and Thomas (1995) reveal an almost identical pattern in North Yorkshire, and Thomas *et al.*'s (1997) survey produced a similarly consistent profile of employment, in that 45 per cent of the sample employed only one full-time worker in addition to the owner manager, and 75 per cent employed five or fewer. In Cornwall (Williams *et al.*, 1989), some 70 per cent of tourism businesses were in the private ownership of a single individual, and the survey by Thomas *et al.* (1997) revealed just over 80 per cent of the businesses to be independently owned by a sole or joint owners. As noted by Williams *et al.* (1989, p. 1643),

> This is, therefore, a small scale, locally owned business sector with little separation of ownership and management. The implications of this are important: entry thresholds to business ownership are relatively low ... and decision making may rest on highly person-alised criteria.

The second major characteristic relates to the fact that many tourism and hospitality owner-managers appear to lack industry-specific expertise or business ownership experience. Shaw and Williams (1990) describe the operators in their survey as predominantly ex-employees with no directly relevant managerial experience. Danvers and Thomas (1995) also identify 76 per cent of the sample as lacking any previous industry-specific business ownership expertise or employment experience.

The third major feature of the sector relates to the sources of capital used to finance the business. Williams *et al.* (1989) identified personal and family savings as the main source of capital, and these were used exclusively by 50 per cent of the entrepreneurs. Thomas *et al.* (1997) profile an almost identical picture, with 56 per cent of small business owners relying on personal capital for the funding of business development initiatives. The comments of Shaw and Williams (1990, p. 77), with reference to Schwaninger (1986), are relevant here, as they state:

> The predominance of informal sources of capital is strongly suggestive of businesses controlled by entrepreneurs who may have only a limited conception of the need to draw up management strategies or business plans.

The available evidence as to the nature and characteristics of the small firm owner-manager in the tourism and hospitality industries thus provides a consistent, albeit still emerging, picture. The majority are individuals who are not motivated by a desire to maximize economic gain, who operate businesses often with very low levels of employment and in which managerial decisions are often based on highly personalized criteria. Many are reliant on personal capital and lack managerial and/or industry-specific experience or expertise.

The findings detailed above have led Shaw and Williams (1990) to conclude that the theoretical or conceptual qualities of entrepreneurship, including innovation, responding to uncertainty and adjusting to disequilibrium, are precisely the qualities that appear to be poorly developed among small tourism firms. However, with reference to arguments advanced earlier, such characteristics are acknowledged as rare among *all* small firms, so this should not be an unexpected conclusion. More notably, these authors (see Williams *et al.*, 1989; Shaw and Williams, 1994) have utilized one of the generic small firm typologies in an attempt to begin to relate the generic to the specifics of small firms in the tourism and hospitality industries. Using Goffee and Scase's (1983) typology, they note that the 'few studies of hotel businesses that have been undertaken suggest that many in the UK would fall into either the first or second groups' (Shaw and Williams, 1994, p. 134). This typology defines the entrepreneurial middle class as consisting of four sub-categories: the self-employed, small employers, owner-controllers and owner-directors. The first two categories are considered the most marginal in terms of the 'entrepreneurial middle class'. Furthermore, they add that 'within this broad framework one type of business seems particularly noteworthy: those which are only partly commodified and driven as much by social as economic motives' (Williams *et al.*, 1989). The work reported by Danvers and Thomas (1995), Horobin and Long (1996) and Thomas *et al.* (1997) provides further evidence to support these conclusions. Thus, a clear starting point for the investigation of the nature and characteristics of small firm owner-managers in the tourism and hospitality industries exists.

CHARACTERISTICS OF OWNERSHIP: A NEW PERSPECTIVE

The previous section has revealed an evident need to set the broad body of work on the nature and characteristics of the small firm owner-manager within a tourism and hospitality context, an issue which has also been explored in more detail in Chapter 1.

With this in mind it is worthwhile drawing on generic studies in order to first consider the process by which businesses are initially created and subsequently managed.

The strategic management process

An individual's personal characteristics (Stanworth and Gray, 1991), coupled with environmental and other external variables (Chell, 1985; Goss, 1991), serve to influence or trigger a decision to create a new business (Burns and Dewhurst, 1989). The emerging business owner-manager is spurred in his or her decision-making by his or her motivations (Stallinbrass, 1980; Brown, 1987; Shaw and Williams, 1987). These may then be translated into mission statements and/or goals for success:

> Increasingly organisations have attempted to encapsulate the purpose of their activity, as much as the direction they wish to take, in a single short statement. This statement represents the 'vision' or 'mission' of the organisation. (Hannagan, 1995, p. 121)

> Goals are the broad, long-range attributes that a business seeks to accomplish; they tend to be general and sometimes even abstract. Goals are not intended to be specific enough for a manager to act on, but state the general level of accomplishment sought.' (Scarborough and Zimmerer, 1996, p. 104)

The identification of a firm's goals is inevitably followed by the development of specific objectives which represent 'more specific targets of performance' (Scarborough and Zimmerer, 1996). Strategies are then devised which are intended to set out the means for achieving the organization's mission, goals and objectives (Stacey, 1993; Hannagan, 1995). There follows a series of stages in which the strategies are translated into actions which are controlled and monitored, and which ultimately result in outcomes or rewards (Johnson and Scholes, 1993). All these stages may be explicitly or only implicitly expressed. A diagrammatic representation of this strategic management process is provided (see Figure 2.1), which is derived from a model originally presented by Johnson and Scholes (1993).

The strategic management model (Figure 2.1) has two particular strengths. First, it can be argued that the model provides a valuable visual interpretation of the differing foci of concern for those involved in small firms research. Indeed, the preceding text has suggested that the psychologists have tended to concentrate their attention on the personality traits of the small business owner-operators (area 1 of the model), while the economists have explored the outcomes or relative rewards of small business activity (area 3 of the model). In contrast, the sociologists have chiefly concerned themselves with the actions of owner-managers in seeking to satisfy their aspirations (area 2 of the model). The second strength of the model is the generally accepted vision it presents of the business start-up and strategic management process. Both elements have been cited as being of direct relevance to the owner-managers of small firms (Bennett, 1990; Scarborough and Zimmerer, 1996). The approach depicted in the model has also been advocated by those working within the tourism industry (Swarbrooke, 1995).

The strategic management model will therefore be used as the starting point for a fresh insight into tourism and hospitality-specific small businesses. The insight will rely heavily on the sociological approach as typified by the work of Chell *et al.* (1991), but it will also draw on facets of the existing psychological and economic approaches to the study of small firms.

A focus on motivations and goals

It is broadly recognized that individual characteristics and personality traits, which are the focus of the psychologists' studies, serve to shape and influence both the decision to start a small business and the motivations behind the decision. In other words, the motivations can be said in some way to reflect the individual characteristics of the small business owner-manager. Yet difficulties have emerged with attempts that have been made to measure and explore the impacts of individual characteristics, including personality traits. The difficulties stem from the sheer range and diversity of pertinent variables. As previously stated, such difficulties have prevented the widespread acceptance of classifications based upon personality traits. Some academics have proposed an alternative approach by suggesting that the assessment of business start-up motivations can serve as a valuable means of categorizing the owner-managers of small

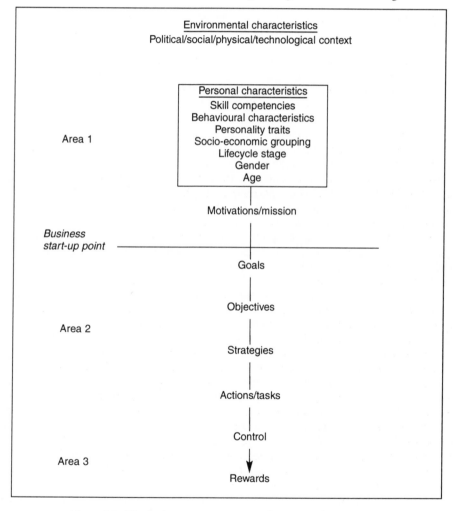

Figure 2.1 The business start-up and strategic management process
Source: Adapted from Johnson and Scholes (1993).

businesses. Studies of business motivations can however, be fraught with difficulties, with the passage of time following a business start-up potentially dealing a double blow to the utility of such an approach. Indeed, the original motivations for a small business start-up may have been forgotten or be of little or no contemporary relevance to businesses which have entered a different stage of their development cycle (Burns, 1989). Additionally, the motivations may be only implicitly recognized, with many small business owner-managers having failed to focus explicitly on them through the use of mission statements.

A study of organizational goals offers an alternative basis for the differentiation and classification of small business owner-mangers. The focus on an organization's goals offers a similar insight into the small business owner-manager to that provided by a study of their motivations. This much is made clear in statements by Dewhurst (1996) and Carson *et al.* (1995):

> those who are ultimately responsible for an organization will ... ensure that their perceptions of success are translated into policy goals. (Dewhurst, 1996, p. 91)

> the goals of the organisation will reflect, in considerable measure, the aspirations of the owners. (Carson *et al.*, 1995, p. 70)

In addition, a study into the goals for success of small businesses is unlikely to suffer from the shortcomings of the motivational studies as expressed above. They are also likely to carry with them the benefit of providing what can be a clear and incisive insight into the nature of the small business, something which is not necessarily a feature of those studies that are expressly concerned with start-up motivations (see Storey and Strange, 1993). An emphasis on the envisaged goals for success consequently lies at the heart of Carland *et al.*'s (1984) classification of small firms, and was also used in Dewhurst's (1996) study of England's most visited tourist attractions. The classificatory value of organizational goals, therefore, makes it necessary to examine the goals for success of small tourism and hospitality businesses.

In addressing the subject of goals for success, it must first be recognized that the goals of any business are likely to be both diverse and varied. Support for this assertion is provided in Dewhurst's (1996) work, which revealed the managers of England's most visited tourist attractions to be generally concerned with goals which were focused on their sites' visitors or customers, their investors and proprietors, as well as the communities within which the sites are located. These categories may be usefully adapted and applied to the small firms operating within the tourism and hospitality industries (see Figure 2.2).

Figure 2.2 is comprised of two distinct areas, with a peripheral set of community-oriented goals surrounding a core area of customer-, investor- and owner-manager-oriented goals. The juxtaposition of each category is significant, with the peripherally located community-oriented goals, including possible commitments to increased levels of local employment, being of only limited relevance to most small business owner-managers. In contrast, within the central core, the customer-oriented goals are likely to include references to both demand and volume satisfaction (Dewhurst, 1996). The investor-oriented goals apply in instances where small business operators have secured external financial support and so are obligated to take heed of either the formal or informal conditions of their loan agreements. Finally, the owner-manager-oriented goals reflect the personal motivations and priorities of the small business owner-managers themselves. It is this last category of goals which is of paramount importance, as it is the owner-manager whom Wynarczyk *et al.* (1993, p. 50) recognize as 'the major

Figure 2.2   Goals for success of small firms

strategic policy maker within the firm' and so, as Carson *et al.* (1995, p. 70) have intimated, it is these goals which 'reflect ... the aspirations of the owner'.

Foley and Green (1989) have identified the owner-managers' personal goals as focusing on financial considerations, creativity and independence as well as job satisfaction. Other studies have suggested a more bipolar dichotomy, with Carland *et al.* (1984) identifying what they consider to be profit- and growth-oriented goals, as well as personal goals associated with 'family needs and desires'. Carland *et al.* have used their dichotomous categorization of goals as the basis for the classification of small business people as either 'small business owners' or 'entrepreneurs'. Implicit support for this goals-based two-point classification is provided by the study conducted by Shaw and Williams (1987), in which a sizable proportion of owner managers refer to non-economic motivations and goals. This latter group were identified as having a 'lifestyle' orientation (Williams *et al.*, 1989).

Chell *et al.* (1991) and Shailer (1994) have criticised Carland *et al.*'s (1984) classification, with Shailer in particular highlighting the 'nonsensical position' which has been adopted in separating commercially oriented and 'personal', or as Williams *et al.* (1989) have called them, 'lifestyle', goals. Shailer's belief that the two types of goal are intrinsically linked is compelling, yet his implied conclusion that they can not therefore provide the foundations for a classification is a false one. Small business owner-managers have their own perceptions of what is important to them, and will prioritize their own particular goals. It can, therefore, be argued that this prioritization should permit owner-managers not only to identify a variety of goals for the success of their operations, but also to rank them in order of their relative significance. Support for this assertion is provided by Dewhurst (1996), who used a five-point Likert scale as the basis for an analysis of the comparative significance of the goals for success, as cited by the managers of England's most visited tourist attractions. The work resulted in a rank ordered listing of prioritized goals. By using such a procedure it should be possible to devise a simple test which can be used to position individual small business owner-managers along what can be regarded as the base axis of a subjective goal orientation model (see Figure 2.3). Those small business owner-managers who choose to empha-size financially oriented goals, including the desire as expressed by Carland *et al.* (1984) for 'profit' and 'business growth', are likely to be positioned towards point *A* of the goal orientation model (see Figure 2.3). A position approximate to point *B* is likely to be the location of those who choose to interpret success less in terms of commercially oriented goals and more in terms of what Williams *et al.* (1989) have expressed as lifestyle goals. This latter grouping of goals utilize both social and environmental criteria as a measure of success, and so they could include what Foley and Green (1989) have referred to as personal 'creativity' and 'independence'. For those small business owner-managers who fall within this category, their businesses success might best be measured in terms of a continuing ability to perpetuate their chosen lifestyles.

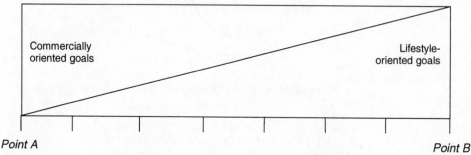

Point A   *Point B*

Figure 2.3   A subjective goal orientation model

The conceptual model as manifested in Figure 2.3 has a number of strengths, not least its potential for simply yet accurately representing the goals orientation of individual small business owner-managers. More particularly, it emphasizes the two all-important ends of a taxonomic spectrum which has been the subject of much debate (Carland *et al.*, 1984; Hornaday, 1990). In emphasizing the commercially oriented owner-manager (located towards point *A*) and the lifestyle-oriented owner manager (located towards point *B*), the model focuses on the two key groups of small business people as revealed in the tourism and hospitality-specific work of Shaw and Williams (1987), Thomas *et al.* (1997) and others. Yet, in focusing on these two categories, the model does not seek to deny the existence of other owner-manager profiles, and so it offers a multi-point scale between points *A* and *B*. The scaling enables the model to provide a vital step towards the synthesis of many of the existing classifications, a process which is much needed and which has recently been advocated by Day and Reynolds (1995). An example of the model's unifying potential is revealed by its compatibility with Hornaday's model (Hornaday, 1990), Chell and Haworth's tax-onomy (Chell and Haworth, 1990) and Carland *et al.*'s (1984) two-point classification of small business owners. An additional strength is the model's potential to serve as the basis for a viable test of subjective goal prioritization which would be resistant to the criticisms that have been levelled against many existing categorization procedures (Chell *et al.*, 1991).

The goal orientation model and associated test has a notable shortcoming, however, which limits its appropriateness as the basis for a taxonomic classification of small business owner-managers: the model presupposes that the owner-manager-oriented goals (see Figure 2.2) will provide the basis for their management strategies. The model therefore fails to take account of those owner-managers who may be able to express their goals for success readily, but who may be failing to implement strategies which are designed to satisfy the goals. Such a situation is possible in instances where owner-managers feel compelled either by the emphasis which is placed on entrepreneurial dynamism (Goss, 1991) or by, for example, their need to consider the terms and conditions of any lending agreement. Thus, they may instigate commercially oriented management strategies which do not accurately reflect their personal aspirations. Alternatively, owner-managers, while keen to pursue particular goals, may not have either the knowledge or the skills to develop pertinent strategies for their attainment (Shaw and Williams, 1997).

A focus on management strategies

An ideal method of addressing the weakness in the goal orientation model is to extend the focus of study to include those strategies which are used to achieve the owner-manager goals for success. Such an approach could replicate that outlined above, with those owner-managers who adopt commercially oriented strategies for the attainment of their personal goals being positioned at or close to point *A* of a management orientation model, while those who choose to emphasize lifestyle-oriented strategies would be positioned towards point *B* (see Figure 2.4). Again, it is envisaged that this model could provide the basis for an actual test of small business owner-managers' strategies for success, with their individual positioning along a base axis being plotted according to their prioritized ranking of specified strategies.

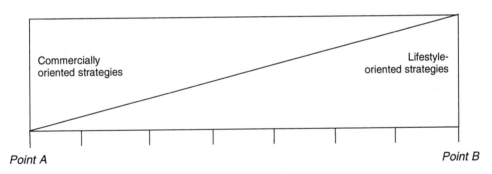

Figure 2.4   Management orientation model

By combining the two models outlined above, it is possible to devise a more rigorous taxonomy of small business owner-managers (see Figure 2.5). At a conceptual level, this model serves as a sophisticated bridge between several of the previously cited classifications which seek to categorize small business owner-managers.

A test could be devised which utilizes multivariate statistical procedures in an analysis of goal and management-oriented survey data. The result would be the positioning of individual owner-managers within a two-dimensional model of owner-manager tendencies (see Figure 2.6).

This model identifies two points where both the owner-managers' goals and management orientations are in harmony. Those owner-managers who espouse commercially

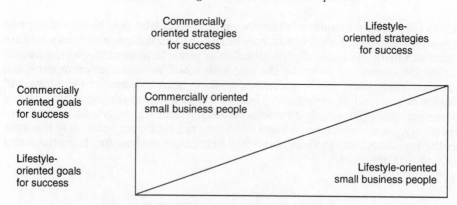

Figure 2.5   A taxonomy of small business owner-managers

oriented goals and who *do* implement sympathetic strategies for their attainment are likely to be positioned at or close to point *A* of the model. Conversely, those who hold to the lifestyle goals and choose to implement appropriate strategies are likely to be located at or close to point *B*. However, a note of caution must be expressed with regard to any such attempt to apply practically the model of owner-manager tendencies. Carson *et al.* (1995, p. 70) have stated that: 'It is ... recognised that after a certain stage of development a comfort factor becomes important to business owners and many run "lifestyle" firms.' This point is significant, as it suggests that owner-managers may alter their business perspectives over time and as a result of changes in their personal or environmental circumstances (see Figure 2.1). Fortunately, such shifts, which have been discussed by Chell *et al.* (1991) and Storey (1994), among others, can be accommodated within an operationalized version of the model of owner-manager tendencies, if it is seen as offering only a time-specific snapshot of an individual's profile. The model therefore provides a level of flexibility within its broad two-point typology which is not a feature of all classificatory options.

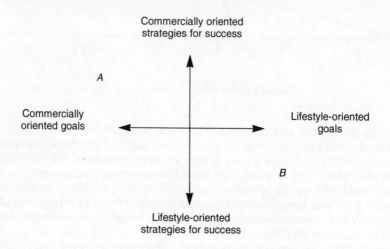

Figure 2.6   Model of owner-manager tendencies

The recognition of a bipolar multi-point classification, as set out in the taxonomy and the model of owner-manager tendencies, is quite distinctive, irrespective of its obvious links to other existing generic classifications. Indeed, it offers a fresh, dynamic insight which can be applied to the owner-managers of small tourism and hospitality businesses. It can be argued, on the basis of existing research (Stallinbrass, 1980; Brown, 1987; Williams *et al.*, 1989; Danvers and Thomas, 1995; Horobin and Long, 1996; Thomas *et al.*, 1997), that many owner managers in the tourism and hospitality industries might be positioned towards point *B* on the model of owner-manager orientations. This neither denies the existence of the 'entrepreneur' in a classical sense nor allocates the entrepreneur to a separate and, often by implication, elite grouping.

IMPLICATIONS FOR POLICY

This new insight does bring with it certain policy implications, especially for those agencies that are charged with providing support for small tourism and hospitality businesses.

Many of the support systems currently necessitate a high degree of commitment and involvement on the part of the small business operators. Yet many of the lifestyle-oriented owner-managers may be reluctant to make such a commitment, and they may be unwilling to search out the support which is available (Shaw and Williams, 1997). This reticence may stem from the fact that their businesses simply represent a means to a lifestyle-oriented end. Consequently, while their targets for success might be modest, the attainment of those targets might be hampered by a reluctance to engage actively in strategies for ensuring even the survival of their businesses. It is, therefore, necessary for support agencies to take the lead by seeking to engage these business owners. They should also endeavour to tailor their provision to the individual needs of the small business owner-manager by a process which begins with an assessment of the individual profiles of those whom they seek to assist. More particularly, they should begin with an evaluation of the owner-manager's goals and use these as the basis for devising tailored strategies for their attainment. Advocates of such an approach include Brownlie (1994, p. 38), who has stated that:

> in the context of finding a way to help small tourism enterprises ... it is not enough to promote a particular analytical technique or research method, leaving individual managers with the choice of trying to implement it themselves, or employing a consultant to do so. Practicable results can be achieved by working with the managers of small tourism enterprises to help them discover what approach best suits their needs and available resources.'

Of course, it can be argued that such a rigorous approach is not merited for those lifestyle-oriented owners who have no interest in growing their businesses. However, such an argument must be countered, not least because of the apparent numeric significance of such non-growth-oriented businesses operating in the tourism and hospitality industries. More significantly, it should be stated that, without such support, many of the small businesses may not be capable of long-term survival: this in turn could serve to jeopardize seriously both the economic health and the social fabric of those communities, resorts and regions which are becoming increasingly reliant upon tourism and hospitality-related activities.

CONCLUSIONS

This chapter has reviewed the existing generic and subject-specific work which seeks to provide an insight into the characteristics of small firm owners. In particular, it has brought together a variety of findings which have been used to construct a clearer picture of the small firm owner-manager in the tourism and hospitality industries.

This has been used as the starting point for a fresh insight based upon an individual's motivations and goals, which, when combined with a consideration of management strategies, have been used in the development of a model of owner-manager orientations. The significance of this model is twofold. First, it suggests a multi-point, dynamic classificatory framework which is not limited by either a drive to separate the 'entrepreneur' from the 'small business owner-manger', or the false hypothesis that a business will progress in a 'staged' manner. Second, the model offers the basis for an actual measurement scale which could be used by support agencies to engage more effectively the owner-managers of small firms.

Future research will therefore seek to develop a viable testing procedure based upon the model of owner-manager orientations. A procedure can be envisaged which would utilize data survey and multivariate statistical techniques in order to position the small business owners along what could be considered to be the base axis of the motivational model. A more rigorous procedure could then be developed which additionally focuses on the 'strategies for success' of the small business owners. It is possible that such an operationalized version of the model could be used for evaluating small businesses prior to the tailored application of support agency services. Ensuing research programmes will also focus on the nature of any observed dissimilarities between the goals and management strategies of small business owners.

The true significance of sectoral and spatial dimensions (highlighted in the work of Shaw and Williams, 1987) must also be assessed. For example, are those with a 'lifestyle' orientation likely to favour certain sectors of the tourism and hospitality industries (e.g. small-scale bed and breakfast) and/or certain geographic locations (rural, 'picturesque' destination areas)? Any variations in the scale of 'lifestyle' and 'commercially' oriented businesses (e.g. are 'lifestylers' likely to content themselves with smaller businesses?) should also be established.

REFERENCES

Bennett, R. (1990) *Successful Big Business Strategies for Small Firms*. London: Kogan Page.

Bird, B. (1988) 'Implementing entrepreneurial ideas: the case for intention', *Academy of Management Review*, **13(3)**, 442–53.

Brockhaus, R.H. (1980) 'Psychological and environmental factors which distinguish the successful from the unsuccessful entrepreneur: a longitudinal study'. *Paper presented at an Academy of Management meeting*.

Brockhaus, R.H. (1982) 'The psychology of the entrepreneur', in Kent, C.A., Sexton, D.L. and Vesper, K.H. (eds) *Encyclopaedia of Entrepreneurship*. Englewood Cliffs, NJ: Prentice Hall.

Brown, B. (1987) 'Recent tourism research in S.E. Dorset', in Shaw, G. and Williams,

A.M. (eds) *Tourism and Development: Overviews and Case Studies of the UK and SW Region, Discussion paper number 4. Exeter: Tourism Research Group, Department of Geography, University of Exeter*, 57–66.

Brownlie, D. (1994) 'Market opportunity analysis', *Tourism Management*, **15(1)**.

Burns, P. (1989) 'Strategies for success and routes to failure', in Burns, P. and Dewhurst, J. (eds) *Small Business and Entrepreneurship*. Basingstoke: Macmillan Education Press.

Burns, P. and Dewhurst, J. (eds) (1989) *Small Business and Entrepreneurship*. Basingstoke: Macmillan Education Press.

Caird, S. (1990) 'What does it mean to be enterprising?', *British Journal of Management*, **1(3)**, 137–45.

Carland, J.W., Hoy, F., Boulton, W.R. and Carland, J.A.C. (1984) 'Differentiating entrepreneurs from small business owners: a conceptualisation', *Academy of Management Review*, **9(2)**, 354–9.

Carland, J.W., Hoy, F. and Carland, J.A.C. (1988) 'Who is an entrepreneur? is a question worth asking', *American Journal of Small Business*, Spring, 33–9.

Carson, D., Cromie, S., McGowan, P. and Hill, J. (1995) *Marketing and Entrepreneurship in SMEs*. London: Prentice Hall.

Carsrud, A.L. and Johnson, R.N. (1989) 'Entrepreneurship: a social psychological perspective', *Journal of Entrepreneurship and Regional Development*, **1**, 21–31.

Casson, M. (1982) *The Entrepreneur – An Economic Theory*. Oxford: Martin Robertson.

Chell, E. (1985) 'The entrepreneurial personality: a few ghosts laid to rest?', *International Small Business Journal*, **3(3)**, 43–54.

Chell, E. and Haworth, J.M. (1988) 'Entrepreneurship and entrepreneurial management: the need for a paradigm', *Graduate Management Research*, **4(1)**, 16–33.

Chell, E. and Haworth, J.M. (1990) 'Profiling entrepreneurs: multiple perspectives and consequent methodological problems', *paper presented at the 4th Workshop on Recent Research in Entrepreneurship, EIASM/ECSM, Cologne*, 29–30 November.

Chell, E., Haworth, J.M. and Brearley, S.A. (1991) *The Entrepreneurial Personality: Concepts, Cases and Categories*. London: Routledge.

Collins, O.F. and Moore, D.G. (1970) *The Organization Makers*. New York: Appleton-Century-Crofts.

Collins, O.F., Moore, D.G. and Unwalla, D.B. (1964) *The Enterprising Man*. East Lansing, MI: East Lansing Graduate School of Business, Michigan State University.

Danvers, H. and Thomas, R. (1995) 'Small firms and sustainable tourism', *paper presented at the 4th Annual CHME Research Conference*, Norwich, April.

Danvers, H. and Long, J. (1996) 'All in the mind? The attitudes of small tourism businesses to sustainability', *paper presented at the IAHMS Spring Symposium*, Harrogate, March.

Davis, W. (1991) *Planning for Success*. London: English Tourist Board.

Day, J. and Reynolds, P. (1995) 'The importance of correctly defining entrepreneurs when studying SMEs', *paper presented at the 18th ISBA National Small Firms Conference*, Paisley, November.

Dewhurst, P.D. (1996) *England's most visited tourist attractions: an evaluation of success and taxonomic review*, unpublished PhD thesis, Manchester Metropolitan University.

Drucker, P.F. (1985) *Innovation and Entrepreneurship: Practice and Principles*. London: Heinemann.

Dunkelberg, W.C. and Cooper, A.A. (1982) 'Entrepreneurial typologies', in Vesper, K.H. (ed.) *Frontiers of Entrepreneurial Research*. Wellesley, MA: Boston College Center for Entrepreneurial Studies.

Foley, P. and Green, H. (1989) *Small Business Success*. London: Paul Chapman Publishing.

Goffee, R. and Scase, R. (1983) 'Class entrepreneurship and the service sector: towards a conceptual clarification', *Service Industries Journal*, **3**, 146–60.

Goss, D. (1991) *Small Business and Society*. London: Routledge.

Hampson, S.E. (1982) *The Construction of Personality*. London: Routledge and Kegan Paul.

Hannagan, T. (1995) *Management Concepts and Practices*. London: Pitman.

Harper, M. (1984) *Small Businesses in the Third World: Guidelines for Practical Assistance*. Chichester: Wiley.

Hebert, R.F. and Link, A.N. (1988) *The Entrepreneur – Mainstream Views and Radical Critiques*, 2nd edn. New York: Praeger.

Hornaday, R.W. (1990) 'Dropping the E-words from small business research', *Journal of Small Business Management*, **28(4)**, 22–33.

Horobin, H. and Long, J. (1996) 'Sustainable tourism: the role of the small firm', *International Journal of Contemporary Hospitality Management*, **8(5)**, 15–19.

Hotel and Catering Training Company (HCTC) (1994) *The Catering and Hospitality Industry – Key Facts and Figures*. London: HCTC.

Johnson, G. and Scholes, K. (1993) *Exploring Corporate Strategy*. London: Prentice Hall International.

Kanter, R.M. (1983) *The Change Masters*. New York: Simon and Schuster.

Katz, J. and Gartner, W.B. (1988) 'Properties of emerging organisations', *Academy of Management Review*, **13(3)**, 429–41.

Keeble, D. and Wever, E. (1986) 'Introduction', in Keeble, D. and Wever, E. (eds) *New Firms and Regional Development in Europe*. Andover: Croom Helm, 1–34.

Knight, F.H. (1921) *Risk, Uncertainty and Profit*. New York: Houghton Mifflin.

McClelland, D.C. (1961) *The Achieving Society*. Princeton, NJ: Van Nostrand.

McClelland, D.C. (1987) 'Characteristics of successful entrepreneurs', *Journal of Creative Behaviour*, **21(3)**, 219–33.

Scarborough, N.M. and Zimmerer, T.W. (1996) *Effective Small Business Management*. Englewood Cliffs, NJ: Prentice Hall.

Scase, R. and Goffee, R. (1980) *The Real World of the Small Business Owner*. London: Croom Helm.

Scase, R. and Goffee, R. (1982) *The Entrepreneurial Middle Class*. London: Croom Helm.

Schumaker, E.F. (1973) *Small Is Beautiful*. London: Abacus.

Schumpeter, J.A. (1934) *The Theory of Economic Development*. Cambridge, MA: Harvard University Press.

Schumpeter, J.A. (1961) *The Theory of Economic Development: An Inquiry into Profits, Capital, Credit, Interest and the Business Cycle*. New York: Oxford University Press.

Schwaninger, M. (1986) 'Strategic business management in tourism', *Tourism Management*, **7(2)**, 77–85.

Shailer, G. (1994) 'Capitalists and entrepreneurs in owner-managed firms', *International Small Business Journal*, **12(3)**, 33–41.

Shaw, G. and Williams, A.M. (1987) 'Firm formation and operating characteristics in the Cornish tourism industry – the case of Looe', *Tourism Management*, December, 344–8.

Shaw, G. and Williams, A.M. (1990) 'Tourism, economic development and the role of entrepreneurial activity', in Cooper, C.P. (ed.) *Progress in Tourism, Recreation and Hospitality Management, Volume 2*. London: Bellhaven, 67–81.

Shaw, G. and Williams, A.M. (1994) 'Tourism and entrepreneurship', in Shaw, G. and Williams, A.M. (eds) *Critical Issues in Tourism: A Geographical Perspective*. Oxford: Blackwell, 120–37.

Shaw, G. and Williams, A.M. (1997) 'The private sector: tourism entrepreneurship – a constraint or resource?, in Shaw G. and Williams, A.M. (eds) *The Rise and Fall of British Coastal Resorts: Cultural and Economic Perspectives*. London: Pinter, 117–36.

Shaw, G., Williams, A.M. and Greenwood, J. (1987) *Tourism and the Economy of Cornwall: A Firm Level Study of Operating Characteristics and Employment*. Exeter: Tourism Research Group, Department of Geography, University of Exeter.

Smith, N.R. (1967) *The Entrepreneur and His Firm: The Relationship between Type of Man and Type of Company*. East Lansing, MI: Michigan State University Press.

Stacey, R.D. (1993) *Strategic Management and Organisational Management*. London: Pitman.

Stallinbrass, C. (1980) 'Seaside resorts and the hotel accommodation industry', *Progress in Planning*, **13**, 103–74.

Stanworth, J. and Curran, J. (1976) 'Growth and the small firm: an alternative view', *Journal of Management Studies*, **13**, 95–110.

Stanworth, J. and Curran, J. (1982) 'Growth and the small firm', in Gorb, P., Dowell, P. and Wilson, P. (eds) *Small Business Perspectives*. London: Armstrong.

Stanworth, J. and Gray, C. (eds) (1991) *Bolton 20 Years on: The Small Firm in the 1990s*. London: Paul Chapman Publishing.

Stevenson, H.H. and Sahlman, W.A. (1986) 'The importance of entrepreneurship in economic development', in Hirsch R.D. (ed.) *Entrepreneurship, Intrapreneurship and Venture Capital*. Lexington, MA: Lexington Books, 1–26.

Storey, D.J. (1994) *Understanding the Small Business Sector*. London: Routledge.

Storey, D.J. and Strange, A. (1993) *Entrepreneurship in Cleveland 1979–1989*. Warwick: Warwick Business School, University of Warwick.

Swarbrooke, J. (1995) *The Development and Management of Visitor Attractions*. Oxford: Butterworth-Heinemann.

Thomas R., Friel, M., Jameson, S. and Parsons, D. (1997) *The National Survey of Small Tourism and Hospitality Firms: Annual Report 1996/7*. Leeds: Centre for the Study of Small Tourism and Hospitality Firms, Leeds Metropolitan University.

van Harssel, J. (1994) *Tourism: An Exploration*. Englewood Cliffs, NJ: Prentice Hall International.

Wild, C.N. (1995) 'Fragmentation in the tourism industry', in Witt, S.F. and Moutinho, L. (eds) *Tourism Marketing and Management Handbook*. Hemel Hempstead: Prentice Hall International.

Williams, A.M. and Shaw, G. (1990) *Tourism Entrepreneurs: A Leisured Class?* Exeter: Tourism Research Group, Department of Geography, University of Exeter.

Williams, A.M., Shaw, G. and Greenwood, J. (1989) 'From tourist to tourism entrepreneur, from consumption to production: evidence from Cornwall, England', *Environment and Planning A*, **21**, 1639–53.

Woo, C., Cooper, A.C. and Dunkelberg, W.C. (1988) *Entrepreneurial Typologies:*

Definitions and Implications. Wellesley, MA: Boston College Center for Entrepreneurial Studies, 165–76.

Wynarczyk, P., Watson, R., Storey, D., Short, H. and Keasey, K. (1993) *Managerial Labour Markets in Small and Medium-sized Enterprises*. London: Routledge.

THREE

An assessment of small business failure

Andrew Boer

The fundamental characteristic, other than size per se, which distinguishes small firms from large is their higher probability of ceasing to trade ... no policy can be formulated for small firms without a central understanding of the importance of business failure. (Storey, 1994, p. 78)

Given the economic significance of the small firm sector, it comes as a surprise to note that little rigorous research has been done into the causes and nature of small firm failure. This chapter reviews the definitions of 'failure' which have been used, and provides a brief statistical overview of the extent of small firm failure. The differing 'schools of thought' regarding the causes of small firm failure are then analysed, and the chapter concludes with an assessment of the likely causes of failure in the tourism and hospitality industries.

DEFINITION OF SMALL FIRM 'FAILURE'

The understanding of small business 'failure' has been impeded by several problems, not least the lack of generally agreed definitions of the terms 'small business' and 'failure'. In theory, it would seem that agreed definitions of both these terms would be prerequisites for both policy-making and research, but, in practice, agreement on the interpretation of these terms does not exist, and a variety of different definitions are available.

When one reviews the current literature, it becomes apparent that the terms 'business death', 'discontinuance', 'insolvency', 'failure' and 'bankruptcy' are often seen to be synonymous, and that the clarity of these terms is further confused by the emotive and frequently negative nature of perceptions regarding this subject. Cochran (1981) attempts to overcome these differing definitions by developing a continuum of business failure, with, at one extreme, businesses which have been declared bankrupt and, at the other end of the spectrum, businesses which have discontinued owing to 'extraneous' factors, such as retirement, illness or alternative opportunities being pursued. Although this may be seen to be an attempt to overcome the emotive aspects of the term 'failure', Cochran carefully avoids identifying any point at which the business can be deemed to have 'failed' or even ceased to exist. Instead, he suggests that Ulmer and Nielsen's (1980) definition – '*firms that were disposed of (sold or liquidated) with losses or to avoid losses*' – is that which '*comes closest to capturing the intuitive sense of failure*'. Cynically, it may be observed that, 'intuitive' or 'aesthetic' sense of appeasement aside, this definition lacks the practical value of being able to be objectively quantified using currently available data.

A major preoccupation of many researchers is the ability to use a definition of 'failure' which is both practical and quantifiable, and this may explain the widespread usage and popularity of accounting definitions of 'failure'. Foremost among these is the definition suggested by Altman (1983). Failure, he suggests, is the state when '*the realised rate of return on invested capital is significantly and continually below prevailing rates on similar investments*' (Altman, 1983, p. 6). However, it may be observed that many small firms (as compared to large firms) may continue to function for a considerable time while still fulfilling this condition.

For practical purposes, it would be useful to differentiate between the various types of 'failure', but currently collated government statistics do not reflect this. Instead the statistics only differentiate between insolvencies ('compulsory' or 'creditors' voluntary' liquidations) and bankruptcies. 'Insolvencies' include only the firms registered at Company House (and thus exclude partnerships, sole traders and all the small unregistered firms in the economy), whereas the term 'bankruptcies' includes reference not only to individuals but also to a majority of the smaller firms in the economy. Consequently, the government statistics referring to bankruptcies can be seen to be only an approximation to the failure of unlimited firms.

Stewart and Gallagher (1986) argue that the government statistics are also subject to serious detrimental time lags, and can thus provide only an approximate measure of 'failure', whereas VAT data can give a more immediate overview of the number of firms deregistering, a figure which they believe is a close approximation to business dissolution. Although VAT data have the benefit of encompassing a greater range and number of firms, Stewart and Gallagher concede that there is likely to be a difference between bankruptcies and VAT deregistrations.

This disparity can be explained by suggesting that the government statistics tend to be preoccupied with either 'limited liability' companies or 'bankruptcies', whereas Stewart and Gallagher (1986, p. 46) suggest that a majority of firms (both limited and unlimited liability) cease trading not through insolvency or bankruptcy, but because '*the majority simply choose to stop trading, the owners changing to another activity*'. This view may be challenged as being a simplistic interpretation of 'deregistration', but estimates of firms which voluntarily choose to stop trading vary between 50 (Stewart and Gallagher, 1986) and 90 per cent (Daly, 1990).

The Dun and Bradstreet International (1982) definition of company failure is widely referred to and recognized by many authors as being one of the more competent definitions available:

> business failure includes those businesses that ceased operations following assignment of bankruptcy; ceased with loss to creditors after such actions as execution, foreclosure or attachment, voluntarily withdrew leaving unpaid obligations; were involved in actions such as receiverships, reorganisation or arrangement; or voluntarily compromised with creditors.

The complexity of this definition should not in itself imply that the Dun and Bradstreet definition is the best or most appropriate. Instead, it may be that its adoption in research projects has more to do with Dun and Bradstreet's consistent set of statistics in this subject area, which span over a century. The practical ability to apply theories directly to the compiled statistics may be more important to researchers than minor definitional disparities.

The work of Ganguly (1985) and, latterly Daly (1990) is frequently cited as some of the most comprehensive statistical treatment of small firm failure in the United Kingdom. In both instances, VAT registrations and deregistrations are used as a proxy for firms' 'births' and 'deaths', although, as Ganguly (1985, p. 29) points out,

> new registrations are not all genuine births and not all births are registered, similarly traders deregistering are not all firms going out of business and not all the firms going out of business were registered for VAT purposes.

It is consequently suggested that these statistics are used with caution, in that many small firms may never register for VAT (either because their financial turnover may not warrant it or for fraudulent reasons), and consequently the estimates may fall short of the real total number of 'births' and 'deaths'. Similarly, as Daly (1990, p. 563) observes, *'there are a number of reasons for "deregistering", not all of them implying a "failure"'*.

These criticisms should not be seen to invalidate the use of VAT registrations and deregistrations as a database of company activity in the United Kingdom. Indeed, as with the American Dun and Bradstreet statistics, the collation of VAT statistics provides a contemporary and easily accessible overview of company 'birth' and 'failure', and may be considered to be a rich source of business information, as well as providing a sound and ongoing guide to small business trends.

EMPIRICAL AND STATISTICAL ANALYSIS OF SMALL FIRM FAILURE

As far back as 1965, Brooker commented upon the inadequacy of the United Kingdom insolvency statistics, and noted that *'it seems that the insolvency statistics have very limited economic application'* (Brooker, 1965, p. 142). This problem has, to a certain extent, continued to the present day, with both the Bolton Committee and more contemporary authors such as Storey (1994) drawing attention to the fact that there is a dearth of timely, reliable and relevant information on small business failure rates. More recently, there has been greater interest and research carried out in the area of small business management, but comparatively few empirical and quantitative pieces of research have been completed in the area of small firm failure.

The empirical research that has been published falls into two main categories: that which gives a regular periodic and ongoing overview of small firm failure; and individual, 'one-off', pieces of research into a specific aspect of small firm failure. Although the latter are more prevalent, it is the former which form the statistical 'core' of research into this area.

Small firm failure: statistical overview

The past decades have been characterized by a marked growth in the number of small firms in the economy. Using Central Statistical Office data, it is possible to identify an increase of 9 per cent in the number of companies registering for VAT in the decade 1984 to 1994, with the largest industrial increases occurring in the financial and telecommunications industries. It is also notable that most of this growth occurred between 1987 and 1991, with a subsequent steady decline until 1994 (see Figure 3.1). Although this decline may be treated with some surprise, given the recent media coverage of the 'revival' of the economy, it must be remembered that the deregistration of firms may represent companies which ceased to trade in previous years but which have only officially deregistered in a later year.

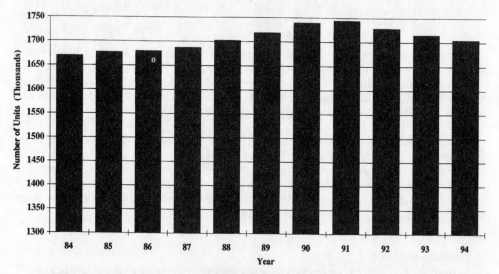

Figure 3.1 Number of legal units registered for VAT by year, all industries, 1984 to 1994
Source: Central Statistical Office (1995).

Although, over the same period, the stock of hotel and catering companies registering for VAT has declined, it may be noted that this industry bears a strong resemblance to the profile of firms in the national economy generally (see Figure 3.2). If one investigates these statistics further, it is notable that between 1987 and 1994 this total figure does not represent an increase in deregistrations, but a lower number of companies registering for VAT. This may have several interpretations, not least that companies in this industry have low turnovers (consequently they are not required to register for VAT) or, alternatively, that potential entrepreneurs are being dissuaded from investing in the industry.

It may also be observed that, although registrations have declined, the proportion of deregistrations (and consequently 'failures') has remained comparatively constant over this period. From this it may be surmised that, despite changes in the market concentration, the failure rate remains consistent irrespective of economic or other factors – again justifying the need to review the failure rates of this industry. Indeed, the net change in the number of hotel and catering firms in the decade ending in 1979 is considerably smaller than in most other industries, and may be seen as indicative of a

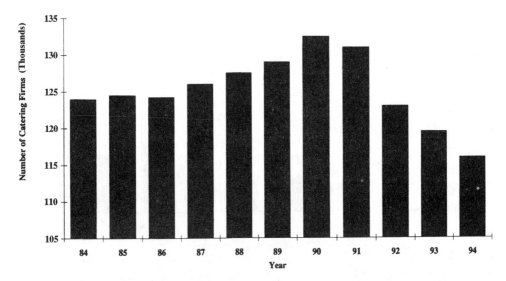

Figure 3.2   Number of hotel and catering firms registered for VAT, 1984 to 1994
Source: Central Statistical Office (1995).

saturated market, a declining industry or, as previously stated, an industry with an exceptionally high failure rate.

Small firm failure by industry

If the individual industries are scrutinized, it is noticeable that some of the industries which exhibited marked growth during the decade 1980 to 1990 (in particular, construction and transport) have a correspondingly high percentage of bankruptcies. However, using Central Statistical Office data, it is also notable that the tourism and hospitality industries had a consistently high bankruptcy rate during the same decade (usually being the second highest after the construction industry), but did not exhibit the same proportionate growth.

Using the same statistical source, it is evident that there has been a marked increase in the number of 'failures' in the past five years, and that a majority of the firms ceasing to trade do so because of bankruptcy (as opposed to insolvencies) (see Figure 3.3). This, in turn, demonstrates a tendency for the failures to originate from individuals and their companies, as opposed to registered companies, again indicating the high proportion of small firm failures in this industry.

It may be concluded, therefore, that the level of failure in this industry is less affected by external economic constraints and stays at a characteristically high level on a constant basis.

Small firm failure by age

Several individual pieces of research have been carried out into the 'lifespan' of small firms in an attempt to gauge their 'life expectancy'.

Altman (1983, p, 421) noted that '*it is well documented that there is greater propensity*

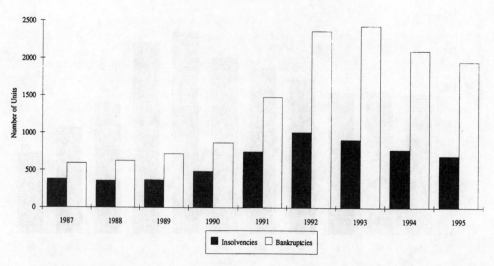

Figure 3.3 Bankruptcies and insolvencies in the hotel and catering industries, 1987 to 1995
Source: Central Statistical Office (1996).

for younger firms to fail than for more mature companies', and he went on to suggest that a majority of firms failed within the first five years of their life. This conclusion seems to be largely upheld by other authors researching the same area, and Figure 3.4 represents a compilation of the research results of four different surveys into the 'lifespan of firms'.

The Dun and Bradstreet (1982) results were compiled over a ten-year period and were related to companies in the United Kingdom which conformed to the Dun and

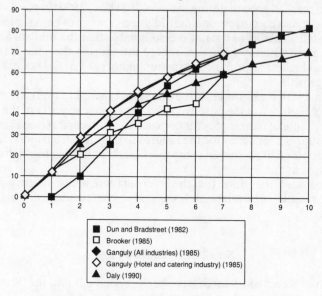

Figure 3.4 Lifespan of firms by cumulative percentage
Source: Various, see key.

Bradstreet definition of 'failure'. They suggest that a majority of small firms (53 per cent) will have failed within five years of starting up, and that over 80 per cent can expect to have failed within ten years of starting up.

Brooker (1985), taking his source of 'failure' from the English insolvency statistics of the 1960s, revealed a slightly different profile, with a generally longer lifespan and with 60 per cent of the firms having a life expectancy of up to seven years.

Ganguly's (1985) analysis of the life expectancy of small firms spanned only seven years. However, using VAT registrations and deregistrations as a basis, this research presented a more pessimistic perspective on the likely length of survival of small firms. Ganguly concluded that just over 50 per cent of small firms would fail within four years, after which the 'failure rate' would be reduced, with 30 per cent of small firms surviving more than seven years. It is of particular interest to note that his conclusions regarding the expected lifespan of an 'average' firm (i.e. a representation of the 'mean' of all industries) closely correlates with the expected life span of a firm in the 'hotel and catering' catering (so closely, in fact, that in Figure 3.4 the series points of 'all industries' are obscured by the 'hotel and catering' series points).

Daly's (1990) more recent research, using a similar database to Ganguly, depicts a more positive image of the small firm's lifespan. In this he reports that, in common with the Dun and Bradstreet results, 53 per cent of all firms will have ceased to trade by their fifth year, but thereafter their demise is less likely to be as swift, with 30 per cent of firms surviving through to their tenth year. This is not only the most recent of the surveys selected but also the most optimistic.

When these pieces of research are compared, obvious disparities emerge, such as the type of economic environment affecting the sample, the locations and the times at which the surveys were carried out. None the less, the fact that is clearly common to all of them, irrespective of the disparities, is the relatively restricted lifespan of the sample firms, with most of the research reports indicating that firms with a lifespan of above five years are in a minority.

Small firm failure by region

Ganguly's (1985) study of 'births and deaths' of firms in the early 1980s indicates that the region with the highest company 'births', as a percentage of all businesses registered for VAT, was the South-east of England, and the region having the highest percentage of 'deaths', as a percentage of all businesses registered for VAT, was the North-west.

Significantly, Daly's research in 1990, which largely replicated that of Ganguly, gives an identical result despite the regionalized assistance provided by the government in the intervening period. Neither of the pieces of research, however, ventures to give explanations for these figures, and both authors seem content with reporting their findings.

In more recent research, Keeble *et al.* (1993) report that there appears to be a correlation between the urban density of an area and a high rate of small firm failure. This, it is suggested, may be owing to a higher number of new firm formations and the consequent vulnerability of firms at this stage of their development. Thus, a high amount of competition and a lack of appropriate financial or skill resources are likely to have a more significant detrimental effect on firms at this stage of their development than at a later stage, when, usually, additional resources have been accumulated.

CAUSES OF SMALL FIRM FAILURE

The UK authorities, unlike those in the USA, do not collate reasons for small firm failure, and the commercial banks' and liquidators, codes of conduct on confidentiality further hinder the analysis of this area. In order to get an accurate overview of the subject, it is consequently important to differentiate between information which is of a subjective, anecdotal nature and that which is based on credible research. Of the former, there is an abundance, much of which reflects the authors, 'experience' or a particular perspective which they wish to highlight, and, although they are sometimes naive and simplistic, these articles do tend to represent much of the 'conventional wisdom' of the subject.

There is a need to highlight the complexity of compiling information in this area, as there is no common definitional 'frame of reference' available. Consequently, one author may refer to 'reasons' for small firm failure, whereas another may refer to 'causes', and yet another to 'initiators of bankruptcy'. Similarly, 'poor management', as a cause of small firm failure, may be defined as 'management incompetence', 'management neglect' or even 'insufficient managerial financial knowledge'. Some authors do not even attempt to distinguish between the 'symptoms' and the 'causes' of small firm failure. One of the few points on which there seems to be agreement is that small firm failure is often attributable to several different factors. However, this does not prevent many of the authors from propounding or focusing on one particular factor to the exclusion of the others.

In an attempt to overcome some of these difficulties, Bunn (1987) divides the reasons for small business failure into 'primary' and 'contributory' factors, with which he attempts to distinguish between the critical and less important problems. Fredland and Morris (1976), however, classify the causes of business failure as either 'endogenous' (internal and within the firm's control) or 'exogenous' (external to the firm and outside its control). This, they suggest, will assist in allocating responsibility in policy-making for small firms. Thus, if the main factors are 'exogenous', the main responsibility for help is placed on the government, and if the main factors are 'endogenous', it is the firm's responsibility to help itself, perhaps with minor government support in the form of training programmes. Using this as a framework, it is possible to focus on particular causes of small firm failure in greater depth.

Endogenous causes of small firm failure

A large proportion of both the subjective and empirical research in the area of the 'causes of small firm failure' concentrates on the endogenous (or internal) factors, the main one of which is often perceived to be 'poor management', followed by 'undercapitalization'. It may be argued, however, that all the 'internally generated' causes of failure may be seen as a subset of poor management, and that factors such as 'under capitalization', 'lack of planning or control' and 'inexperience' are frequently accentuated by 'managerial incompetence'.

Poor management
Much of the literature regarding 'start-ups' of small firms refers frequently to the personal characteristics of the individual starting up the small firm, and the managerial shortcomings of the entrepreneur.

Research published by Dun and Bradstreet (1991) is unequivocal in stating that the primary cause of business failure in the USA is 'management incompetence' of the owner of the business. In their survey of reasons for failure, 66 per cent of the failures were attributed to managerial incompetence, which was considered to include aspects of owners' inability to plan, analyse, control or direct the operation of the business.

Gibb and Webb (1980), in their examination of the records of over 200 bankrupt firms, similarly concluded that the main cause of failure in small firms in the UK was a lack of knowledge and 'neglect' by management. There are several other pieces of empirical research which support this finding (Lauzen, 1985; McNight, 1990). However, it is notable that few of these go into any great detail in defining the meaning of management incompetence or neglect.

One exception is McKinlay (1979), who attempted to define management short-comings by considering the likely components of such a state (inept financial management, little control over inventories, absence of planning, lack of consultation, etc.). He concludes:

> few insolvencies are primarily and fundamentally caused by the inability to obtain necessary financing, instead it is usually inadequacies in administrative functions ... specifically manifest by the absence of even rudimentary knowledge of financial planning and control. (McKinlay, 1979, p. 21)

This emphasis on the knowledge of the manager is further investigated by Larson and Clute (1979), who, in a sample of 359 small firms in Chicago, noted that a large proportion of the units experiencing difficulty tended to 'denigrate' management education and training, leading to their suggestion that '*perhaps the most common management problem is the assumption that all problems, especially financial ones, are exogenous in nature*' (Larson and Clute, 1979, p. 39).

Peterson *et al.* (1983), in a survey covering over 1000 small firms in the USA, are unequivocal in reporting that the primary cause of failure is the 'lack of management expertise', to which, they suggest, the solution is to provide better management education. In a more recent survey in the USA, Bates (1990) suggests that higher levels of education might be associated with higher survival rates, a finding generally reflected by Cressey (1992) in the UK. Although this may initially be perceived to be a simplistic interpretation and response to the high number of small firm bankruptcies in both the USA and the UK, it is one which tends to predominate in much of this subject literature and also illustrates one of the main difficulties in this form of analysis – that of individual perspective.

A multitude of articles and references review the small business owner's inability to handle the business aspects of the firm, but they seem to ignore the owner's perspective on or explanations of the causes of failure. On the other hand, it could equally be suggested that to review merely the owner's perspectives would lead to a biased view, where blame may be allocated not to management incompetence, but to a range of other 'external' factors and, as Hall and Young (1991, p. 58) observe, '*owners may well lack objectivity and probably expertise in interpretation of their own business failings*'.

Undercapitalization

In his survey of 437 small firms, Bunn (1987) reports that undercapitalization was cited as a primary cause of failure in 54 per cent of cases and as a contributory factor in 77 per cent of cases. Although providing the right level of capital could be seen as the task of the manager, Bunn concedes that there might be an element of bias in the survey, given that the data were derived from bank managers and not the small firms concerned.

In a research project looking at small firms and Enterprise Agency assistance, Smallbone (1990) endorses Bunn's finding and suggests that a large proportion of small firms which fail within their first year of operation fail due to undercapitalization. He does, however, go on to point out that, in common with Bunn's conclusions, the second most cited cause of failure (which tended to be prevalent in firms which had been operational for more than one year) was '*a lack of motivation or ability needed to run a successful business*' (Smallbone, 1990, p. 42).

Two of the most notable pieces of research conducted in this area were studies by Hall and Young (1991) and Brough (1970). Although the latter is now over 25 years old, it is notable as the first rigorous attempt to analyse the causes of failure in this way, and it is also useful as a basis for comparison with Hall and Young's research, which duplicated its methodology some twenty years later.

Brough reviewed the reports of the official receivers for over 100 English companies and compared the official receivers' views of the reasons for failure with those of the directors of the companies concerned. Not surprisingly, perhaps, they differed. The directors perceived the lack of working capital and undercapitalization as the principal causes of failure, whereas the official receivers were overwhelmingly of the view that most of the failures were due to mismanagement (see Figure 3.5).

This may be seen to be a natural reaction from the directors in trying to apportion blame away from their own managerial skills, and there are a wide range of other causes given by the directors which may have been interpreted by the official receivers as indications of mismanagement (poor labour, shortage of materials, increasing over-heads, etc.). Nevertheless, although the official receivers do acknowledge the lack of capital as being of importance, the term 'mismanagement' may again be seen as a convenient term with which to cover a multitude of factors, even though the official receivers do list some factors, such as bad debts and overtrading, separately.

Both sets of respondents seemed to agree that a majority of the causes of failure were internal to the companies, with the directors listing only bad weather and competition as being factors which were outside the control of the companies.

Hall and Young (1991) conducted a similar piece of research by reviewing 300 companies' files and comparing both directors' and official receivers' views of the causes of company failure. Again, the directors' perception of the single principal cause of failure was undercapitalization. However, it is noticeable that there is a heavier emphasis on, and recognition of, mismanagement, perhaps indicating a more realistic perspective from the directors (see Figure 3.6). Of this, Hall and Young (1991, p. 59) observe that '*one might have expected a bias from owners towards factors beyond their control, but there is no evidence of this*', external or 'environmental' factors (fire, theft, interest and exchange rates, etc.) are seen largely as a matter of 'bad luck', rather than factors which can be controlled by either the company or the government.

Perhaps the largest difference between the two pieces of research is that the official receivers' perception of the main reason for failure changes from management (according to Brough) to undercapitalization, with over 52 per cent of the official receivers noting this as the principal cause. Little explanation is given for this finding, beyond the comment that:

> the emphasis on purely financial factors cannot easily be dismissed as the preoccupation of accountants [and the] adequacy of the capital market may need to be reviewed in light of the needs of small firms. (Hall and Young, 1991, p. 61)

Taking into account differences in terminology and research methodology (which in themselves could invalidate any conclusions), a comparison of these surveys illustrates not only the emphasis which has been placed upon mismanagement and under-capitalization as causes of small firm failure, but also a potential change in the role and significance of the lending institutions in providing financial support for small firms. It would be both an interesting an useful exercise to repeat these surveys for the purpose of comparison, but in view of changes in codes of confidentiality and differences in reporting requirements, such research would be complex, if not impossible.

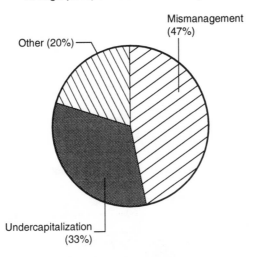

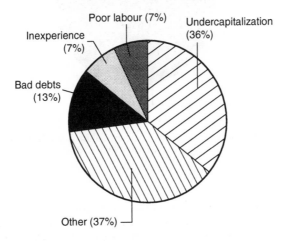

Figure 3.5 Views of reasons for company failure from Brough's research
Source: Brough (1970).

Hall (1995) Official Receivers' Opinions

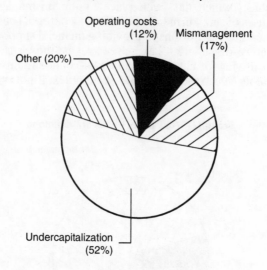

Hall (1995) Directors' Opinions

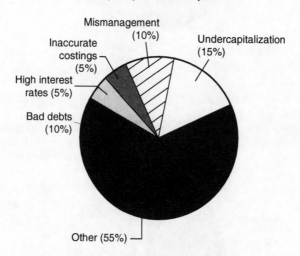

Figure 3.6 Views of reasons for company failure from Hall's research
Source: Hall (1995).

Inexperience

Inexperience as a cause of small firm failure is sometimes listed and perceived as a distinct entity, separate from poor management. Certainly, Dun and Bradstreet (1991) considered it to be the second most important cause of business failure, accounting for 29 per cent of their sample of failed firms. This lack of experience may be caused by 'lack of managerial experience', 'lack of line experience' or 'unbalanced previous experience', although this does not reveal, in any depth, its exact definition or its manifestations when applied to small firms.

Williams (1985) in a survey of retail firms, noted that 82 per cent of the failed firms' owners had no previous experience in the industry, whereas of the surviving firms, 85 per cent had directly related managerial experience in the retail industry. A supposition that can thus be made is that there is a positive correlation between related previous managerial experience and the survival of the firm, a view that is supported by the work of Townroe and Mallalieu (1993), who suggest that the experience of managing others and the opportunity to learn from previous mistakes can be a positive influence on small firm survival. This complements the earlier work of Stanworth *et al.* (1989), who identified that a history of involvement in a family firm, even if indirect, can be crucial in avoiding difficulties, owing to access to business advice and even financial and moral support.

Lack of planning and control

These are causes which are cited as being of importance by several authors, yet which have little objective or empirical research to support them.

Eversley *et al.* (1983) comment on the importance of credit control, while Hartigan (1976) concentrates on the importance of a coordinated system of record keeping, and Lauzen (1985, p. 37) observes, perhaps somewhat obviously, that without adequate planning and control, *'the likelihood of failure is greatly increased'*. Whereas the importance of these skills is undeniable to any firm, it may be observed that this category may have been subsumed into 'poor management' by other researchers, hence accounting for its lack of recognition in empirical studies.

Other causes

While there is a plethora of other causes of failure which are fleetingly mentioned by many of the authors, very few of these 'contributory' factors are recognized or analysed in any great depth. Abelsamad and Kindling (1978) attempt to supplement the literature with an analysis of causes which, they feel, are given insufficient attention in the available texts.

In a largely subjective article, they cover several operational reasons for failure (failure to grow with the company, negligence in developing subordinates, etc.) and conclude by suggesting 14 'financial pitfalls' to avoid. This generalized approach is typical of a wide range of articles and books, which either propose unsubstantiated causes of failure or skim the surface of the reasons and offer advice on how to avoid getting into these situations. Whereas these texts have a place in the literature covering the subject, it is felt that they contribute little of significance to a serious review.

Exogenous causes of small firm failure

While managerial incompetence may continue to be perceived as one of the primary causes of small firms going bankrupt, it can also be argued that many small firms are, at present, being incompetently managed, yet still continue to survive. A manager may thus be able to manage a hotel or restaurant incompetently in an economic boom, but may not be able to manage the business in this manner during an economic recession. The former may lead to continued survival, the latter to failure. It may consequently be argued that it is the owner's ability to manage in face of specific economic environmental variables that determines the firm's success or failure, and that it is, in fact, these economic variables which are often the 'initiators' of small firm failure.

Relatively little research has taken account of these additional variables, with many authors preferring to analyse the factors which seem to remain constant in the situation (i.e. the managers or the operation itself). Two researchers who do attempt to take these variables into account are Fredland and Morris (1976), who not only suggest dividing the causes of small firm failure between endogenous and exogenous factors, but further suggest subdividing the latter into macroeconomic and microeconomic factors.

Evidence concerning the impact of the microeconomic variables is, they consider, scarce, although they concede that economic factors of specific relevance to particular small firms (such as the food hygiene laws in the tourism and hospitality industries) will obviously have some effect. Instead, it is the macroeconomic variables (such as credit controls, loan security requirements and interest rates) which, they feel, will have the greatest impact on small firms and their rate of failure.

To a certain extent this is not an innovative idea. The impact of a recession and its effect on the small firm failure rate have been relatively well documented, even if not empirically proved. Fredland and Morris, however, set out to prove a statistical link between firm size and failure, taking aspects such as loan security requirements into account. They concluded that 'failure' is not strongly correlated to the size of a firm; however, *'there is considerable statistical evidence that economic aggregates do influence the number of business failures'* (Fredland and Morris, 1976, p. 7).

In a later study, Clute and Garman (1980) considered the relationship between the rate of business failure and US economic policies, such as variations in the volume of bank loans and fluctuations in the amount of money supply and interest rates. Using an econometric model, they reported that a reduction in the volume of bank loans or money supply was likely to lead to a short-term increase in business failure, while such a co-relation between interest rates and business failure did not exist. This conclusion is further supported by the work of Hudson (1986), who found that higher interest rates are associated with a lower level of company liquidations.

These latter findings may be considered by many to be surprising, as some categories of business, such as hotel and catering firms, will, by their very nature, require high investment in fixed assets, much of which is likely to be dependent on long-term loans from commercial lending institutions. As a consequence, changes in interest rates are likely to have a comparatively larger effect on small firms that are more highly geared than on those with a lower gearing ratio. Clute and Garman's observation may thus be technically correct but, in the instance of the tourism and hospitality industry, may not apply in its totality, and the work of Keeble *et al.* (1993) supports the view that the effect of interest rates will vary according to the nature and characteristics of the industry under scrutiny.

Exogenous and endogenous causes of small firm failure

Only two pieces of research have been found which give equal consideration to both internal and external factors.

Di Petro and Sawhrey (1977) used an econometric model to assess the theoretical effects of both managerial competence and economic variables upon firm failure. They concluded that both factors will have an influence on the rate of small firm failures. However, with an increase in managerial knowledge, the influence of external factors in determining failure rates is likely to diminish. This is not a novel conclusion, and it bears resemblance to Peterson's view that a better trained managerial workforce will have a greater comprehension of the economic environment and the ability to alter and adapt the organization to changes within the economy.

Miller (1977) analysed environmental variables and organizational factors to try to find 'syndromes' of business failure and, in common with many other authors, considered that causes of failure invariably stem from 'poor management', as opposed to external influences. However, although both Di Petro and Sawhrey and Miller come to similar conclusions, the nature and basis from which Miller derives his conclusions is, at best, suspect, and the article concludes with a prescriptive list of 'warning signs of failure' which does little to enhance either its academic depth or its credibility.

Causes of small firm failure in the tourism and hospitality industries

In hotel and catering small firm failures, it can be seen that several disparities exist, not least the differing natures, structures and characteristics of the types of enterprise.

Hotels have a tendency to be more capital intensive, with higher initial investment requirements and a consequently longer-term payback period than catering companies. This is because, in the main, hotel firms operate out of buildings which are owned or mortgaged by the operators and which, in smaller firms, often double as the owners' domestic accommodation. As a consequence, the value of assets, specifically fixed assets, per employee is considerably higher than that of catering firms, with a far higher proportion of fixed costs. Hotels are also likely to have a higher proportion of debtors than catering establishments owing to the fact that hotels are more likely to extend credit and thus may be seen to be more susceptible to cash flow problems.

In addition, hotels (and particularly those outside major towns) have a tendency to be reliant on a seasonal demand from transient customers who have a wide variety of alternative options (holidays abroad, other resorts, etc.) and who may be dissuaded from returning by uncontrollable factors such as the weather.

This should not be perceived to mean that catering operations are not in a similarly competitive market. However, their customers tend to differ, in that catering operations supply a comparatively local and less seasonal demand. Equally, catering firms frequently operate out of premises which are leased, thereby requiring less initial investment and lower fixed costs. The knowledge and training requirements for the two types of operation are different and, although an element of catering is usually found in hotels, the level of skills required in the different establishments varies (e.g. food handling and service compared to reception and housekeeping skills). With this in mind, any results obtained from research in the tourism and hospitality industries should be considered to be of a general nature because of the diversity of the types of operation contained under this heading.

Boer (1996) suggested that the characteristics of the industry may have an influence upon the nature of funding of hotels and on the subsequent failure rate experienced in this sector. He argued that, given the capital-intensive nature of hotels and the consequent dependence on long term loans, firms in this industry are likely to be heavily dependent on the buoyancy (or otherwise) of the banking sector.

This becomes more evident when it is noted that, in the United Kingdom, four banks control in excess of 65 per cent of the funding to small firms. Thus, should the investing institutions suffer from economic difficulties (as the banking sector has done in the past decade), these difficulties may be passed on to more vunerable clients, namely the small firms that are dependent on their longer-term financial support.

Bunn (1987) whose analysis of reasons for small business failure includes a brief overview of the tourism and hospitality industries, identifies the reasons shown in Table 3.1 as being the most important 'primary' factors in causing hotel and restaurant failures. It should be remembered that these findings form only a small part of the total sample (12 per cent), and that little detailed analysis is given of them. Despite this, all the listed reasons are plausible and can be logically explained in view of the characteristics of the industry.

Table 3.1 Bunn's reasons for small business failure

Reason	Sector rank	Global rank
Undercapitalization	1	1
Poor operations management	2	2
Poor state of local economy	3	7
High gearing	4	6
Poor chief executive officer	5	5

Source: Bunn (1987).

As previously observed, the comparatively high investment in fixed assets and the consequent high break-even point in hotels and restaurants will often mean that only a small amount of funding is available for working capital, thus resulting in operations which have a tendency to be both highly geared and, at times, undercapitalized. Equally, the low knowledge barriers to entry and the emphasis in the industry on 'vocational' and 'skills' training (as opposed to 'business' training) may help to explain the relative importance of 'poor operations management' and the citing of a 'poor chief executive officer' as reasons for small hotel or restaurant failure. Certainly, the geographically limited market for each unit, together with the inseparable nature of the service that hotels and restaurants offer, illustrates the crucial importance that the state of the local economy plays in the survival of small hotel and catering operations.

It is also worth noting that one of the other reasons, 'short-term liquidity problems', which is ranked as third most important in the 'global ranking' (the average of all firms in all the sectors surveyed) comes comparatively low down the list of importance for the tourism and hospitality industry, being placed seventh. Again, this can be explained by reference to the characteristics of the industry, which traditionally demands payment prior to or immediately after the service has been delivered. This stands in marked contrast to many other industries, in which small firms are required to offer or extend longer credit terms to their clients in order to secure business.

Boer (1992a) undertook research into the survival of hotel companies and catering companies in Dorset, in which owners of the companies were asked to rank a list of factors as to which they considered to be most positive influences on the long-term survival of their firms. Each list was developed from a pilot study. It is interesting to note that most of the factors chosen by the sample were almost exclusively endogenous, implying that the owners perceived company survival to be largely in their own hands.

It is also interesting to note that there is considerable duplication of factors identified as being of importance to the two sample groups, although, as can be seen, the ranking of the factors varies between the two samples. Factors such as 'reputation' and 'value for money', despite often being dismissed as clichés, seem to be of significance to both samples, and it would be useful to gain a greater insight into the true interpretation of these factors. Similarly, the samples seem to share the pragmatic view that 'luck' was of little relevance to small firms, and often survival in both samples was attributed to a considerable amount of hard work.

Table 3.2 Positive influences of long-term survival (owners' views)

Hotel sample	Rank	Catering sample
Reputation	1	Value for money
Value for money	2	Control of cash needs
Good customer communication	3	Reputation
Location	4	Control of costs
Control of cash needs	5	Location
Control of costs	6	Staff
Management skills	7	Catering skills
Low borrowing needs	8	Good suppliers
Limiting firms growth	9	Luck
Access to other finance	10	
Luck	11	

Source: Boer (1992a).

An area in which the two groups differ is 'financial awareness', with the hotel sample placing a lower emphasis on 'cash needs' and 'cost control' than the catering sample, perhaps owing to the more immediate working capital needs imposed by a business needing to replenish its food and beverage stocks on an ongoing basis.

CONCLUSIONS

Although the results of the above research help to illuminate an area which has been largely neglected in the past, it should not be assumed that the findings can be transferred to other areas of the tourism and hospitality industries or even to any other industry. Indeed, in view of the foregoing analysis, it is possible to conclude that the ability to identify the 'causes' of small firm failure in the tourism and hospitality industries or any industry, is largely a reflection of the perspective and frame of reference used by the researcher.

As may be seen from a comparison between the categories obtained from the hotel and catering samples and the available literature on small firm failure, there are distinct differences between the proprietors' perceptions of small firm survival and failure and the perceptions of researchers. The former have a tendency to focus on the operational and day-to-day functions of the business, which is hardly surprising, as, like many owners of small firms, they may have entered the sector with the motivation of being involved in a particular trade or profession. Consequently, they may adopt a more 'tactical', short-term approach in the analysis and operation of their business.

Researchers, however, have tended to adopt a more 'detached', 'strategic' or longer-term approach, not only to conform to their own research methodologies, but also because of the complexity of accounting, in academic terms, for the varying characteristics of different industries. By taking a more remote stance, analysts may present broader, more generalized findings, which, although academically sound, have lacked the detail to be utilized or applied to any great extent.

To suggest that one single factor (whether strategic or tactical) is likely to be the main cause of failure in all industries would be simplistic. There are likely to be several factors, both endogenous and exogenous, which will cause small firm failure, and their relative significance will depend on the individual nature and characteristics of the industry concerned. It is thus incumbent on the next generation of researchers to take up the challenge of not only continuing the research in this important area, but also becoming more closely involved with particular sectors, so that their findings may provide useful, applicable and relevant vocational analysis for small firms rather than the more general conceptualized information that exists at present.

REFERENCES

Abelsamad, M. and Kindling, A. (1978) 'Why small businesses fail', *SAM Advanced Management Journal*, **43(2)**, 24–32.

Altman, E. (1983) *Corporate Financial Distress*. New York: John Wiley and Sons.

Bates, T. (1990) 'Entrepreneurial human capital inputs and small business longevity,' *Review of Economic and Statistics*, **72(4)**, 551–9.

Boer, A. (1992a) 'A review of small firm failure in the United Kingdom hotel and catering industry', unpublished thesis.

Boer, A. (1992b) 'The banking sector and small firm failure in the United Kingdom hotel and catering industries', *International Journal of Contemporary Hospitality Management*, **4(2)**, 13–16.

Brooker, R. (1965) 'Business failures – the English insolvency statistics', *Abacus*, **1(2)**, 131–49.

Brough, R. (1970) 'Business failures in England and Wales', *Business Ratios*, 8–11.

Bunn, D. (1987) 'A study to determine the reasons for failure of small businesses in the UK', unpublished project.

Central Statistical Office (1995) *Size Analysis of United Kingdom Businesses*. London: Government Statistical Service.

Central Statistical Office (1996) *Size Analysis of United Kingdom Businesses*. London: Government Statistical Service.

Clute, R. and Garman, G. (1980) 'The effect of US economic policies on the rate of business failure', *American Journal of Small Business*, **5(1)**, 6–12.

Cochran, A. (1981) 'Small business mortality rates: a review of the literature', *Journal of Small Business Management*, October, 50–9.

Cressey, R. (1992) *Loan Committments and Business Starts: An Empirical Investigation on UK Data*' SME Centre Working Paper No. 12. Warwick: Warwick Business School.

Daly, M. (1987) 'Lifespan and firm registration', *British Business*, April, 14–18.

Daly, M. (1990) 'The 1980s – a decade of growth in enterprise', *Employment Gazette*, November, 558–64.

Di Petro, W. and Sawhrey, B. (1977) 'Business failures: managerial competences and macroeconomic variables', *American Journal of Small Business*, **2(2)**, 4–15.

Dun and Bradstreet International (1982) *American Business Failure Record*. New York: Dun and Bradstreet.

Dun and Bradstreet International (1991) Press release, June.

Eversley, J., Craven, D. and Dyson, J. (1983) *Be Your Own Boss*. Durham: National Extension College.

Fredland, J. and Morris, C. (1976) 'A cross section analysis of small business failure', *American Journal of Small Business*, July, 7–18.

Ganguly, P. (1985) *UK Small Business Statistics and International Comparisons*. London: Harper & Row.

Gibb, A. and Webb, T. (1980) *Policy Issues in Small Business Research*. Andover: Teakfield.

Hall, G. and Young, B. (1991) 'Factors associated with insolvency amongst small firms', *International Small Business Journal*, **9(2)**, 58.

Hall, G. (1995) *Surviving and Prospering in the Small Firm Sector*. London: Routledge.

Hartigan, P. (1976) 'Why companies fail', *Certified Accountant*, **68(6)**, 400–2.

Hudson, J. (1986) 'An analysis of company liquidations', *Applied Economics*, **18**, 219–35.

Keeble, D., Walker, S. and Robson, M. (1993) 'New firm foundation and small business growth: spatial and temporal variations and determinants in the United Kingdom', *Employment Department, Research Series* No. 15.

Larson, C. and Clute, R. (1979) 'The failure syndrome', *American Journal of Small Business*, **4(2)**, 35–43.

Lauzen, L. (1985) 'Small business failures are controllable', *Corporate Accounting*, **3(3)**, 34–8.

McKinlay, R. (1979) 'Some reasons for business failures', *Cost and Management*, May, 17–21.

McNight, C. (1990) 'Business and bankruptcy: a review', *Journal of Finance*, November, 16.

Miller, D. (1977) 'Common syndromes of business failure', *Business Horizons*, **20(6)**, 43–53.

Peterson, R., Kozmersky, G. and Ridgway, N. (1983) 'Perceived causes of small business failures', *American Journal of Small Business*, **8(1)**, 15–19.

Smallbone, D. (1990) 'Success and failure in new business start ups', *International Small Business Journal*, **8(2)**, 34–47.

Stanworth, J., Blythe, S., Granger, B. and Stanworth, C. (1989) 'Who becomes an entrepreneur?', *International Small Business Journal*, **8(1)**, 11–22.

Stewart, H. and Gallagher, C. (1986) 'Business death and firm size in the UK', *International Small Business Journal*, **4(1)**, 40–6.

Storey, D. (1994) *Understanding the Small Business Sector*. London: Routledge.

Townroe, P. and Mallalieu, K. (1993) 'Founding a new business in the countryside', in Curran, J. and Storey, D. (eds) *Small Firms in Urban and Rural Locations*. London: Routledge.

Williams, A. (1985) 'Why so many small businesses fail', *Real Estate Journal*, in Flahvin, A. 'Why small businesses fail', *Australian Accountant*, **55(9)**, 17–20.

FOUR

Financing small businesses

Stephen Taylor, Jim Simpson and Helene Howie

INTRODUCTION

A major issue for all small firms concerns the raising of the necessary finance to resource the start-up and subsequent growth of the operation. In this chapter, the financing decision is examined from both a theoretical and an empirical perspective. Initially, the general theory relating to financing the firm is examined, before we move on to look at the key issues related to financing small firms, with a specific focus on those in the tourism and hospitality industries, where empirical data permit. The main emphasis of the chapter is upon sources of external finance for small tourism and hospitality firms, and this includes an examination of debt finance (as provided by banks) and equity finance (as provided by both formal and informal venture capitalists). The chapter concludes with a discussion of the government funding initiatives that might be applicable to small tourism and hospitality firms in their frequently highly challenging quest for finance.

FINANCING THE FIRM: GENERAL THEORY

In this initial section, we briefly outline the general theory relating to capital structure and financing the firm. While this in itself provides a useful conceptual framework, it also provides a basis for subsequently highlighting how small firms differ from larger firms in respect of their financing decision-making.

Considerable progress has been made over the past forty years with regard to our understanding of the financing decision. A seminal contribution was Modigliani and Miller's (1958) analysis of capital structure, which marked a move away from the descriptive approaches to understanding the financing decision that had hitherto dominated the field, to a much more rigorous, analytical approach. Modigliani and

Miller challenged the then dominant assumption that there existed an optimal capital structure (i.e. a particular mix of debt and equity) that provided a lower cost of capital than any other given combination which maximized the value of the firm. While this early work by Modigliani and Miller excluded the effects of corporate taxation and the advantages of interest relief on debt finance, and assumed the existence of competitive capital markets, it did result in significant and productive debate on the issue of a firm's capital structure.

In subsequent work, the original model was enhanced to include corporate taxes (Modigliani and Miller, 1963), and latterly this was extended to include personal taxes (Miller, 1977). This has led to the general view that, although there are some corporate tax advantages in employing debt, these are largely offset by the personal tax on interest income. The value of debt financing to a firm will be dependent upon its ability to utilize the tax shield afforded by interest payments. A detailed discussion on capital structure theory is beyond the scope of this text (see, for example, Brealey and Myers, 1988), but it is a pertinent issue when considering how one should finance the small tourism and hospitality business. The critical finding is that there is no optimum capital structure *per se* for firms that will increase their value to investors. Nevertheless, there are a number of caveats regarding the use of debt finance as opposed to equity finance that are particularly relevant to the smaller firm.

Capital structure and small firms

It is generally considered wise to limit the amount of debt finance in a firm's capital structure where certain conditions prevail concerning taxes, risk, asset type and financial slack. Clearly, the advantage of tax relief on interest payments can only operate if a firm is in a non loss-making situation. Therefore, unless the firm is achieving a sufficient income over the life of the debt to take advantage of interest tax shields, then the firm is likely to be disadvantaged by debt finance. An additional factor to consider is that tax shields might also be available to the firm via, for example, capital allowances. Where there is a high level of business risk (and typically there *is* in new small businesses), debt finance should generally be minimized owing to the high costs of financial distress and bankruptcy. For firms whose value is largely based upon intangible assets (as is frequently the case in the tourism and hospitality sectors), the costs of financial distress are likely to be higher – owing to the lack of opportunity to leverage upon tangible assets – and therefore debt finance should be utilized less, on average, than in those firms consisting of largely tangible assets (such as manufacturers). The final variable to be considered in relation to the use of debt finance concerns the amount of financial slack available for future growth opportunities. If a firm is too highly geared, it will not have access to financing when it wishes to capitalize on emerging growth opportunities. For this reason, those firms with high growth strategies, all things being equal, will tend towards conservative capital structures (Brealey and Myers, 1988, pp. 434–5).

In summarizing the discussion above, the main point is that there is no optimum capital structure that small firms should strive to achieve. This said, however, the level of business risk experienced by small firms generally, coupled with a likelihood – in the case of small firms in the tourism and hospitality industries – of firm value being based upon a predominance of intangible assets, suggests, other things being equal, that, from a theoretical perspective at least, debt finance should be used cautiously by these firms.

SMALL FIRMS AND THE FINANCING DECISION

The discussion so far has tended to assume that small firms and large firms *are equal* in respect of their ability to access funding. Unfortunately, this would appear not to be the case in actuality, with financing decision-making for small firms being constrained by a number of issues which are specific to this sector of the economy. This includes the apparent difficulty small firms face in obtaining long-term capital. Examination of this issue has tended to focus predominantly upon the supply side: the availability of capital. An enduring theme has been the existence of a 'gap' which results in small firms being discriminated against in their efforts to raise capital. There is, however, another aspect of this problem that receives much less attention. This concerns the demand side and the nature of decision-making regarding raising capital on the part of small business owners. An examination of both these dimensions is critical if we are to begin to understand the nature of financing the small firm.

Supply-side issues

The Macmillan Committee (1931) detected that smaller firms experienced problems when attempting to source long-term capital in amounts of £200,000. This has subsequently become known as the 'Macmillan gap', and its continued presence has been noted by the Radcliffe (1959), Bolton (1971) and Wilson (1979) committees, though the value of the gap does appear to be falling (Storey, 1994). However, for small firms, this apparent difficulty in obtaining smaller sums of equity capital results in many owners claiming that they are being forced to rely upon high interest loans.

One immediate issue that requires to be tackled is what is actually meant by a 'gap' in the provision of finance for small firms. Different authors have attributed different meanings to this term. Thus, the term gap has been applied variously, according to Hall (1989), to describe:

1. The difficulty experienced by small firms in raising small amounts of capital, usually in the form of equity as described by the Macmillan Committee.
2. The situation (even though no blanket minimum amount might exist) whereby small viable firms experience unjustified prejudice from the capital market. One possible source of this is the application of inadequate credit assessment procedures. Here the gap could perhaps be more accurately described as *market failure* (Aston Business School, 1991).
3. In order to raise capital, small firms may be required to accept inequitable conditions compared to larger firms, in the form of punitive interest rates or the security they are required to provide.
4. The perception of the capital market that small firms represent a higher risk than large firms. There is, of course, evidence, as Hall (1989) cites, that supports this view. For example, Ganguly's (1983) study found that only 43 per cent of the businesses registered for VAT in 1973 survived over a ten-year period. Additionally, research by Hall and Stark (1986) has demonstrated that the probability of business failure is inversely related to company size.
5. The tendency for financial markets to be very narrowly focused on achieving the highest possible financial returns as opposed to the generation of employment. Small firms might be effective in creating new jobs but this might be allied to low financial returns.

Another type of gap concerns the issue of *credit rationing*, which, as Stiglitz and Weiss (1981) argue, can result in equally meritorious projects being treated differentially, in so far as one receives a loan while another does not, regardless of whether this firm was willing to pay a higher rate of interest to obtain the loan. Stiglitz and Weiss also use the term credit rationing to describe the situation whereby some firms are unable to obtain credit (regardless of the rate of interest they are willing to pay) because of a limited supply of credit. The finance gap, then, can take a number of forms, but they share a common implication for small firms – that is, they generally experience greater difficulty than large firms in raising capital. Why does this situation arise? In respect of equity capital, we suggest below that certain demand-side characteristics may play an important role in explaining the apparent difficulty of raising equity. With regard to debt finance, we suggest that considerable insight on this issue is provided by examining the nature of the transaction involved in business lending.

The nature of business lending

The fundamental issue, as Binks and Ennew (1996) discuss, surrounding business lending concerns the presence of information asymmetries between the lender and the borrower. The lending situation can be viewed as being an agency problem whereby the bank (the principal) advances monies to the firm (the agent), which in return is expected to provide the bank with a stream of income that yields a 'profit' on this advance. The difficulty in this seemingly straightforward transaction is that it takes place under what is characterized as conditions of imperfect and asymmetric information (Berger and Udell, 1993; Keasey and Watson, 1993). This is the difficulty that the bank has in evaluating at the outset (*ex-ante*) the proposed project and the entrepreneur. The issue here concerns the problem of *adverse selection*, i.e how can the bank assure itself that it does not lend to a poor quality proposal? Another aspect of the problem concerns the subsequent (*ex-post*) monitoring of the firm's performance. This is the issue of *moral hazard* whereby, having advanced the monies, the bank faces the difficulty of obtaining sufficient information to assure itself that the firm is behaving in a way that will protect its (the bank's) interest. The issue then becomes: how does the bank cope with the level of information asymmetry?

In practice, the bank has two principal mechanisms for tackling the problem of information asymmetry: the first is to demand collateral as a condition of advancing the loan; the second is to develop a close working relationship with the borrower. In respect of collateral, there are strong theoretical grounds for supporting this as an effective means of overcoming information asymmetry with respect to the problem of adverse selection (see for example, Stiglitz and Weiss, 1981). Essentially, the argument is that those borrowers who perceive their projects to be of low risk are willing to communicate (signal) this to the lender by their readiness to offer an appropriate level of security. This, according to Dempsey and Keasey (1993), is a rational means by which banks, facing high project appraisal costs, can facilitate good proposals to self-select effectively. Highly risky projects are unlikely to induce small firm owners to offer up security – often in the form of a charge over their personal residence. Collateral can also help with the issue of moral hazard. This is because, as Bester (1987) observes, it provides a significant incentive for small firm owners to ensure that their best efforts are focused upon achieving the desired outcome in respect of firm performance.

There are, however, at least two situations where collateral will not be an effective mechanism. In some instances collateral might not be available or might be available in insufficient amounts. This could result in a viable project being rejected. A particular problem arises where a business consists of largely intangible assets and the bank assesses the business on its 'carcass' value (i.e the value likely to be obtained in a distress sell-off). In this type of scenario, such a business would find it extremely difficult to secure debt finance. Another situation where the use of collateral will be ineffective is when a small business owner is unwilling to compromise his or her limited liability status by offering a guarantee in the form of personal assets. Where these types of problems occur, the bank must either forgo the opportunity to invest in a viable project or apply another mechanism to overcome the problem of information asymmetry. One means of doing this is for the bank to develop a closer working relationship with the small business. Although this will not result in the availability of perfect information, it will, according to Berger and Udell (1993), have a positive influence upon both the quality and quantity of the information made available. The value of getting to know a customer's business is being increasingly recognized by the banks. The British Bankers' Association has recently begun to make efforts to promote the message that its members are making more use of a knowledge of a company's prospects when assessing loan requests and less use of security (Houlder, 1996).

Demand-side issues

There has been a tendency in respect of small business finance to overlook the 'demand side' of the equation and to focus exclusively on supply-side problems. This approach, however, is based upon a naive view of the small business owner, where, implicitly, he or she is seen as operating from within the neo-classical economic model of rational, maximizing, decision-making. Although a convenient assumption for research purposes, it ignores the complex behaviour that actually characterizes the financing decision-making of the small business owner. For example, an issue which should not be overlooked concerns the not uncommon desire of many small business owners to maintain full control of their venture. This could be a critical factor in the apparent sub-optimization investment behaviour of firms, resulting in slower growth, owing to their reluctance to cede control in return for growth capital – so-called equity aversion (Hutchinson, 1995). Additionally, as discussed above, the higher the debt: equity ratio, the greater the impact on the business of any financial downturn. Thus, as Chamberlin and Gordon (1989, 1991) have suggested, small business owners are likely to operate their business with a lower debt: equity ratio (and thus operate the business below the theoretical maximized market value level) in order to afford the business the best survival opportunity through a lower risk investment strategy.

Thus, a further explanation of the difficulties facing small firms in raising capital is the efforts of owners to avoid risk – as they perceive it – and to maintain full control over their venture. In this scenario, small businesses owners minimize the use of equity and rely more heavily upon debt finance in both the short and the long term – regardless of the strong theoretical argument against this behaviour. Where a firm wishes to retain flexibility to pursue growth opportunities as they arise, a very conservative level of gearing (i.e. the ratio of debt to equity) will be maintained to provide the necessary scope for raising additional debt finance. If a small firm owner is pursuing this sort of financing strategy, this can have implications for the subsequent decision-making regarding investments in the form of the product market opportunities chosen. Of particular relevance here is the agency problem, introduced above, which will impact on the firm's financing decision-making.

SOURCES OF FINANCE FOR SMALL FIRMS

Small firms have a number of options for raising finance. These include the owner's own funds, family and friends, the banks, venture capital providers, government loans and grants, as well as arrangements such as lease agreements, debt factoring and even trade credit. All these are potential sources of finance for small firms. Figure 4.1 shows the breakdown of external finance sources for UK service sector small and medium-sized enterprises in 1994–5. The findings of a large scale survey in 1996 by the Centre for the Study of Small Tourism and Hospitality Firms at Leeds Metropolitan University (Thomas *et al.*, 1997) provides some insight into sources of capital utilized by small tourism and hospitality firms (Figure 4.2). This shows that, like most small firms, the sector relies primarily upon owners' funds and debt finance from the clearing banks. In this chapter, we focus on what are typically considered the three main sources of *external* finance for small firms: (a) the clearing banks; (b) venture capital providers (both formal and informal sources); and (c) governmental sources of funding (European, national and local).

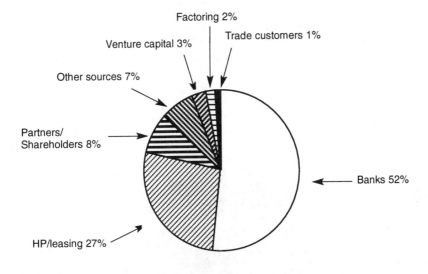

Figure 4.1   Sources of external finance for service sector SMEs, 1994 to 1995
Source: Bank of England (1996b).

Banks and small firms: an overview

Within the UK, banks represent the primary source of external financing for small businesses, both past and present (Bank of England, 1996a). The evolution of the British banking system has had a profound effect on the nature of the relationship between the banks and their small business clients. As Binks (1991) notes, unlike their counterparts in many other countries, such as Germany and Japan, where there is a tradition of industrial banking which exists to provide a system to channel private sector savings to industrial investment, the UK banks have emerged as primarily deposit protection services.

The main effect of this has been a more distant relationship between UK banks and their small business clients than is found in many other countries where an industrial banking system exists (Yao-Su Hu, 1984; Edwards, 1987). Fundamentally, it is this British banking system that underpins the agency problem previously highlighted and the consequent emphasis upon securing collateral. Those countries where industrial banking is practised utilize the closer relationships with their small business clients, which is inherent in this system, to focus upon the income-generating potential of the project when assessing the likelihood of repayment. Clearly, this latter approach requires banks to have a detailed knowledge and 'feel' for the client's business and its potential.

The heavy criticism of clearing banks (see Keasey and Watson, 1992, for an overview) for adopting an unhelpful, risk-adverse stance towards small firms has arguably emanated from a perspective of bank practices which is not fully conversant with the commercial pressures faced by the UK banks today. For example, increased competition in the sector during the 1980s and economic pressures in the early 1990s (e.g. the impact upon banks of the recent recession upon their property and small business portfolios; Gapper, 1993) and regulatory changes (such as the imposition of new capital loan requirements by the Bank of International Settlements; Plender, 1993) have forced the clearing banks to adopt policies of charging economic rates for many

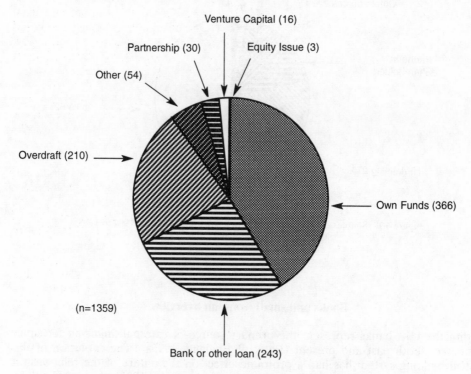

Figure 4.2 Small tourism and hospitality firms: where do they seek the capital?
Source: Thomas *et al.* (1997).

business service elements which were in effect previously cross-subsidized by their more 'profitable' activities. Thus, in many ways, the banks are themselves as much victims of a more demanding commercial environment as are their small firms customers. The combination of the nature of the UK banking system (i.e. its origins and focus as outlined above), the frequent unwillingness of small firm owners to cede control in return for equity finance and/or difficulties in obtaining this type of finance creates a dynamic in the relationships between banks and small firms which is extremely difficult for both parties.

This is further exacerbated by the fact that debt finance is essentially an unsuitable instrument for the long-term financing of firms. This is the role of equity finance. A situation where small firms rely heavily upon short-term bank loans and overdrafts for their financing (for both the short and long-term) is, in the final analysis, attractive to neither the firm nor its lenders. For the small firm, which typically experiences volatile cash flows coupled with a low equity base, debt finance is extremely risky and unsuitable as a substitute for long-term risk capital, owing to the uncertainty of its continuing availability – i.e. it may be recalled at short notice, in the case of overdrafts, or the debt facility might not be renewed. This creates an unattractive scenario for both the borrower and the lender. From the bank's perspective, the absence of sufficient equity funding creates a high-risk investment position whereby they are effectively assuming a risk that equity sources have refused to accept. For the small firm, it creates a great deal of uncertainty in respect of future debt finance.

An additional factor which should not be overlooked when examining bank lending is the fact that debt repayment requirements are unaffected by actual firm performance. Therefore, debt-holders do not benefit from any of the gains from a good financial performance (these accrue to equity holders), but in instances of financial distress could experience a loss. There is, in effect, an inherent conflict between debt and equity holders owing to the relative pay-offs to each that can be exacerbated by any imprudence in the activities of highly leveraged small firms. These could expose debt-holders to a greater level of risk or otherwise impact negatively on their financial claims (Keasey and Watson, 1994). Bearing this in mind, and recognizing the small margins which banks apply to small firm debt finance – where one bad loan could wipe out the profits from many other loans – the apparent reluctance or caution on the part of banks in providing finance to the small firm sector becomes more understandable.

Bank lending and small firms: empirical evidence
Given the inherent difficulties in the relationship between banks and small firms, what is the actual nature of the involvement of UK banks in the small business sector? One estimate suggests that UK clearing banks are responsible for around 90 per cent of lending to small firms (Batchelor, 1989). However, another source, the ESRC Centre for Business Research at the University of Cambridge estimates that banks accounted for some 61 per cent of external finance to small firms in the period 1987 to 1990 and that this fell to 49 per cent in 1991 to 1993 (Bank of England, 1996a). Since 1992–3 there has been a steady drift away from overdrafts towards term loans (predominantly on a variable rates basis), with the latter now accounting for approximately 63 per cent of total bank lending to the small firm sector. The extent to which this represents a trend is, as yet, unclear. None the less, overdrafts still remain an essential element of finance for small firms, particularly as a source of working capital (Bank of England, 1996a).

A study by Keasey and Watson (1994), focusing on the period 1986 to 1990, utilized a sample of 110 small firms in Yorkshire, which – based upon findings of previous UK studies (Bradford, 1993) – is broadly representative of the UK as a whole in terms of both its financial and sectoral characteristics. They found that bank finance and owners' equity provided almost equal proportions (approximately 31 per cent each) of total funding. Additionally, trade credit represented an important element of short-term finance for the sampled firms. The finance from the banks broke down into 17 per cent short-term (in the form of overdrafts) and 14 per cent longer-term loans. Keasey and Watson found that, on average, some 55 per cent of the total funding of the firms was short term – roughly a third of which was provided by the banks. In respect of longer-term finance from the banks, around a third was unsecured. For the majority of both overdrafts and term loans there was a security (collateral) requirement in the form of a charge over the personal assets of directors or a combination of personal and business assets. Interestingly, Keasey and Watson's finding of an average security ratio of assets to loans in the region of three to one is very similar to those reported in previous studies by Cowling *et al.* (1991) and Binks *et al.* (1992).

Bank lending and small tourism and hospitality firms

The authors' own clearing bank survey, carried out in late 1996, which specifically focused upon bank lending to small tourism and hospitality firms, unfortunately provides little additional information. The heavy criticism levelled at the banks in respect of their treatment of small firms during the 1990s (see, for example, the most recent Forum of Private Business survey, 1996 – this has been undertaken every two years since 1988 and provides an excellent barometer of the relationship between small firms and the banks) has, understandably, made the banks very reluctant to divulge details regarding their dealings with small firms. Of the eleven banks approached, only five were willing to participate in the survey. One of the primary aims of this research was to establish the extent to which the banks perceived small firms in the tourism and hospitality industries to be less attractive than small firms in other sectors and, if so, whether they subsequently treated them differently. All the respondents claimed to lend to the industries but only two banks had a specialist who dealt with the tourism and hospitality industries, although all the banks had specialists for other industry sectors. When asked whether the industries were seen as being as attractive as other industries, four said they were and one stated that they were less attractive owing to poor cost control by operators.

Another issue of particular interest was to determine the amounts lent to the industries by the banks as a percentage of total lending. Three banks were unable/ unwilling to specify this, but the two banks which did stated that these industries accounted for between 3 and 5 and less than 1 per cent respectively of their total business lending. There were indications that some of the banks utilized lending criteria which were specific to the hospitality and tourism industries. Interestingly, the two which stated that this was the case were the same two which had a tourism and hospitality industries specialist. In one of the cases, this simply involved utilizing occupancy figures (current and historical) when lending to hotels. In the second case, there was a specification of 'most attractive segments' – for hotels this was town house hotels and those targeting commercial travellers, while for public houses, themed bars were seen as being particularly attractive. Additionally, there was a specific sector policy of a maximum loan to a value of 70 per cent and a ceiling of five times earnings for advances.

The level of collateral sought is an issue that frequently attracts attention when one looks at bank lending behaviour towards small firms. Of those surveyed, one bank stated that it required a higher level of collateral from small firms in the tourism and hospitality industries than from small firms in other industries. Based upon the responses received, it would appear that 75 per cent of small firms in tourism and hospitality are required to provide collateral. This is probably towards the higher end of the average for all small firms which is typically cited (see, for example, Keasey and Watson, 1994). All the banks surveyed were involved in the Small Firms Loan Guarantee Scheme (SFLGS), and the reported percentage of these loans made to the tourism and hospitality ranged from under 1 to less than 5 per cent. The most frequent response was fewer than 1 per cent of all loans under the scheme. This figure is considerably lower than one might expect, given that the official Department of Trade and Industry figures reported for 1995–6 indicate that the catering category *alone* accounted for 8.5 per cent of all advances made under the SFLGS during this period. This suggests that either the banks surveyed are underreporting the advances made to the tourism and hospitality industries or the majority of advances under the scheme are being made by banks which did not participate in the survey.

Given the limited amount of empirical evidence, it is dificult to draw any definitive conclusions regarding bank lending to tourism and hospitality small firms. There is, however, some limited evidence that tentatively suggests that banks may view small tourism and hospitality firms as being less attractive than small firms in other sectors. That this is indeed the case is far from clear, and the work by Thomas *et al.* (1997) indicates that the majority of small tourism and hospitality firms they questioned experienced little difficulty securing capital and that, after personal funds, bank loans and overdrafts represented the primary source of finance (see Figure 4.2).

Venture capitalists and small firms

As the preceding section has highlighted, bank (i.e. debt) financing is primarily suited for funding the short- to medium-term needs of the small firm. Where there is a requirement for longer-term financing, it becomes necessary for the small firm to consider equity finance. This involves the small business operator offering an owner-ship stake in the firm in return for equity capital. In practice, after family and friends, this can be obtained from two principal sources: (a) the formal equity market, whereby an ownership stake is taken by a venture capital firm; or (b) the informal equity market, which involves a private individual (or syndicate of private individuals) injecting capital into the firm in return for an ownership stake. In both cases, the net result will be that the small firm will have traded some control in return for additional funding. As we have highlighted above, this can represent a significant psychological barrier for many small firms. However, it is far from being the only potential barrier to small firms seeking equity capital.

Formal equity capital

Where a small firm has aspirations and opportunities for significant growth, it is likely that additional equity finance, over and above that which the owner is likely to be able to access from personal sources, will be required. Equity investment, in the form of venture capital, is frequently cited as a source of finance for the growth-oriented small firm. There are, however, likely to be difficulties in qualifying for this type of financing source for the majority of small firms, as we highlight below.

The formal venture capital providers, such as members of the British Venture Capital Association (BVCA), invested a total of £2140 million in British companies in 1995 (Bank of England, 1996b). However, only 4 per cent (down from 12 per cent in 1990) of this was invested in early stage financing, with some 23 per cent being invested in the expansion stage. The vast majority of the total amount invested in 1995, some 73 per cent, was to support management buy-outs/buy-ins (MBOs/MBIs). The formal venture capital sector is therefore not a major provider of equity finance to the small firm sector. Venture capital firms have a preference for investing larger rather than smaller amounts in companies, owing to the fact that management costs attached to an investment of £50,000 are much the same as those attached to one of £5 million. Indeed, venture capital lending is a numbers game with a vengeance: required annual rates of return can vary from 25 to 80 per cent, depending on the stage of investment (Bygrave, 1996). As a general rule of thumb, it is considered uneconomic to lend less than £250,000 owing to the high fixed costs involved. For example, the initial professional fees (accounting and legal) will typically be in the region of £50,000 to £70,000, regardless of the proposed size of investment (Batchelor, 1993). The basic objective of the venture capital firm is to back those firms with the potential at least to double their asset base over an average period of three to five years. This strategy is seen as being essential if their profits are not to be wiped out by those firms which ultimately do fail.

The economics of this form of financing results in venture capital firms having a fairly well defined set of preferences for investments in terms of preferred sectors, amounts invested, stage of investment, timescales and even geographic area. A survey by accountancy firm Levy Gee (1995), which maintains a venture capital database, reveals that the preferred investment sectors are predominantly manufacturing/technology based. The leisure/recreation sector is ranked tenth (out of twenty), while hotels and restaurants are ranked eighteenth, just above property and construction and the film industry. The basic ranking of preferred business activity reported by Levy Gee is (1) manufacturing, (2) services, (3) wholesale/distribution and (4) retail. The extent to which tourism and hospitality businesses are classified as retail operations in this ranking is unclear, but the low ranking of hotels and restaurants would suggest that they, at least, probably fall under retailing.

As suggested earlier, the majority of venture capitalists impose a minimum amount which they are willing to invest. The 1993 survey by Levy Gee revealed that only 35 per cent of venture capital firms would consider investing less than £100,000. The most preferred locations were the South East of England and Yorkshire and Humberside. The least preferred areas were Scotland and Northern Ireland. As a generalization, in terms of stage of investment, it is fair to say that venture capital firms are biased towards providing development capital and to financing MBOs and MBIs. Levy Gee's 1995 survey supports this, and indicates that the start-up stage is ranked seventh, just ahead of mezzanine and seedcorn finance in terms of preferred investment stage. The preferred timescale for the realization of investments is three to five years, although periods up to and beyond ten years are sometimes considered. What does all this mean for small tourism and hospitality businesses? In order to assess the level of venture capital financing activity within the sector, the authors surveyed those members of the BVCA who indicated (in the BVCA directory) an interest in investing in the leisure sector (some 72 out of a total membership of 108). We discuss these findings below.

Venture capital and the small tourism and hospitality firm
Of the 72 firms surveyed by the authors, 56 returned completed questionnaires, a 78 per cent response rate. This represents a sizable majority of those venture capital firms active in the sector. Some 90 per cent of respondents (51 firms) stated that they would consider projects within the hospitality and tourism area. Only one firm indicated that it discriminates against the sector by applying lower investment limits. Of those firms

which indicated that they would consider projects from the sector, 32 were actively involved in investing in hospitality and tourism firms. This amounted to a total of 99 projects accounting for a total investment of £273 million (see Tables 4.1 and 4.2). To put this into some context, the BVCA membership currently has an aggregated investment portfolio in the region of £25 billion. This means that hotel and tourism projects represent only a fraction over 1 per cent of their total investment in the UK. Of this, almost exactly half of the number of projects were below £2 million, with only three projects attracting more than £10 million. The breakdown by project type (Table 4.3) shows that hotels and food outlets accounted for 58 of the projects backed. Only eight projects were clearly identifiable as being tourism-oriented. The 'other' category included outlets such as nightclubs.

Table 4.1 Venture capital and small tourism and hospitality firms: breakdown by average funds provided (BVCA membership)

Average investment per project (£ million)	Number of projects
Less than 1	19
1–2	31
2–3	17
3–4	8
4–5	4
5–6	9
6–7	0
7–8	2
8–9	6
9–10	0
10–11	1
15–16	2

Table 4.2 Venture capital and small tourism and hospitality firms: breakdown by project involvement (BVCA membership)

Number of projects funded	Number of venture capital companies	Total number of projects
1	7	7
2	9	18
3	6	18
4	4	16
5	2	10
6	1	6
7	0	0
8	3	24
Total	32	99

The general conclusion that can be drawn from this survey was that, although venture capitalists were not discriminating against the tourism and hospitality industries *per se*, the characteristics of both – mainly small, low growth enterprises – have inevitably created limited opportunities for this type of financing. If a project does meet the basic criteria of venture capital firms (as outlined above) then there is every chance that it will attract the necessary equity injection. There is, however, owing to the almost craft nature of much of both industries, a high probability that most tourism and hospitality projects will be unattractive to the large-scale investment, high-growth

Table 4.3 Venture capital firms: breakdown by category (BVCA membership)

Project category	Number of projects
Hotels	31
Food outlets	27
Contract caterers	5
Tourism projects	8
Others	28
Total	99

preferences of formal equity investors. Moreover, this is as true for the small firm sector generally as it is for tourism and hospitality. It is owing to this apparent equity gap that informal venture capital investment has begun to gain increased attention, from both academics (e.g. Mason and Harrison, 1992a, b) and politicians, in the UK.

Informal equity capital: 'business angels'

Business angels are private investors who provide informal venture capital to firms. Given the intrinsically private nature of the involvement, little is known about the true extent of this type of financing in the UK. The BVCA has estimated that in 1994–5 some £16 million was invested by business angels using networks listed in the BVCA's own directory (Bank of England, 1996a). This is almost certainly a fraction of the total amount of informal equity financing that took place during this period. The most extensive research into the UK informal equity market has been undertaken by Colin Mason (University of Southampton) and Richard Harrison (University of Ulster).

Mason and Harrison have estimated that UK small and medium-sized enterprises (SME) have raised around £2 billion from informal equity sources. Their calculation is based upon an estimate of the number of companies who have raised finance from business angels in the UK, some 5.45 per cent of companies, which is an average drawn from two studies (Mason and Harrison, 1993; Small Business Research Trust, 1991). The estimated average investment per investor is £20,000, and approximately 39 per cent of deals are syndicated with an average of 3.25 investors (Mason and Harrison, 1992a, b). Like the formal venture capitalists, these investors appear to prefer manufacturing-based activities (Mason and Harrison, 1994). A major difference is that they prefer to invest in projects in the range of £10,000 to £100,000, the zone most formal venture capital firms prefer to avoid. Sometimes a business angel will bring together a syndicate of investors. This type of individual is known as an 'archangel'. An angel who invests in a firm and then eventually takes control is known as a 'devil' (see Gatson, 1989, for an expanded listing of types of angels found in the USA). The business angel has a preference – unlike the formal equity sector – for the start-up and early stages of an investment. The preferred criteria are a entrepreneurial start-up with forecasted growth potential in excess of 20 per cent per annum, a turnover in excess of £5 million per annum within five years and a 15 per cent pre-tax return on equity (Mason and Harrison, 1994).

In addition to their willingness to lend smaller sums than venture capital firms and a tendency to focus upon the start-up and early stages of a firm's development, business angels have a number of other characteristics that make them more attractive to small firms. These include the fact that they are often motivated not just by financial considerations, although these remain extremely important. This can lead to business angels being willing to accept a lower rate of return (this is perhaps one reason why business angels have a lower rejection rate than venture capitalists) than the formal equity sector. Frequently, business angels become more involved in the firms in which they invest than venture capitalists, and can provide an invaluable input to management decision-making in areas such as product and market development (Harrison and Mason, 1992b). Additionally, there is evidence that this type of investor is geographically widespread, with a tendency to invest in their local region, which helps to overcome the venture capitalists' geographic emphasis upon the South East of England (Mason and Harrison, 1991, 1995). Thus, informal equity goes some way in helping to overcome the deficiencies of the formal sector from a small firm's perspective.

There are, of course, potentially negative aspects to utilizing informal equity sources (Mason and Harrison, 1994). As individuals, business angels have less financial resource than venture capitalists and may be unwilling or unable to meet additional financing needs of the firm. Even though a business angel takes a minority stake in a small firm, he or she is likely to want to have a significant say upon strategic issues. It is therefore likely that this source of equity will have a proportionally greater impact on the small firm owner's control than formal equity sources. Ultimately, this may manifest itself in the shape of a hostile attempt to seize control of the firm, i.e. the angel turns out to be a 'devil'. Over and above these 'caveats', another potential difficulty in utilizing business angels involves sourcing a suitable investor. The very nature of this source – its informality – means that the referral network for putting interested parties in touch is less developed and efficient than might be wished. Most angels depend upon referrals to place them in touch with a potential investment opportunity, but available evidence (Mason and Harrison, 1992a, b) suggests that there is a high level of dissatisfaction with the effectiveness of current systems. An additional difficulty is that the independent nature of most business angels means that firms seeking informal equity are unlikely to receive referrals from one angel to other potential angels. This can create an entry barrier, in the form of lack of information and relatively high 'search' costs in terms of time, for small firms trying to tap into this particular source of funding.

Government and small firms

Governments, at European, national and local levels, have some degree of involvement in the financing of small firms. Fundamentally, regardless of the level, this involvement is motivated by a belief that the 'market' has failed to meet the financing needs of some small firms. In this section we briefly review the government support for small firms, including an overview of the grants available from European sources, the financing initiatives devised by the UK government and, finally, the local government support that is available to small tourism and hospitality firms.

European funding

As part of its efforts to remove economic disparities between member states, the European Union (EU) has established a number of funding schemes in the form of grant aid and soft finance. For example, in 1996–7 a total budget of approximately £60–65 billion was fixed. Although this budget covers a total of seven different funding areas, the most relevant, the 'business and industry' section, is a substantial element in its own right, but other funded areas might be applicable in some circumstances to small tourism and hospitality firms. Tourism and hospitality projects which have attracted European funding – which can vary from 10 to 100 per cent of total project costs, in the SME sector (defined by the EU as those employing fewer than 250 and having a turnover of less than £28 million) – include a museum in Portugal (£1 million), a hotel refurbishment in Italy (£800,000) and a winter ski resort in Crete (£2 million), among many others (McKeon, 1996). Obtaining EU funding is a complex business, but not impossible, for UK small firms. Successful bids must meet a stringent criteria and specialized Euro-consultants exist to guide applicants through the various criteria. A good starting point for anyone interested in this area is one of the increasing number of books and guides that have been written on this issue. The Internet can be used to access current EU funding initiatives: the web address is *http:www.cordis.lu/*.

UK government funding

Within the UK, the government has sought to stimulate the small business sector by creating financing schemes that it perceives will overcome market deficiencies. This includes initiatives such as the Small Firms Loan Guarantee Scheme (SFLGS), the Business Expansion Scheme (BES) and more recently the Enterprise Investment Scheme (EIS) and venture capital trusts (VCTs). At this time it is impossible to comment on the effectiveness of the latter two initiatives – although the EIS is effectively a replacement for the BES – because of their newness, but the first two schemes were first introduced in the 1980s, and therefore it is possible to make some assessment of their impact upon the small firm sector. It is interesting to note that recent EU statistics suggests that the UK lags significantly behind its European counterparts in the amount of government funding it attracts per employee, £520 against the EU average of £1485 per annum. One UK clearing bank, the Royal Bank of Scotland (RBoS), believes this is due to a lack of awareness on the part of UK small firms of the 1500 government funding schemes (grants, loans and subsidies) that exist at present. The RBoS has now launched a service for small firms that matches their characteristics with a database of all available government funding.

The SFLGS was first introduced as a pilot scheme in June 1981 to address the perceived gap in loan financing for small firms. This was in line with the recommendations of the Wilson Committee (1979) but, as Storey (1994) points out, this was despite the subsequent inability of the National Economic Development Office to uncover any substantive evidence that such a loan scheme was required. The SFLGS involves the government guaranteeing a percentage of the loan made by a bank (this percentage has varied over the life of the scheme from 70 to 85 per cent) to small firms considered to be viable, which would otherwise not normally qualify for debt finance on commercial terms. The types of firms eligible has varied over the scheme's lifetime and, as of 1996–7, catering businesses have been excluded, although hotels and untied public houses with accommodation remain eligible. In economic terms, the success of the SFLGS is questionable on a number of dimensions. For example, the latest figure for the number of loans sanctioned, 7484 in 1995–6, represents only a fraction of the total number of small firms in the UK. As Storey (1994) notes, if we take the conservative figure of one million small businesses operating bank accounts in the UK, then this figure of 7484 – the highest achieved in any one year since the scheme's inception – represents less than 1 per cent of small firms. Recent research by Cowling and Clay (1995) provides evidence that the SFLGS parameters (loan premium and percentage of loan guaranteed) are the most significant influences in determining take-up rates. Additionally, Cowling and Clay assert that the scheme fulfils a valuable role and that the government needs to do more to publicize the scheme to the small firm sector.

The impact of the SFLGS upon the tourism and hospitality industries is difficult to assess owing to the absence of any detailed research. Our own research, which is looking at the number of loans and their value made to tourism and hospitality firms under the SFLGS, is currently ongoing. However, available information is suggestive of a relatively high utilization of the scheme by the sector. For example, in 1995–6, of the 7484 loans made, some 634 were to catering businesses (Conway, 1996), which represents 8.5 per cent of the total loan volume. This figure excludes hotels and tourism projects. Given that the Department of Trade and Industry (DTI) estimates that hotels *and* restaurants constitute 3.7 per cent of the smaller firm sector, with fewer than 100 employees (DTI, 1996), there are perhaps grounds for suggesting that the sector may have a proportionally higher reliance upon the SFLGS than other sectors. It may well be the case that the perceived riskiness of the sector, the relatively low level of tangible assets upon which to secure loans and the typically low levels of growth experienced have combined to make it relatively more difficult for tourism and hospitality businesses to obtain external finance (both debt and equity) than small firms in other sectors. If this hypothesis is true, then a strong case emerges for arguing that the finance 'gap' for small tourism and hospitality firms may well be greater than that which exists for small firms generally. This would have significant implications for both the sector and government policy towards funding small tourism and hospitality firms. At this time, however, we are still some way from being able assess the validity of this conjecture.

Another government initiative, the BES, was introduced in 1983 and was effectively a follow-up to the Business Start-up Scheme (BSU). The BES existed to provide tax incentives for individuals to invest in qualifying unquoted companies. It was anticipated that this would stimulate investments of equity in the range of £10,000 to £50,000 in small firms – typically the sums business angels would invest. The reality of this scheme was that it became a vehicle for wealthy individuals to avoid taxation, and it is highly questionable that it came near to achieving its objective of injecting equity into productive small enterprises (Storey, 1994). Although Mason (1993) suggests that there were a number of benefits to the BES, such as raising the profile of small firms as being equity investment opportunities for both financial institutions and private investors, Storey (1994) is less charitable, and expresses incredulity that the government effectively reintroduced the BES in 1993 in the form of the EIS. The extent to which the EIS becomes another tax avoidance mechanism instead of an effective vehicle for equity investment in small firms remains to be seen.

Specific government funding for tourism-related businesses

In addition to general government support for UK small firms there are a number of initiatives targeted at specific areas, such as employment and training, research and development, exporting and so on. These can provide a source of funding for small firms generally where the necessary criteria are met. There are also a number of sector-specific funding schemes. The tourism and recreation area (tourism, sport, countryside recreation, historic buildings and museums) is one such sector, and there is potential for small tourism and hospitality firms to obtain funding for certain qualifying initiatives. Examples include the British Tourist Authority (BTA), which provides financial support for overseas marketing activities, and schemes operated by the Rural Development Commission (England), the Wales Tourist Board, the Scottish Tourist Board and the Northern Ireland Tourist Board. Generally, each offers a funding scheme that enables firms to undertake capital expenditure in order to develop tangible assets for tourism purposes. Specific requirements and levels of funding vary across the UK, and therefore it is difficult to generalize too much about the nature of the support that might be available to small firms in the sector. An excellent and comprehensive source on UK government funding for businesses is Walker *et al.* (1993).

Local government funding

In addition to funding sources at the European and national levels there are specific initiatives that operate at regional and local levels in the UK. These frequently take the form of grants for purposes such as capital investment, improving premises, marketing, business start-ups, management consultancy and so on. Local government is thus a potentially fruitful source of funding for small tourism and hospitality firms. What is specifically available in any given geographic area can be found by contacting the local government economic development or planning section.

CONCLUSIONS

As this chapter has highlighted, financing the small tourism and hospitality business can represent a major challenge. The primary source of external finance for small firms in the sector continues to be debt finance provided by the banks. There is currently limited research which specifically focuses upon bank lending to small tourism and hospitality firms, and consequently the emphasis is upon the general practices of bank lending to the small firm sector. There is some limited evidence, derived from the authors' own research, that the tourism and hospitality industries are looked upon less favourably than other sectors by the banks. That this is indeed the case is far from clear, but it is an issue worthy of further research.

In the examination of the formal venture capital sector it was highlighted that this is a source of funding available to very few small firms, owing to the highly specific and demanding criteria utilized by this type of lender. Evidence was provided that demonstrates that some tourism and hospitality projects do attract venture capital, but that the characteristics of both industries are such that this will be an avenue open to only a very small minority of firms. The extent to which the informal venture capital sector, as represented by business angels, can plug the equity gap is not entirely clear, but it certainly offers small tourism and hospitality firms more potential than the formal sector.

The final part of the chapter focused upon government sources of funding. Particular emphasis was given to the SFLGS scheme, which appears, based upon the limited evidence available, to have been utilized by a relatively high proportion of firms in the hospitality industry. We have suggested that this may reflect the unattractiveness of small firms in the tourism and hospitality industries to other providers of funding. This is an issue that certainly demands further investigation. If this scenario is an accurate one, it suggests that the recent move by the UK government to exclude catering businesses from the scheme could have potentially serious implications for these industries. One thing that is very clear from this chapter is that there is significant scope for further research into the financing of small tourism and hospitality firms.

REFERENCES

Aston Business School (1991) *Constraints on the Growth of Small Firms*. London: Department of Trade and Industry.

Bank of England (1996a) *Finance for Small Firms: A Third Report*. London: The Bank of England.

Bank of England (1996b) *Quarterly Report on Small Business Statistics*. London: Business Finance Division, The Bank of England.

Batchelor, C. (1989) 'The banks fight off their critics', *Financial Times*, 14 February, 21.

Batchelor, C. (1993) 'From lender to investor', *Financial Times*, 23 March, 15.

Berger, A.N. and Udell, G.F. (1993) 'Lines of credit, collateral and relationship lending in small firm finance', Working Paper (S-93/17), Saloman Brothers Center for the Study of Financial Institutions, New York University.

Bester, H. (1987) 'The role of collateral in credit markets with imperfect information', *European Economic Review*, **31**, 887–99.

Binks, M.R. (1991) 'Small business and their banks in the year 2000', in J. Curran and R.A. Blackburn (eds) *Paths of Enterprise: The Future of the Small Business*. London and New York: Routledge.

Binks, M.R. and Ennew, C.T. (1996) 'Growing firms and the credit constraint', *Small Business Economics*, **8**, 17–25.

Binks, M.R., Ennew, C.T. and Reed, G. (1992) *Small Business and Their Banks*. London: Forum of Private Business.

Bolton, J.E. (1971) *Report of the Committee of Inquiry on Small Firms*, Cmnd 4811. London: HMSO.

Bradford, J. (1993) 'Banks and small firms: an insight', *National Westminster Bank Review*, May, 13–16.

Brealey, R.A. and Myers, S.C. (1988) *Principles of Corporate Finance*. New York: McGraw-Hill.

Bygrave, W.D. (1996) 'How venture capitalists work out the financial odds', *Financial Times Supplement: Mastering Enterprise, Part 3*, 2 December, 6–7.

Chamberlin, T. and Gordon, M. (1989) 'Liquidity, profitability and long-run survival: theory and evidence on business investment', *Journal of Post-Keynesian Economics*, **11**, 589–609.

Chamberlin, T. and Gordon, M. (1991) 'The investment, financing and control of the firm: a long-run survival view', *Cambridge Journal of Economics*, **15**, 393–403.

Conway, H. (1996) 'Government cuts aid to caterers', *Caterer and Hotelkeeper*, 25 April, 7.

Cowling, M. and Clay, N. (1995) 'Factors influencing take-up rates on the Loan Guarantee Scheme', *Small Business Economics*, **7**, 141–52.

Cowling, M., Samuels, J. and Sugden, R. (1991) *Small Firms and Clearing Banks*. London: Association of British Chambers of Commerce.

Dempsey, M. and Keasey, K. (1993) 'Small firms and the provision of bank finance', *Accounting and Business Research*, **23**, 291–9.

Department of Trade and Industry (1996) *DTI Statistical Bulletin*. London: HMSO.

Edwards, G.T. (1987) *The Role of Banks in Economic Development*. London: Macmillan.

Forum of Private Business (1996) *Private Business and Their Banks: 1996*. London: Forum of Private Business.

Ganguly, P. (1983) 'Lifespan analysis of business in the UK, 1973–82', *British Business*, August, 12.

Gapper, J. (1993) 'The equation that did not add up', *Financial Times*, 2 February, 15.

Gatson, R.J. (1989) *Finding Private Venture Capital for Your Firm: A Complete Guide*. New York: Wiley.

Hall, G. (1989) 'Lack of finance as a constraint on the expansion of innovatory small firms', in J. Barber, J.S. Metcalf and M. Porteus (eds) *Barriers to Growth in Small Firms*. London: Routledge.

Hall, G. and Stark, A. (1986) 'The effects of the Conservative government as reflected in the changing characteristics of bankrupt firms', *International Journal of Industrial Organisation*, **4**, 23–30.

Houlder, V. (1996) 'Act of goodwill', *Financial Times*, 8 October, 14.

Hutchinson, R.W. (1995) 'The capital structure and investment decisions of the small owner-managed firm: some exploratory issues', *Small Business Economics*, **7**, 231–9.

Keasey, K. and Watson, R. (1992) *Investment and Financing Decisions and the Performance of Small Firms*. London: National Westminster Bank report.

Keasey, K. and Watson, R. (1993) *Small Firm Management*. Oxford: Blackwell.

Keasey, K. and Watson, R. (1994) 'The bank financing of small firms in UK: issues and evidence', *Small Business Economics*, **6**, 349–62.

Levy Gee (1993) *UK Venture Capital Survey 1993*. London: Levy Gee Chartered Accountants.

Levy Gee (1995) *UK Venture Capital Survey 1995*. London: Levy Gee Chartered Accountants.

McKeon, A.J. (1996) *Where and How to Raise Finance*. Chalford: Management Books 2000.

Macmillan Committee (1931) *Report of the Committee on Finance and Industry*, Cmnd 3897. London: HMSO.

Mason, C.M. (1993) Private communication with D.J. Storey, 25 August, cited in Storey, D.J. (1994) *Understanding the Small Business Sector*. London and New York: Routledge.

Mason, C.M. and Harrison, R.T. (1991) 'Venture capital, the equity gap and the north–south divide in the UK', in M. Green (ed.) *Venture Capital: International Comparisons*. London: Routledge.

Mason, C.M. and Harrison, R.T. (1992a) 'The supply of equity finance in the UK: a strategy for closing the equity gap', *Entrepreneurship and Regional Development*, **4**, 357–80.

Mason, C.M. and Harrison, R.T. (1992b) 'Promoting informal investment activity: some operational considerations for business introduction services', *Venture Finance Research Project working paper no. 4*, Urban Policy Research Unit, University of Southampton.

Mason, C.M. and Harrison, R.T. (1993) 'Strategies for expanding the informal venture capital market', *International Small Business Journal*, **11(4)**, 23–38.

Mason, C.M. and Harrison, R.T. (1994) 'Informal venture capital in the UK', in A. Hughes and D.J. Storey (eds) *Finance and the Small Firm*. London and New York: Routledge.

Mason, C.M. and Harrison, R.T. (1995) 'Closing the regional equity capital gap: the role of informal venture capital', *Small Business Economics*, **7**, 153–72.

Miller, M.H. (1977) 'Debt and taxes', *Journal of Finance*, **32**, 261–76.

Modigilani, F. and Miller, M.H. (1958) 'The cost of capital, corporation finance and the theory of investment', *American Economic Review*, **48**, 261–97.

Modigilani, F. and Miller, M.H. (1963) 'Corporate income taxes and the cost of capital: a correction', *American Economic Review*, **53**, 433–43.

Plender, J. (1993) 'Caught in a double blind', *Financial Times*, 6/7 March, 8.

Radcliffe Committee (1959) *Report of the Committee on the Working of the Monetary System*, Cmnd 827. London: HMSO.

Small Business Research Trust (1991) 'Small business finance', *Natwest Quarterly Survey of Small Business in Britain*, **7(4)**, 19–21.

Stiglitz, J. and Weiss, A. (1981) 'Credit rationing in markets within imperfect information', *American Economic Review*, **71**, 393–410.

Storey, D.J. (1994) *Understanding the Small Business Sector*. London and New York: Routledge.

Thomas, R., Friel, M., Jameson, S. and Parsons, D. (1997) *The National Survey of Small Tourism and Hospitality Firms: Annual Report 1996–97*. Leeds: Centre for the Study of Small Tourism and Hospitality Firms. Leeds Metropolitan University.

Walker, R., MacDonald, L. and Allen, K. (1993) *Government Funding for United Kingdom Business*, 8th edn. London: Kogan Page.

Wilson Committee (1979) *The Financing of Small Firms*, Interim Report of the Committee to Review the Functioning of the Financial Institutions, Cmnd 7503. London: HMSO.

Yao-Su Hu (1984) *Industrial Banking and Special Credit Institutions: A Comparative Study*. London: Policy Studies Institute.

FIVE

Small firms and the state

Rhodri Thomas

INTRODUCTION

Small business policy in the UK has come of age. Indeed, it is now such an established feature of the political landscape that during the 1997 general election all main political parties were at pains to demonstrate their enthusiasm for supporting small business development. Barbara Roche – then Shadow Minister for Small Business – for example, noted that 'Labour is dedicated to providing the right conditions in government for small firms to grow and thrive ... [we] want strong small businesses because they are crucial to this country's success' (Labour Party, 1997a, p. 4). Such declarations can also be found in earlier official documents which relate specifically to tourism and hospitality firms (see, for example, DNH, 1995).

This concern to promote the development of small firms is not new – what some described as a 'steady stream of measures' during the 1970s became a torrent during the 1980s (Stanworth and Gray, 1991, p. 16) – or unique to the UK. The European Union (EU) has, since the mid-1980s, also sought to ensure that small (and medium-sized) enterprises are assisted rather than stifled by the state (Thomas, 1996a).

As has been argued elsewhere (Thomas, 1995a), it is reasonable to suppose, *prima facie* at least, that the impact of small business policy would be particularly marked on industries which remain – despite increased trends towards concentration – characterized by fragmentation (see Chapter 1). Yet, to date, little energy has been expended by researchers in examining how public policies designed to influence the behaviour of, *inter alia*, small tourism and hospitality firms impacts upon them. This is lamentable, for it suggests that the deliberations of policy-makers may not be as fully informed by sector-specific considerations as many might consider desirable.

This chapter will review and evaluate state policies to support small business development. Here, the 'state' refers to UK government initiatives and to the supranational small business policies of the EU. The chapter begins by outlining the main strands of small business policy in the UK.[1] This is followed by an assessment of their impact on small tourism and hospitality firms. Of necessity, the chapter draws heavily on the general small firms literature, particularly where research has been undertaken in the context of comparable services. This is followed by a critical review of EU policy interventions. Finally, the chapter concludes by arguing that although important insights may be gleaned from available studies, sector-specific research is long overdue.

SMALL BUSINESS POLICY IN THE UK

Small business policy is, at least according to the political rhetoric, determined in the light of detailed consultation with the representatives of small businesses. Thus, prior to leaving office, the Conservative government instigated the 'Your Business Matters' consultation exercise which brought together the Institute of Directors, the Confederation of British Industry, the British Chambers of Commerce, the Training and Enterprise National Council, the Federation of Small Businesses and the Forum of Private Business (see DTI, 1996a, b). The incoming Labour government has plans to engage in similar activity. As a consequence, governments invariably claim that they are responding to the needs of the small business community.[2]

As Table 5.1 illustrates, small business policy in the UK has four main themes: creating a favourable economic environment for small firms to thrive; initiatives to encourage financial investment in small businesses; the provision of business information and support; and sponsoring programmes to encourage business and management development. The table enables readers to compare the policies of the Conservative Party when in office with those of the newly elected Labour government. At the time of writing (the immediate aftermath of the general election), few details of Labour government small business policy have emerged. Table 5.1, therefore, contains pre-election pledges. Despite the political rhetoric, the most striking feature of the table is undoubtedly the similarity of approach between the two parties. With the exception of initiatives to encourage financial investment (which have already been discussed in Chapter 4), each of these themes is discussed separately below.

The business environment

The creation of a favourable economic environment, in terms of low inflation and reduced taxation, is an important feature of the government's attempt to create a business environment conducive to the development of small firms. The rationale for this rests on the premise that small (and large) firms will be better able to plan their future and more likely to invest for long-term growth given these conditions. It is beyond the scope of this chapter to examine the impact of general economic variables on small business performance.

Since the mid-1980s, deregulation has been a central plank of efforts to improve the business environment for small firms. Official enthusiasm for deregulation is based on the notion that smaller firms face an unreasonable regulatory burden which, crucially, stifles enterprise; easing that 'burden' will result in increased growth and employment as owners and managers have more time to devote to their businesses and become less risk-averse as the consequences of breaching regulations are more readily understood.

The then Conservative government created a Deregulation Task Force, an advisory body consisting of private sector members, including some from the hospitality industry. The Task Force will be maintained by the government, but with greater representation from small firms (Labour Party, 1997a). The aim of the Task Force is to review the current regulatory system with a view to making recommendations for its improvement. Thus, for example, its 1995–6 annual report made recommendations which included exemption from unfair dismissal legislation for newly created jobs in small firms, the removal of certain building regulations for small projects, improvements to the efficiency of the planning system and increasing flexibility of health and safety regulations (Deregulation Task Force, 1996; Cabinet Office, 1996a).

Specific consideration of the regulatory regime facing small tourism and hospitality firms has not been neglected. For example, the Department of National Heritage (DNH) noted that the 'deregulation initiative has paid special attention to eliminating unnecessary regulation in the tourism field' (DNH, 1995, p. 12). A report presented by the then President of the Board of Trade in 1995 (DTI, 1995c), for example, included proposals to relax liquor licensing requirements, to consider removal of the need to display prices in hotels and to review the Hotel Proprietors Act 1956. Moreover, as part of its consultative process, the Conservative government hosted a seminar to help to

Table 5.1 Major themes of UK small business policy[a]

Conservative government (until May 1997)	Labour government (from May 1997)
The business environment	
• Control of inflation • Reducing taxation and simplifying procedures • Deregulation • Increasing participation in public procurement contracts • Measures to avoid late payments	• Control of inflation • Lower starting rate of income tax • Deregulation • Statutory right to interest on late payments
Financing small businesses	
• Loan Guarantee Scheme[b] • Measures to encourage investment (including informal investment and venture capital) • Regional policy measures	• Measures to encourage investment • Regional policy measures
Business information and support	
• Business Link services (including personal business advisers, diagnostic and consultancy support, support for start-up)	• Improve Business Links • Internet site ('Enterprise Zone') • Support for high-technology firms • Encourage exports
Management training and development	
• Management skill training • Mentoring • Benchmarking • Quality management	• Flexible management development programmes • University for industry • Guides to high-quality training

Notes: [a] Within each heading there are sometimes a series of specific programmes. [b] Catering firms have been excluded from this scheme since September 1996.

Sources: DTI (1995a, 1996a, b), Labour Party (1997a, b).

identify issues of particular concern to small tourism and hospitality firms. The outcome was a list of 29 issues, ranging from health and safety matters and employment legislation to the licensing of caravan parks and the regulations governing tourism signs (Cabinet Office, 1996b).

Tourism and hospitality industry representative associations are generally supportive of this aspect of government policy. Even casual observers of the British Hospitality Association's (BHA's) journal *Voice* will not have missed their enthusiasm (see, for example, BHA, 1994, 1995). The Tourism Society appears to be more circumspect. Although a recent report from the President of the Society noted the 'over-regulated British business environment', he also suggested that some aspects of state intervention – including the planning system – were operating acceptably and that new regulation, such as statutory registration of tourist accommodation, was desirable (Robinson, 1996, p. 18). The remainder of this part of the chapter seeks to assess the veracity of assertions that the current level of government regulations is burdensome and, in turn, stifles enterprise.[3]

Bannock and Peacock (1989) are among the few academics who present a systematic case in favour of deregulation. Two main arguments emerge from their international review of empirical studies. First, they cite survey evidence which highlights a general concern among firms relating to government regulation. Second, and more importantly, they point to studies which estimate that compliance costs amount to some 3 to 4 per cent of gross national product (GNP); these resources could more productively be used by businesses. Moreover, they argue that compliance costs are regressive, falling disproportionately on smaller firms. For example, in a study conducted in Britain and Germany, compliance costs as a percentage of turnover were 2.5 and 7.8 per cent respectively for the smallest firms in the sample but declined to 0.07 and 0.02 per cent for slightly larger firms.

Advocates of deregulation in the context of the tourism and hospitality industries might point to the closure of many small establishments in the 1970s following the introduction of more stringent fire regulations as an example of a possible detrimental effect of regulation on smaller firms. Further, one survey of small businesses in Cornwall, which included a high proportion of hospitality and tourism firms, noted that: 'In almost all cases firms complained about unnecessary rules and regulations' (Restormel Economic Development Service, 1994, p. 17). More recently, a survey of almost 1400 small tourism and hospitality firms found that some 30 per cent of businesses felt constrained by regulations, which rose to 50 per cent among those organizations employing fewer than ten people (Thomas *et al.*, 1997).

Thorough evaluation of the impact of state regulation is, however, extremely complex. As Storey (1994) has made clear, any analysis must consider the purpose of each regulation. Therefore, measures designed to improve the environment, to encourage job security or to protect consumers may well provide benefits to society which outweigh the private costs to firms. Clearly there are difficulties in excluding smaller operators from many of these requirements. Crudely, it would seem unacceptable that those visiting small cafes were more at risk of food poisoning as a result of their not having to comply with hygiene regulations than consumers in an establishment owned by a multinational corporation.

Stanworth and Gray (1991) offer a robust *theoretical* critique of deregulation. They present three interrelated arguments. First, they anticipate that any preferential treatment of smaller firms in relation to labour market regulations may initially reduce costs, but is likely, in the longer term, to lower wages and other conditions of employment. Consequently, the competitive position of these firms may in fact be reduced as high-calibre employees became more difficult to attract. Second, they suggest that the immediate benefits associated with deregulation may in the longer term lead to complacency among smaller operators. The removal of the necessity to compete on innovation and market development, replaced by the possibility of competing on price, may not ultimately result in enhanced performance by these firms. Finally, significantly different cost structures between smaller and larger firms may simply cause increased subcontracting. Although this is potentially beneficial to small firms, there may be no net gains in terms of overall economic activity or, in this case, the development of the sector.

Arguably, many of their criticisms do not apply as forcefully to an industry which does not generally require skilled personnel and is not predominantly technologically driven. However, the possibility of increased subcontracting if smaller firms become increasingly exempt from compliance with regulations is more persuasive. There is evidence that the cost-cutting strategies of some hospitality firms incorporate subcontracting of certain functions, including the use by large city-centre hotels of smaller firms operating in the informal economy (Thomas and Thomas, 1994; Williams and Thomas, 1996). Naturally, the latter is limited by factors such as potentially adverse publicity or poor quality. However, with the legitimacy afforded by deregulation, smaller businesses may flourish, but at the expense of large-firm activity, resulting in no net benefits to the sector.

Available empirical evidence of the impact of state regulation is equivocal. It has been noted that surveys often appear to support official assertions, but the picture is not uniform. For example, almost two-thirds of Curran *et al.*'s (1993) sample did not consider that employment legislation made a major impact on their business. It is interesting that there appeared to be greater concern among hospitality firms, but their perceptions were often based on ignorance of the law, implying that a programme of education would be more appropriate than further deregulation.

In a detailed critique of five surveys which also focused on the impact of employment law, it is significant that Westrip (1986) found considerable variation in their methodological rigour, which, she argues, goes some way to explaining apparently contradictory findings. Nevertheless, there does appear to be some consensus that small firms tend to be hostile to government intervention in the employment process. Often, commentators part company when attention is turned to the likely effect of the removal of particular regulations; naturally, if asked, it is not surprising that small employers do not generally see regulation as helpful to the development of their businesses, but there may be a sharp contrast between general dispositions and consequent actions. Westrip's analysis suggests that current survey evidence in the UK provides little support for the notion that deregulation in this sphere would stimulate greater employment.

In the context of the hospitality industry, Thomas and Thomas (1992) have examined the impact of planning regulation on hot food take-aways. The evidence from their study showed that despite moves to deregulate and simplify the planning process, small firms in that sector tended to be confused by the deliberative process of planning authorities and faced geographical variation in how regulations were implemented. The main recommendation was not further deregulation, but clarification of the criteria used and an encouragement to greater consistency of decision-making.

Finally, Goss (1991) questions the appropriateness of deregulation in relation to health and safety at work. He argues that moves to reduce the requirements on smaller firms to comply with legislation and the encouragement of inspectors to be more sympathetic to small firms sit uncomfortably with the varied evidence he provides that smaller firms are more prone to industrial injuries than larger ones. Although not considered specifically from the perspective of the tourism and hospitality industries, it nevertheless highlights another legitimate concern which cautions against a bifurcated approach to state regulation.

It should be clear that what is being argued here is not a defence of regulation *per se*. Clearly, the government *should* consider the implications of regulations for the development of smaller firms. Equally, it is desirable that proposals should be amended where the aims can be achieved without imposing significant compliance costs. What is at issue is the extent to which smaller firms currently face an unreasonable burden, the removal of which would encourage enterprise; available evidence suggests that a degree of ambivalence is appropriate in evaluating such a claim. Above all, perhaps, it is clear that further sector-specific research is required before informed judgements can be made.

Business information and support

The second major component of small business policy discussed in this chapter is the provision of business information and support. In England, great emphasis has been put on the Business Link Network.[4] Business Links enable small firms to access a variety of services from one location. The network – which is a partnership between chambers of commerce, training and enterprise councils (TECs), enterprise agencies, local authorities and the government – now has more than 220 outlets which cover 96 per cent of VAT registered firms in England (DTI, 1996a, p. 44). Each Business Link offers the following: an enquiry and information service, a personal business adviser service, assisted diagnostic and consultancy support, innovation and technology services, international trade services, services for start-up and micro-enterprises and access to a regional supply network. In addition, many Business Links have developed services which are said to be relevant to their locality, as well as offering marketing and financial advice, training and management development, and guidance on issues relating to premises and planning (DTI, 1995d, 1996a).

The main issue for the purposes of this chapter is not to describe in detail the services offered by Business Links (readers are referred to the sources cited above), but instead to examine the extent to which they are likely to achieve their objectives. The government's actions in promoting information and advisory services are predicated as a perceived market failure which necessitates public sector involvement. The argument is that small firms are not likely to have the resources and internal structures to gather and process information as effectively as their larger counterparts. The creation of public sector mechanisms which generate appropriate business information and assist firms in the development of suitable strategies (as a result of advice) should, therefore, ensure that smaller organizations can prosper in an increasingly competitive environment.[5]

The rationale for the provision of business information and support certainly has an intuitive appeal, and a range of evidence might be drawn upon in its support. For example, there is widespread acceptance that tourism and hospitality organizations need business information to operate effectively, with some commentators pointing to increasing empirical evidence which links environmental scanning with enhanced business performance (Costa and Teare, 1996). Moreover, the few studies which specifically address information gathering and processing in small businesses point to great areas of uncertainty in their approach (Sharkey, 1992). However, taken alone, these factors do not represent an endorsement of the government's actions; more substantial evidence is required before it can be supposed that the public provision of information and advice will lead to the development of small firms in general, and those in the tourism and hospitality industries in particular.

One review of studies which examined the value of information and support services before the creation of Business Links is provided by Haughton (1993). He notes that participation rates are generally low (and there are no *a priori* reasons for expecting tourism hospitality or industry rates to be at variance with this finding) and that the perceptions of clients vary significantly: in some studies up to 65 per cent of the sample considered the support available to be very useful or crucial to the development of their businesses, whereas others show predominantly negative perceptions. Perhaps the variation is not surprising, since the agencies studied had differing aims and objectives. Generally, it appears that there is some consensus in the literature that greater coordination of activity at a local level and careful targeting would improve the effectiveness of support agencies. Indeed, some go further, arguing that sector-specific initiatives are most likely to yield positive benefits (Curran, 1993).

The 'lessons' revealed by the work of Haughton (1993) and others (indirectly) form part of the philosophy which informed the development of Business Links. Since the network's inception in 1993, fewer small businesses have faced a potentially confusing panoply of provision, and some Business Link companies have targeted specific sectors, including tourism and hospitality (DNH, 1995; DTI, 1996b).

Such a positive outlook appears to be corroborated by a recent study of Business Link services. It noted that 'in 80% of cases ... services had totally or partially met the firms' needs and over half of these firms had taken actions to improve their business performance' (DTI, 1996a, p. 49). The optimism implicit in such remarks is perhaps diluted when it is recognized that few businesses – some 9 per cent according to one estimate – avail themselves of the services on offer (*Financial Times*, 1 October 1996, p. 9).

It is instructive at this stage to consider some of the research which has focused specifically on business advisers or consultants, since they form an integral part of the services offered by Business Links. Although it is too early to assess current arrangements, there is material on which to draw which evaluated an earlier scheme.

The Consultancy Initiative (CI) was a major feature of small business policy during the 1980s. The intention was that if the benefits of engaging consultants were demonstrated (by the provision of a subsidy), small firms would continue to use such expertise, resulting in greater efficiency and effectiveness. Support was available to improve areas of business activity such as marketing, quality assurance, financial and information systems and business planning (Segal Quince Wickstead, 1989).

The most prominent evaluation of the Consultancy Initiative has been undertaken by Segal Quince Wickstead (1991a, b). The findings of their work are generally positive. For example, the majority of participant firms had implemented or were intending to implement the recommendations of the consultants, and 84 per cent were satisfied with the scheme. Further, value added as a result of participation was estimated to be on average £2800, with significantly higher benefits expected. However, as has been argued elsewhere (Vance *et al.*, 1996), the research did not satisfactorily isolate a number of variables likely to have an impact on business performance nor make a comparison with non-participating firms, which suggests that the work has serious limitations (see also Storey, 1994; Molian and Birley, 1995).

In the context of the hospitality industry, it is interesting to consider a project undertaken by researchers at the University of Portsmouth (*Caterer and Hotelkeeper*, 2 March 1995, p. 14). Perhaps predictably, they found small hotel owners reluctant to use the services of consultants. However, in contrast to Ford and Ram's (1995) findings, which revealed that small-scale consultancy projects often create expectations which are not satisfied, many of the firms in the Portsmouth study which had utilized external advice were positive about the outcomes. Thus, almost three-quarters were satisfied with the advice, all claimed they would use consultants again and 15 of the sample (17 firms) had recouped the financial outlay within two years.

The main weakness of much of the research cited above, however, is its failure to address fundamental, but methodologically more complex, questions. To what extent do smaller businesses who do utilize the support or advisory services on offer perform better (or worse) than those who do not? Are they, for example, less likely to fail? These issues become particularly important where direct assistance is offered (perhaps for unemployed business start-up). Clearly, evaluation of such policies must move beyond participation rates and user perceptions and consider possible 'displacement' (the failure of some firms precipitated by the assisted enterprises), 'additionality' and 'dead weight' (consideration of what would have happened anyway in the absence of the policy) (Thomas, 1995a). Some of these issues may be particularly pertinent for a sector which has low entry barriers and, therefore, attracts many new firm formations and numerous cessations.

It is important to recognise that the inferences of the type of studies reviewed above are not borne out conclusively by the literature which seeks to identify determinants of small-firm success or failure. Although a major econometric analysis of small firms in the UK found some positive association between support agency activity and business performance (Keeble and Walker, 1993), Storey's (1994) extensive and highly regarded review suggests that the influence of this variable is relatively minor when compared with factors such as size, age and the previous growth patterns of small firms. Undoubtedly, then, further research is required, some of which should pay particular attention to the structural features of the hospitality industry.

Management training and development

In seeking to support the development of small firms, the Conservative government sponsored a range of programmes for small business owners and managers (DTI, 1996a). The indications are that the new Labour government will continue in similar vein (Labour Party, 1997a). Consistent with the general thrust of government policy, organizations such as the Hospitality Training Foundation (HtF) and DNH (now the Department of Culture, Media and Sport) are keen advocates of increasing levels of training in the tourism and hospitality industries (see for example HCTC, 1995; DNH, 1996; HtF, 1996). Although much of the discourse in these publications emphasizes employee training (not an issue for this chapter), there is often implicit and sometimes explicit reference to the desirability of improving the business and management skills of small tourism and hospitality operators (see also Thomas, 1995b).

Two themes emerge from the government's perspective. The first is that management training and development for small business owners or managers will lead to improved business performance. Second, there are a range of barriers which militate against increased levels of participation in training and, crucially, the government has a role to play in helping small firms overcome these obstacles. Thus, the orthodox view is that if sufficiently flexible, high-quality and relevant provision could be made available, small business owners would realize that management training was an investment which would provide rewards in terms of improved profits and growth. The remainder of this section critically examines the appropriateness of this aspect of small business policy.

Most commentators concur that small tourism and hospitality firm participation in formal management development programmes – whether government sponsored or not – is relatively scarce (Thomas, 1995b). Several reasons may be advanced for this. Perhaps the most obvious starting point in the search for an explanation is the economics literature. There, the debate tends to focus upon the importance of market failure. Although there are several forms which may be relevant (see Chapman, 1993), debate has tended to focus upon the argument that firms may not train because of a fear of having their employees 'poached' – the so-called 'free rider' problem. Crudely, there may be a disincentive for firms to spend on training if the employees in receipt of training leave for employment in other firms. The evidence provided by Wynarczyk *et al.* (1993) supports such a position as far as managerial training in fast growth small firms is concerned. Their findings suggest that the absence of internal labour markets in small firms leads to a situation whereby the expectation of managers is that their next post will be with another employer; providing training may accelerate that process. In such circumstances, there may be a case for government intervention in the form of subsidized training.

The explanation above does not, of course, relate to management training of the *owners* of small firms. Storey and Westhead (1995) suggest additional reasons why levels of training might be low, particularly when compared with levels in larger organizations. As far as demand is concerned, they note, for example, that smaller firms have (perhaps necessarily) short-term horizons, whereas management training may offer longer-term benefits. Additionally, the cost of training – including the opportunity cost of not being at work – may be higher for small firms than larger ones and, finally, small firms may be unaware of management training 'opportunities'. On the supply side, they draw attention to possible difficulties faced by training providers in attempting to sell their courses to a fragmented market, compared with securing fewer (but more rewarding) contracts with larger employers. Again, these propositions suggest a role for the government in supporting managerial skills development for small businesses.

It is also important to recognize non-economic explanations for the level of management training. It is now well established, for example, that not all small firms are motivated to grow. Indeed, as in other sectors, the vast majority of small tourism and hospitality firms are motivated by a range of factors, including those related to lifestyle considerations (Thomas *et al.*, 1997). For these firms, training to improve business performance is unlikely to be attractive. However, if enhancing their managerial skills led to an increased likelihood of survival, there might be a role for government in persuading them to participate.

What should be a central issue in an explanation of training levels, and any resulting public policy is, as Storey and Westhead (1995) point out, often absent: the case for state intervention (and, indeed, private sector investment) is dependent upon there being benefits in terms of business performance for the small business owner. It is frequently taken as axiomatic that such benefits exist, yet there is emerging evidence that the 'benefits' associated with management training in small firms *may* not obtain. Low participation rates may, therefore, be explained not in terms of market failure (which suggests that government action is appropriate) but by the low (or non-existent) returns from engaging in such activity (which suggests that government action is inappropriate). It is to this question that attention is now turned. The issues will be explored in the context of start-up training and the development of existing owners or managers of small firms.

Several commentators support the notion that training for start-up is likely to have a beneficial impact on small firm performance. For example, Reid (1993) points to higher survival rates among firms which have participated in publicly sponsored training initiatives than those which have not. His suggestion that skills such as preparing business plans can be developed to competent levels with relative ease will undoubtedly resonate with those engaged in such training, and is implicit in official support for such programmes. Westhead and Storey (1996) point to some other studies with similar findings to Reid. Contrary to the observations above, however, wider evidence is more equivocal. For example, Storey (1994) examined studies which evaluated the Enterprise Allowance Scheme (EAS), which became the Business Start-Up Scheme (BSUS) in the early 1990s. He argues that training for start-up has little impact on the future survival of new small businesses. Indeed, he notes that in one major study 'there were marginally, but not significantly, higher rates of failure for those who went on the courses than those who did not' (Storey, 1994, p. 283). The inference Storey draws from this empirical evidence is that the orthodox view about the importance of training for start-up may not stand up to close scrutiny, and that the reasons for the survival, growth or failure of new firms may be found elsewhere.

It has already been noted that the government has promoted a number of initiatives to increase the level of small business management training for those already engaged in small business activity. Business Growth Training (BGT) Option 3 is a major example of such a scheme. This provided a subsidy for up to half the cost (subject to a maximum of £15,000) of engaging a consultant for the training and development of managerial staff. The rationale for the programme was that it should expose the value of training to many small firms, who would then continue to invest once public funding ceased because the performance of their business had improved (Marshall *et al.*, 1993).

Marshall *et al.* (1993, 1995) are among the few to have undertaken a detailed analysis of the impact of BGT. In a generally positive assessment, they suggest that the programme caused a 'dramatic boost' to the level of training in small firms, which, in some cases, continued after the subsidy had ceased. Moreover, they observed improved business planning and clearer identification of training needs among the firms which had participated in the scheme. However, since the objective was ultimately to improve business performance, any optimism must be somewhat diluted by the additional observation made by the researchers that it was 'difficult to identify any impact of Option 3 on measures of firm performance (for example, growth in sales, labour productivity, or employment)' (Marshall *et al.*, 1993, p. 341).

Although Storey and Westhead (1994) provide numerous examples of other studies which report the 'benefits' obtained by participants on small business management training schemes, they argue that there are several grounds on which such publications may be criticized. Perhaps most important among these are the concerns that many of the studies have been 'technically primitive and have only measured the impact of management training within a univariate framework' (Storey and Westhead, 1994, p. 13). In addition, they express concern that many ignore sector-specific considerations. Others, such as Stanworth and Gray (1991) and Goss (1991), have also highlighted the difficulty of identifying clear causality between the managerial development of small business owners and improved business performance.

Finally, to avoid confusion it should be recognized that the commentary above does not necessarily suggest that management development should not be sponsored by the government. It *may* be that the market failure explanations for the low level of management training are appropriate and that government-sponsored training initiatives would effectively support the development of small tourism and hospitality firms. However, further questioning of this proposition is required: robust evaluation of the various management development programmes available – which differ in terms of their content, duration and quality – is necessary before one can reach firm conclusions about this aspect of the government's small business policy.

THE EUROPEAN DIMENSION

For those seeking to understand how the state impacts upon the development of small tourism and hospitality firms, it is essential to have an appreciation of the activities of the EU. To a large extent, its small and medium-sized enterprise (SME) policy goals have not differed significantly from those prioritized by the UK. Hence, two central features of policy are its promotion of deregulation and the provision of business information and support. Naturally, these have been undertaken in a European context and, therefore, focus upon EU regulations and the supply of information and support designed to encourage Europeanization (or the encouragement to operate across borders), the third aspiration of enterprise policy. Table 5.2 summarizes the main themes and instruments of the three major areas of policy. The table is intended to be indicative (readers should consult Commission of the European Communities (1996) and Thomas (1996a) for details). Each of the three dimensions of enterprise policy is discussed below.

The Commission's report on Community measures affecting tourism (Commission, 1994b, p. 50) notes that:

> To provide a favourable environment for firms, especially small and medium-sized businesses, Community policy acknowledges the need to simplify legislation and reduce the constraints which it imposes on them ... like firms in other sectors, tourism enterprises, which are overwhelmingly of small or medium size, benefit from this rationalisation of administrative procedures, which is designed to avoid any unwarranted burden being placed on them.

This concern has resulted in the adoption of a formal impact assessment procedure for new legislative proposals and a review of existing regulation. As part of this process it is incumbent upon the Commission to canvass the views of representative associations in the member states. Thus, for measures likely to affect tourism, DG-XXIII has a list of 31 organizations which may be consulted, such as the Confederation of National Hotel and Restaurant Associations in the EC (HOTREC) and the European Tour Operators Association (ETOA). In many cases, these bodies have a federal structure, drawing their membership from national trade or professional associations. The extent to which 'representative' organizations are in reality representative has already been questioned earlier in the chapter (see note 2).

Although it has expressed some disappointment with progress towards deregulation, the Commission has enjoyed some modest 'success'. For example, Anderson (1993) provides a clear illustration of how accounting procedures have been simplified for SMEs, and the administrative requirements on small firms entering exclusive contracts have been eased.

Table 5.2   Major EU themes and policy instruments to support SMEs

Improving the business environment

- Administrative simplification/impact assessment
- Improving the fiscal environment
- Increasing access to public procurement

Encouraging Europeanization

- BC-Net
- Bureau de Rapprochement des Enterprises (BRE)/Business Cooperation Centres
- EUROPARTENARIAT
- INTERPRISE
- SPRINT
- SIMAP
- European Economic Interest Groupings (EEIGs)
- Subcontracting

Information and support

- EICs
- Forums to consider 'best practice'
- Improving management quality: EUROMANAGEMENT, ADAPT
- European Business and Innovation Centres
- Increasing access to finance and credit

Notes: Some measures apply to all enterprises and not only to SMEs. Some of the instruments are under the jurisdiction of directorates-general (DGs) other than DG-XXIII.

Source: Thomas (1996a, p. 19).

Mulhern (1994), however, offers a more critical assessment, arguing that the rhetoric has not been matched by action. As has already been argued in the context of the UK, the real issue is the extent to which deregulation is an appropriate means of promoting small business development. Earlier discussion suggests that this may not be the case.

Europeanization

The Commission's aspirations to create a *de facto* unified European market, another strand of enterprise policy, have led to a number of initiatives designed to increase cross-border cooperation between enterprises. Indeed, some 20 per cent of enterprise policy funding has been allocated to finance measures for this purpose (Commission, 1994b, p. 51).

BC-Net is undoubtedly the flagship of this dimension of policy. Briefly, it is a computerized network of consultants (including European Information Centres, discussed later in the chapter) both within and outside the EU. The consultant draws up a confidential cooperation profile (CP) on behalf of organizations, which contains details of the company and the nature of the partnership it is seeking. The Central Unit in Brussels then attempts to match the profile with CPs submitted from other locations. Where appropriate, the companies are then introduced to each other. Criticisms that potential partnerships may flounder at this stage have led the Commission to propose extending the support available until formal contractual arrangements are made (Thomas, 1996a).

It is difficult to find extensive justification for activity in this area. As is often the case, commentaries concentrate more on describing the details of the initiative than on providing clear policy aims or a rationale. Thus a background report on BC-Net notes only that:

> the project was established to encourage and assist co-operation between small and medium-sized companies (SMEs). Many of these companies need assistance to face the increased competition and to take advantage of the opportunities created by the opening of the Single European Market. (Commission, 1992, p. 1)

Evaluation of this type of policy instrument is difficult because of the lack of published research. Official comment, which tends to focus primarily on usage statistics, is sanguine. For example, the Commission (1992) points out that between BC-Net's inception in 1988 and mid-1992 there were almost 58,000 partnership offers or requests. As far as tourism is concerned, during the period to 1994 there had been 823 requests for cooperation using the network, of which more than half related to the hotel sector (Commission, 1994b, p. 51). As Thomas (1996a) argues, however, what is conspicuously absent is any indication of how many of these requests were translated into successful partnerships. Official publications are also silent on the nature of cooperation which might be encouraged in this sector, which is in sharp contrast to other industries, notably manufacturing. This clearly implies that either less effort is made to promote the service to firms in the hospitality and tourism industries or the network has little to offer.

One small study of a non-confidential partnership search scheme, Eurokom (which utilized the BRE network), found no hospitality sector-specific requests for cooperation or partnership during a two-month period in 1992 (Thomas, 1993). Although official statistics point to higher usage than implied by that project, with 273 tourism-related BRE partnership searches during 1993, the Commission's (1994b, p. 51) bold claim that this demonstrates the effectiveness of the system is inappropriate.

European information and support

As in the case of deregulation and Europeanization, the policy to provide European business information and support has resulted in the creation of a range of instruments and programmes. In budgetary terms, the European Information Centre (EIC) network is the most significant, accounting for some 40 per cent of DG-XXIII's budget (Commission, 1994b, p. 51).

Heinrich von Moltke, Director-General of DG-XXIII, summarized the role of EICs as follows:

> it [a small firm] may not have the time or resources needed to study the wide range of opportunities that are available. The European Information Centres open these doors – doors to local, national and European markets, doors to partnerships across borders, doors to public procurement contracts, to calls for tender, to all manner of opportunities ... the services that EICs provide are essential for SMEs if they are to compete on a level playing field ... in the internal market. (Von Moltke, 1993, p. 93)

The Commission's justification for its actions and the evaluative criteria applied to monitor the effectiveness of policy instruments are, typically, implied rather than explicit. Careful reading of official publications is required to identify the kind of evidence which is used to inform decisions. The following extract is one of a few instances where the Commission is unambiguous:

> it is a fact that good support measures for enterprises greatly increase their chances of surviving and expanding. For example, it is acknowledged that the level and type of initial training for the creator of an enterprise, and the existence or otherwise of external advisory services, greatly influence the possibility of an enterprise closing down or surviving. According to a 1990 survey of 16,000 French enterprises created in 1984/5, the closure rate within five years was 59% in the case of new enterprises which had not used advisory services, compared with 19% for those who had consulted experts. (Commission, 1994a, p. 17)

Elsewhere in the same document, the perceived effectiveness of Business Innovation Centres (BICs) is highlighted by noting that between 1984 and 1993 they had been responsible for the creation of 2726 firms employing 15,953 people. In addition, the seed capital project has since its inception in 1989 apparently resulted in 187 new organizations and over 1700 jobs (Commission, 1994a, pp. 7–10).

As far as EICs are concerned, it is clear that the Commission's primary indicator of success is the number of queries handled by the network. On this measure their performance is impressive. Official estimates for the network as a whole suggest that the number of enquiries grew from approximately 12,000 in 1987–8 to 120,000 by 1991, with the majority of enquiries coming from firms employing fewer than 20 people. Not surprisingly, then, the Commission can claim that it is achieving its objective of reaching SMEs (Commission, 1993). It is likely to be equally positive about its record of encouraging participation from a wide range of sectors; Table 5.3 suggests usage across most industries. Of particular interest for the purposes of this chapter is NACE classification 6, distribution and catering, which accounted in 1991 for 7.5 per cent of total enquiries. As with all aggregated figures, there is a danger of obfuscation; what is not clear, for example, is usage levels by hospitality firms.

Table 5.3   EIC use by industrial sector 1991

NACE sector		Usage (%)
0	Agriculture	8.8
1	Energy, water	2.0
2	Energy, processing of non-energy minerals, chemicals	4.0
3	Metal manufacture, mechanical, electrical engineering	13.0
4	Other manufacture	15.0
5	Building and civil engineering	5.5
6	Distribution, catering	7.5
7	Transport, communication	4.5
8	Banking, financial and business services	13.0
9	Other services	27.0

Source: Cooper (1993, p. 20).

The disaggregated statistics contained in the Commission's report on initiatives affecting tourism (Commission, 1994b, p. 51) suggest significantly lower contact with the sector. The report notes that between 1991 and November 1993 only 136 requests for information and support related to the industry; it somewhat optimistically adds, 'to these should be added the hundreds of oral questions to which a direct answer was given by the various members to the network'.

Thomas's (1994) assessment of UK and Irish EICs also found low usage among hospitality firms. Further, the promotional methods used by centres and the evidently low sector-specific knowledge of EIC personnel revealed by that study suggests that contact between small hospitality firms and EICs is unlikely to increase in the foreseeable future unless there are significant organizational changes. A policy shift whereby EICs concentrate their activities on particular groups of industries which share common features might encourage increased usage and result in greater responsiveness to the needs of hospitality businesses. Clearly, such a move would make the appropriate EIC geographically remote for numerous organizations but, as has been argued elsewhere, many EIC services may be accessed easily by telephone.

It should be noted that official monitoring of EIC performance has also included two generally favourable quality control reports, and there are plans to introduce biannual reports in the future. However, these exercises have been based largely on reports completed by EICs themselves, and did not include sectoral considerations (Thomas, 1996a). Again, it could well be that centres perform a vital function for some industries but not others. Finally, however, it must be noted that the observations made earlier in the context of evaluating support agencies in the UK are pertinent here: methodologically sophisticated studies are required before unequivocal support can be given to this aspect of policy.

CONCLUSIONS

Evaluating the impact of state intervention on the development of small tourism and hospitality firms is complex; this chapter has undoubtedly posed more questions than it has been possible to answer. Although there is a high degree of consensus between policy-makers in the UK and EU, neither provide substantial research-based evidence to support their various initiatives. Unfortunately, this is not yet adequately compensated for by the academic literature. Thus, the conclusions of a review such as this must, necessarily, be tentative.

As far as the first aspect of public policy discussed – deregulation – is concerned, the available evidence suggests that there are dangers in extending the bifurcated approach adopted in some spheres. Although the compliance costs of state regulation are undoubtedly regressive, there is little hard evidence to support the notion that current requirements stifle enterprising small firms in the tourism and hospitality industries. Some regulations may be unpopular, but their removal will not necessarily counter trends towards concentration. As has been argued earlier, this is not to suggest that the UK government or EU should not be mindful of the interests of SMEs when drafting regulations; if their aims can be achieved with minimum impact upon the sector then that is clearly desirable.

The second area of policy examined, business information and support, rests on the notion that there is market failure which necessitates public sector involvement at a UK and European level. However, there are reasons for questioning the validity of research which examines the value of public sector support mechanisms based on usage statistics and users' perceptions of utility; this form of business support appears not to be a key feature of many multivariate analyses which focus upon the reasons for the creation, growth or cessation of small businesses.

Public policy-makers attach significant weight to improving the survival rates and business performance of small firms by providing training in management skills, the third policy area explored here. In this they are supported by tourism and hospitality industry-related organizations. The findings of the relatively limited research conducted among small firms are not, however, unequivocally supportive of such a position. It is clear that participation in management training for start-up and for established businesses is low, but what is not obvious is whether this is the result of market failure (implying a role of the state) or because there are few benefits to be obtained from such activity.

Examination of measures designed to encourage the Europeanization of businesses, the only major component of EU policy which differs significantly from the domestic approach, reveals relatively isolated use of instruments by firms in the tourism and hospitality industries. Although consideration of these is interesting (because they offer the possibility of illustrating their potential value to other firms within the sector), it is not possible at this stage to assess effectively their significance. Lack of participation by firms may signal weaknesses in the promotion of these instruments, but equally, and probably more plausibly, could be a reflection of the fact that the benefits on offer are minimal. A detailed assessment of any advantages accruing to participating firms is required before any valid judgement can be made.

Perhaps above all, this chapter has highlighted lamentable deficiencies in tourism and hospitality management research. Notwithstanding the structural characteristics of these industries, little energy has been expended by researchers in attempting to understand how public policy designed to support small business development impacts upon them. It is to be hoped that a new research agenda will emerge so that the formation of small business policy in the UK and Europe can be informed by sector-specific considerations.

NOTES

1. The discussion which follows is necessarily partial because of the limitations of space. Unfortunately, it is not possible to examine those policies which have a significant impact upon small firms but whose main aims lie elsewhere. For example, it may be argued that, in many instances, aspects of national, regional or local tourism strategies are *de facto* small business policies (see, for example, Lennon and Kaley, 1996; Horobin and Long, 1996). Equally, those elements of competition policy which resulted in interventions by the Office of Fair Trading, as in a case involving small tour operators (*Guardian*, 8 November 1996, p. 3), may be seen in a similar light.

2. It is, of course, debatable whether or not these 'representative' organizations *are* representative of the small business community in general (Storey, 1994). Further, the articulation between the organizations listed and the tourism and hospitality industries is, arguably, even more tenuous. It is unfortunate that little research has been undertaken which examines the extent to which small businesses may genuinely influence the policy-making process. It is interesting that a recent study which examined tourism policy and local governance tentatively suggested that the views and aspirations of small businesses were not as effectively incorporated into the policy-making process as those of their larger counterparts (Thomas and Thomas, 1998). Further, Thomas (1996b) points to evidence of large firms circumventing EU consultative procedures and thereby possibly marginalizing the perspectives of small business owners.

3. Those interested in pursuing the issue of deregulation should note a related debate between those who advocate a public interest theory of regulation and others who advance a private interest perspective. Briefly, the former assumes that those responsible for the introduction of regulations do so out of a desire to achieve collective goals, whereas the latter emphasize the notion that specific groups benefit from their introduction. A corollary of this, of course, is that the motivations to deregulate may be understood in a similar way (for a review, see Ogus, 1996).
4. Similar arrangements have developed in Wales, Scotland and Northern Ireland. For details of the variations in provision, see DTI (1996a, pp. 65–74). The evaluation which follows is relevant to each of these locations.
5. For further discussion of market failure and information provision, see Bennett and Krebs (1993).

REFERENCES

Anderson, C. (1993) *Getting European Community Help for Your Company*. London: Kogan Page.

Bannock, G. and Peacock, A. (1989) *Governments and Small Business*. London: Paul Chapman Publishing.

Bennett, R. and Krebs, G. (1993) 'Chambers of commerce in Britain and Germany: the challenge of the single market', in Bennett, R.J., Krebs, G. and Zimmerman, H. (eds) *Chambers of Commerce in Britain and Germany and the Single European Market*. London Anglo-German Foundation, 1–38.

BHA (British Hospitality Association) (1994) 'Deregulation remains a live issue', *Voice*, **3(8)**, 9.

BHA (1995) 'Europe presses de-reg button', *Voice*, **4(2)**, 24–5.

Cabinet Office (1996a) *The Government Response to the Deregulation Task Force Report 1996*. London: Cabinet Office.

Cabinet Office (1996b) *Cutting Red Tape in the Tourism and Hospitality Industries: Points Raised during the Tourism and Hospitality Deregulation Seminars*. London: Cabinet Office.

Chapman, P.G. (1993) *The Economics of Training*. London: Harvester Wheatsheaf.

Commission of the European Communities (1992) *BC-Net (the Business Cooperation Network) Background Report*. ISEC/B24/92.

Commission of the European Communities (1993) *The Enterprise Dimension Essential to Community Growth*. COM (92) 470 Final.

Commission of the European Communities (1994a) *Integrated Programme in Favour of SMEs and the Craft Sector*. COM (94) 207 Final.

Commission of the European Communities (1994b) *Report From the Commission to the Council, the European Parliament and the Economic and Social Committee on Community Measures Affecting Tourism*. COM (94) 74 Final.

Commission of the European Communities (1996) *Maximising European SMEs Full Potential for Employment, Growth and Competitiveness: proposal for a Council Decision on a Third Multiannual Programme for Small and Medium-sized Enterprises (SMEs) in the European Union (1997–2000)*. COM(96)98 Final.

Cooper, M. (1993) 'EICs: use and users – a statistical review', *EIA Review*, **1**, 19–23.

Costa, J. and Teare, R. (1996) 'Environmental scanning: a tool for competitive advantage', in Kotas, R., Teare, R., Logie, J., Jayawardena, C. and Bowen, J. (eds) *The International Hospitality Business*. London: Cassell, 12–20.

Curran, J. (1993) 'TECs and small firms: can TECs reach the small firms other strategies have failed to reach?', paper presented to the all-party Social Science and Policy Group, House of Commons.

Curran, J., Kitching, J., Abbot, B. and Mills, V. (1993) *Employment and Employment Relations in the Small Service Sector Enterprise – A Report*. Kingston-upon-Thames: ESRC Centre for Research on Small Service Sector Enterprises.

Deregulation Task Force (1996) *Report 1995/6*. London: Cabinet Office.

DNH (1995) *Tourism: Competing with the Best*. London: Department of National Heritage.

DNH (1996) *Tourism: Competing with the Best 3. People Working in Tourism and Hospitality*. London: Department of National Heritage.

DTI (1995a) *Competitiveness: Helping Smaller Firms*. London: Department of Trade and Industry.

DTI (1995b) *Small Firms in Britain Report 1995*. London: Department of Trade and Industry.

DTI (1995c) *Deregulation: The Way Forward*. London: Department of Trade and Industry.

DTI (1995d) *Business Link Services Guide*. London: Department of Trade and Industry.

DTI (1996a) *Small Firms in Britain Report 1996*. London: Department of Trade and Industry.

DTI (1996b) *Your Business Matters: Government Response*. London: Department of Trade and Industry.

Ford, J.M. and Ram, M. (1995) 'Supporting inner-city firms: lessons from the field', in Chittenden, F., Robertson, M. and Marshall, I. (eds) *Small Firms: Partnerships for Growth*. London: Paul Chapman, 182–91.

Goss, D. (1991) *Small Business and Society*. London: Routledge, 128–56.

Haughton, G. (1993) 'The local provision of small and medium enterprise advice services', *Regional Studies*, **27(8)**, 835–42.

HCTC (1995) *Training – Who Needs it? Research Report 1995 (Executive Summary)*. London: Hotel and Catering Training Company.

Horobin, H. and Long, J. (1996) 'Sustainable tourism: the role of the small firm', *International Journal of Contemporary Hospitality Management*, **8(5)**, 15–19.

HtF (1996) *Facing the Future: Report 1996*. London: Hospitality Training Foundation, London.

Keeble, D. and Walker, S. (1993) *New Firm Formation of Small Business Growth in the United Kingdom: Spatial and Temporal Variations and Determinants*. Research Series no. 15. Sheffield: Employment Department.

Labour Party (1997a) *Growing and Prospering: Your Business and a Labour Government*. London: Labour Party.

Labour Party (1997b) *New Labour: Because Britain Deserves Better*. London: Labour Party.

Lennon, J. and Kaley. K (1996) 'Proactive business development strategy for urban tourism locations: Glasgow Development Agency's Tourism Business Partnership Programme', IAHHS Spring Symposium: Issues Relating to Small Businesses in the Hospitality and Tourism Industries, Leeds, March.

Marshall, J.N., Alderman, N., Wong, C. and Thwaites, A. (1993) 'The impact of government-assisted training and development on small and medium-sized enterprises in Britain', *Environment and Planning C*, **11**, 331–48.

Marshall, J.N., Alderman, N., Wong, C. and Thwaites, A. (1995) 'The impact of management training and development on small and medium-sized enterprises', *International Small Business Journal*, **13(4)**, 73–90.

Molian, D. and Birley, S. (1995) 'Decoding a black box? Evaluating marketing consultancy schemes for SMEs', in Birley, S. and Mason, C. (eds) *International Entrepreneurship*. London: Routledge, 273–302.

Mulhern, A. (1994) 'The SME sector, the single market and the appropriateness of DGXXIII policies', *Small Business and Enterprise Development*, **1(1)**, 3–11.

Ogus, A.I. (1996) *Regulation: Legal Form and Economic Theory*. Oxford: Oxford University Press.

Reid, G.C. (1993) *Small Business Enterprise: An Economic Analysis*. London: Routledge.

Restormel Economic Development Service (1994) *Business Needs Survey: Very Small Firms*. St Austell: Restormel Borough Council.

Robinson, K. (1996) 'Deregulation', *Tourism*, **90** (Autumn), 18.

Segal Quince Wickstead (1989) *Evaluation of the Consultancy Initiatives*. London: DTI.

Segal Quince Wickstead (1991a) *Evaluation of the Consultancy Initiatives – Second Stage*. London: DTI.

Segal Quince Wickstead (1991b) *Evaluation of the Consultancy Initiatives – Stage Three*. London: DTI.

Sharkey, G. (1992) 'Information search by small firms', *Business Information Review*, **9(2)**, 42–9.

Stanworth, J. and Gray, C. (1991) *Bolton Twenty Years on: The Small Firm in the 1990s*. London: Paul Chapman Publishing.

Storey, D.J. (1994) *Understanding the Small Business Sector*. London: Routledge.

Storey, D. and Westhead, P. (1994) 'Management training and small firm performance: a critical review', SME Centre Working Paper no. 18, University of Warwick, Warwick.

Storey, D. and Westhead, P. (1995) 'Management training in small firms: a case of market failure?', SME Centre Working Paper no. 29, University of Warwick, Warwick.

Thomas, H. and Thomas, R. (1998) 'The implications for tourism of shifts in local governance', *Progress in Tourism and Hospitality Research*, **4(4)**.

Thomas, R. (1993) 'EICs and sectoral usage: the case of hotels and catering', *EIA Review*, **2**, 18–23.

Thomas, R. (1994) 'European Union enterprise policy and the hospitality industry', *International Journal of Contemporary Hospitallity Management*, **6(4)**, 10–15.

Thomas, R. (1995a) 'Public policy and small hospitality firms', *International Journal of Contemporary Hospitality Management*, **7(2/3)**, 69–73.

Thomas, R. (1995b) 'State support for management training in small hospitality firms: Issues for hospitality and tourism research', CHME Research Conference, Nottingham, April.

Thomas, R. (1996a) 'Enterprise policy', in Thomas, R. (ed.) *The Hospitality Industry, Tourism and Europe: Perspectives on Policies*. London: Cassell, 117–34.

Thomas, R. (1996b) 'Assessing and influencing the policies of the European Union', in Kotas, R., Teare, R., Logie, J., Jayawardena, C. and Bowen, J. (eds) *The International Hospitality Business*. London: Cassell, 3–11.

Thomas, R. and Thomas, H. (1992) 'State regulation and the hospitality industry: the case of hot food take-aways', *International Journal of Hospitality Management*, **11(3)**, 197–211.

Thomas, R. and Thomas, H. (1994) 'The informal economy and local economic development policy', *Local Government Studies*, **20(3)**, 486–502.

Thomas, R., Friel, M., Jameson, S. and Parsons, D. (1997) *The National Survey of Small Tourism and Hospitality Firms, Annual Report 1996–97*. Leeds: Centre for the Study of Small Tourism and Hospitality Firms, Leeds Metropolitan University.

Vance, P., Thomas, R. and Margerison, J. (1996) 'The impact of consultancy schemes on the business performance of small hospitality firms: a framework for research', IAHHS Spring Symposium: Issues Relating to Small Businesses in the Hospitality and Tourism Industries, Leeds, March.

Von Moltke, H. (1993) 'The European Commission view', in Bennett, R.J., Krebs, G. and Zimmerman, H. (eds) *Chambers of Commerce in Britain and Germany and The Single European Market*. London: Anglo-German Foundation, 87–103.

Westhead, P. and Storey, D. (1996) 'Management training and small firm performance: why is the link so weak?', *International Small Business Journal*, **14(4)**, 13–24.

Westrip, A. (1986) 'Small firms policy: the case of employment legislation', in Curran, J., Stanworth, J. and Watkins, D. (eds) *The Survival of the Small Firm, Vol. 2*. Aldershot: Gower, 184–203.

Williams, C.C. and Thomas, R. (1996) 'Paid informal work in the Leeds hospitality industry: unregulated or regulated work?', in Houghton, G. and Williams, C.C. (eds) *Corporate City? Partnership, Participation and Partition in Urban Development in Leeds*. Aldershot: Avebury, 171–83.

Wynarczyk, R., Watson, R., Storey, D., Short, H. and Keasey, K. (1993) *Managerial Labour Markets in Small and Medium-sized Enterprises*. London: Routledge.

Part II

Small Business Management

SIX

Business planning

John Margerison

INTRODUCTION

It is generally agreed that the tourism and hospitality industries in the UK are still dominated by small firms (see Chapter 1). Commenting on small firms in the UK, a recent government report on competitiveness (Cabinet Office, 1996, p. 5) made the following points:

> Small firms have steadily increased their share of output and employment over the last 20 years. Their adaptability to change and closeness to their customers give them a competitive edge in many markets. But smaller firms also face particular obstacles. Smaller firms may be reliant on a small number of customers, they can face difficulties in raising finance and they may also find it difficult to spare time from day-to-day management to the vital task of planning for the future.

Business planning is clearly seen by government as being a 'vital task' for small firms. Furthermore, the importance of business planning appears to be the accepted wisdom put forward by banks and a range of advisory agencies (such as training and enterprise councils). This chapter attempts to assess whether business planning is important in the context of small tourism and hospitality firms. The first four sections of the chapter are designed to give the reader a clear impression of what business planning is generally considered to be: the process and the main parts of a typical business plan, together with an example of business planning in a small hospitality firm. In the fifth part, existing research on small firms and business planning is reviewed. This examines whether there is a link between business planning and small firm success. To date, little research has been carried out on the effect of business planning on small tourism and hospitality firms. Consequently, this chapter draws on the generic small firms literature and tries to draw parallels for the tourism and hospitality industries. It should be noted at the outset that even the generic literature provides mixed evidence on the importance of business planning to small firms.

WHAT IS A BUSINESS PLAN?

A business plan is defined by Williams (1994, p. 68) as: 'merely encapsulating your longer-term objectives, estimates and forecasts on paper'. In more detailed form, Hodgetts and Kuratko (1995, p. 159) explain that the business plan is 'a road map for a would-be entrepreneur [which] shows what the company is going to do, its projected expenses and earnings, and its plan for repaying the loan'. While the first definition allows for a continual process of planning, the second is typical in seeing a business plan as vital to the start-up process and the obtaining of finance.

Fry and Stoner (1985, p. 2) usefully divide business plans into two major types: working plans and investment plans.

> The fundamental purpose of the working plan is to provide information and guidance for making operational decisions about the firm. It prescribes objectives, goals, and targets, and it delineates steps to be taken to achieve those goals ...
>
> The investment plan is designed for the sole purpose of obtaining financing ... Thus, while the investment plan may include strategic information, its focus is clearly financial.

Working plans are the subject of a study by Ackelsberg and Arlow (1985) which draws a distinction between formal plans, which are written and contain budgets, and more informal, active or analytical aspects of planning, which explore strengths and weaknesses and consider alternative courses of action. Some might argue that informal planning goes on in the mind of the 'entrepreneur', and, although this chapter concentrates on formal aspects of business planning, informal planning is considered later by way of an illustrative example of a restaurant business.

The English Tourist Board (ETB), in its 1991 development guide to funding a tourism business, refers to an 'investment plan' in its section about business planning:

> Raising money to start or expand a tourism business needs very careful planning. You need to decide how much money you need, when you need it, how long you need it for, what security you can offer, who to approach and, most importantly, how to present a good case. You must be in a position to persuade others about the prospects for your business – and to do this, you will need a well thought-out business plan containing realistic financial forecasts. (ETB, 1991, p. 7)

There is an implicit assumption that some form of business plan is vital if a business is to persuade a bank to lend it money (the above guide was written in conjunction with Barclays Bank). It is also clear from the emphasis on financial matters that financial planning is an integral part of a business plan.

The business planning process

There is no single agreed model of the process of planning. Typical of what may be found in the literature is the model provided by Martin and Smith (1993), which is reproduced in Figure 6.1. Figure 6.1 illustrates the wide range of activities that make up business planning. Martin and Smith stress that the apparent separation of the activities does not fully represent the reality of the process. In many instances, they state, activities such as marketing and financial forecasting will take place in tandem; and there will also be constant feedback from the 'later' to the 'earlier' stages of the process.

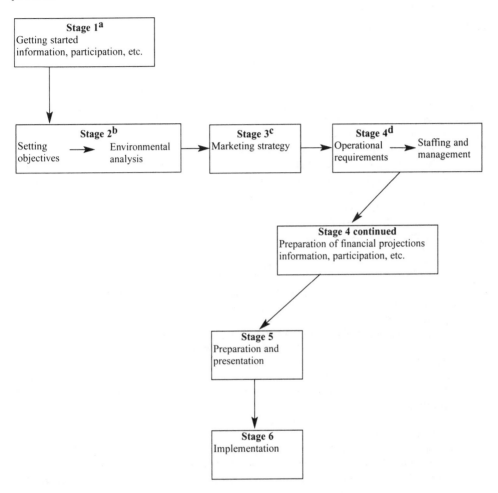

[a] Includes resolving questions such as: 'who is involved in preparing the plan?'
[b] Environmental analysis includes looking at the current conditions (e.g. finance, staffing) facing the organization.
[c] The preparation of a strategy to assist the organization in making the most of opportunities identified in the environmental analysis.
[d] Includes the identification of systems that will be essential for successful implementation of the plan.

Figure 6.1   The business planning process
Source: Martin and Smith (1993, p. 6).

The model in Figure 6.1 is more relevant for investment plans, as it assumes that the plan will be presented to a provider of finance. For working plans it is usually suggested that a similar process is carried out on a cyclical basis: typically annually or at key 'decision points' relating to the future development of the firm. Stage 6 of the model, relating to 'implementation', shows that the business plan is not just a hurdle which has to be jumped in order to obtain finance. Instead, it is argued that it should be used on an ongoing basis, but it is also constantly revised and updated in the light of changing information and circumstances.

Developing a business plan

Having established that business planning is a process with stages which has a cyclical nature, in this section we outline its main components and to relate them to the tourism and hospitality industries where appropriate. It is not intended to give a detailed 'how to' account of the development of a business plan. There are many books and articles which deal with the preparation and the content of a business plan, some of which deal specifically with the tourism and hospitality industries (Small, 1988, pp. 341–62; ETB, 1991; Brush, 1993, pp. 72–82; Williams, 1994, pp. 68–74; Hodgetts and Kuratko, 1995, pp. 158–71).

Business planning is generally agreed to involve both non-financial and financial considerations. The non-financial considerations are usually dealt with first, as they provide the assumptions and parameters on which the financial matters are based.

Non-financial considerations

Brush (1993) and Williams (1994), in outlining the contents of a typical plan, highlight those sections which are non-financial. These should be developed in the light of a detailed review of the business and its prospects.

- *Statement of purpose* (sometimes called a mission statement): a short declaration of the project's overall goals and the plan for attaining them.
- *The past:* an indication of how relevant past performance is to future prospects.
- *Management and employees:* past employment and business record; particular strengths of the management and employee team; weaknesses and how they are to be rectified.
- *The product or service:* why the product or service is distinctive or unique; brief survey of the competition.
- *Marketing:* size, past and future growth potential of the market; identification and analysis of the sector that the business is aimed at; likely customers; detailed analysis of competitors; marketing plan, promotion and advertising, who will sell and how; pricing policy.
- *Operational details:* location and premises; suppliers; equipment and facilities needed; staffing requirements and training plans (together with detailed start up costs for each of these).

The above assumes that the plan will be written down and formal. In practice, this may not be the case, as the business owner might carry out working planning on a day-to-day basis without committing ideas to paper.

Financial considerations

Three financial statements – cash flow forecast, profit and loss account forecast and balance sheet projection – are generally accepted by the financial community as important parts of a business plan. Evidence for this can be obtained by reviewing any of the booklets produced by banks and other financial institutions to help small firms (see ETB, 1991, as a typical example related to the tourism industry). Williams (1994, pp. 268–85) provides an excellent account of the content of forecast financial statements. Readers are referred to that work for detail on the preparation of the forecast financial statements discussed below.

A *cash flow forecast* summarizes future movements in the bank account. Figure 6.2 provides an illustration of a typical layout. Many texts assert that the important benefit of preparing a cash flow forecast is that it shows the business how much funding it will need, together with the timing of anticipated inflows and outflows of cash. If the balance at the end of each month is permanently in overdraft then more long-term funding (such as owner's capital and loans) will be needed. If the balance fluctuates between a positive balance and an overdraft, then there is a case for negotiating an overdraft with the bank which will allow for these fluctuations, without the business having to tie up its own funds during periods when there is a shortfall.

	Jan	Feb	Mar	Apr	May	Jun	Jul	Aug	Sep	Oct	Nov	Dec
Balance at bank at start of the month												
CASH IN DURING THE MONTH												
Capital introduced by the owner												
Loans received from the bank												
Cash sales												
Cash in from credit customers												
Other cash received												
Total cash in during the month												
CASH OUT DURING THE MONTH												
Payments in cash for expenses (itemized)												
Payments to suppliers giving credit												
Payments in cash for fixed assets (itemized)												
Total cash out during the month												
Balance at bank at the end of the month												

Figure 6.2 A typical example of the layout of a cash flow forecast for a small business

Atkinson *et al.* (1995, p. 352) stress that in the tourism and hospitality industries a significant proportion of sales are for cash, as opposed to credit arrangements where a customer is given a period of say 30 days to pay the business for services. They go on to say that tourism businesses are often characterised by seasonality, where the inflows of cash tend to come at a particular period, as opposed to the outflows, which are often spread more evenly over the year (*ibid.*, p. 353). These comments support their contention that the management of cash – both making arrangements for shortfalls and efficient utilization of surpluses – is very important in the tourism and hospitality industries.

Generally, a *profit and loss account forecast* is considered to be a summary of the expected revenues (or sales) and expenses of a business for a particular period. When revenues and expenses have been estimated for a period, the forecast profit or loss is calculated by deducting the expenses from the revenues. If revenues are greater than expenses, a profit is expected, and vice versa for a loss. Typically, the profit and loss forecast is laid out so as to show 'gross profit' and 'net profit', as in Figure 6.3.

At this stage, it is appropriate to reconsider comments in the English Tourist Board publication (ETB, 1991, p. 9):

> Have you prepared a profit and loss account and cash flow forecast? Remember profit and cash are not the same thing. Cash is real and reflects actual cash coming in and going out. Profit and loss is not a real thing but an accounting concept based on set rules.

Although intending to be helpful, the ETB presumes a level of understanding of accounts which, research suggests, small firms do not have. The absence of knowledge such as the difference between cash flow and profit may be important. For example, if a travel agent sells a large number of summer package holidays in November, the profit on these sales could easily be calculated and appear to be very healthy for that month. In cash flow terms, however, perhaps all that has been received to date from the customer is a small deposit which must be forwarded to the tour operator within 30 days. The cash flow benefit from sales only arises late in the following spring, when the customers settle their 'outstanding balances' by paying in full for the holidays six weeks before travel.

The *balance sheet projection* gives the owners of a business a snapshot of the financial position of their business at some future date. In particular, it contains information about the assets (what the business will own), liabilities (what the business will owe) and capital (what the owners' investment will be worth). An example of a projected balance sheet is shown in Figure 6.4.

Numbers have been included to illustrate the principle of balance, i.e. capital equals total assets minus total liabilities. Year on year, as the business makes profits, so the capital or net worth of the business will grow as well. The implication is that a healthy business grows year on year and that this growth can be seen on the balance sheet.

Some suggest that balance sheets are a difficult concept for non-accountants to grasp. Because of this, there is a tendency to downplay their importance. For example, Geoffrey Lightfoot, in a recent review of a small business planning guide, makes the following comments:

> many techniques founded in accounting 'best practice' such as balance sheet and depreciation planning ... are abstractions that the vast majority of small business owners are prepared to live without. There is little evidence that they are wrong to do so. (Lightfoot, 1993, p. 100)

Most of the small business planning guides only recommend that an annual balance sheet projection be prepared. The implication is that a balance sheet projection is only important when one is preparing an investment plan, as it shows the assets which will be used as security by the bank for any loan granted, together with the total levels of funding and indebtedness expected for the business. Further to this, Williams (1994, p. 279) suggests that if the business is small scale and the amount to be borrowed is fairly modest, a forecast balance sheet may not be necessary.

	Jan	Feb	➝	Nov	Dec	TOTAL
Sales (A)						
Less cost of sales						
Purchases						
Labour						
Other direct costs						
TOTAL (B)						
<u>Gross profit (C)</u>						
Take (B) from (A)						
Less overheads						
Rent and rates						
Heating/lighting						
Telephone						
Professional fees						
Depreciation						
Employee costs						
Other overheads						
Interest on loans/overdraft						
TOTAL (D)						
Plus						
Miscellaneous income (E)						
= <u>Net profit</u> (F)						
(C) + (E) - (D)						

Figure 6.3 A typical layout for a profit and loss account forecast, with 'gross' and 'net' profit highlighted
Source: Based on the example in Williams (1994, p. 276).

	£	£	£
FIXED ASSETS			
Freehold property			10,000
Equipment			3,916
Crockery etc.			979
			14,895
CURRENT ASSETS			
Stock of food	3,300		
Debtors	5,875		
Prepayments	1,200		
Bank	6,415		
		16,790	
CREDITORS: amounts falling due in less than one year			
Trade creditors	8,620		
VAT creditor	1,050		
Accruals	85		
Interest payable	40		
		(9,795)	
Net current assets			6,995
			21,890
CREDITORS: amounts falling due after more than one year			
Loan			(4,000)
			£17,890
CAPITAL			
Initial capital			15,000
Less drawings			(500)
			14,500
Add profit for the year			3,390
			£17,890

Figure 6.4   An example of the projected balance sheet of a restaurant at the end of the following year

EXAMPLE OF BUSINESS PLANNING IN ACTION

Those unfamiliar with business and financial planning sometimes find it difficult to relate the theory to practice. What follows is an example – taken from a small restaurant in Leeds – which illustrates the principles of planning. The extent to which planning leads to improved business performance is discussed later in the chapter.

This business has operated from small premises, providing 46 covers, in a busy suburb of Leeds since 1976. It has 35 employees (including ten part-time). Typical of many small tourism and hospitality businesses, this one is managed by a single proprietor. The owner's key objective is to increase profitability from the restaurant by giving the customer an ever higher quality of service and experience. This has led to a decision to rent and expand into the premises next door to the existing restaurant – so increasing the floor area and allowing a bar/waiting area to be created, as well as ten extra places in the restaurant.

The owner has clearly based the decision on a plan. However, there is no formal written business plan – neither about the day-to-day running nor about the proposed expansion of the business. Although a number of financial statements are produced for use by the proprietor, non-financial matters are rarely committed to paper.

In examining the planning process for the expansion, it is interesting to note that, as the literature suggests, sophisticated formal planning techniques were not used. However, as the proposed expansion was described by the proprietor, it quickly became apparent that many of the key sections of a 'typical' plan had been covered, for example:

- *Financial considerations.* A sum of £20,000 was required for the refurbishment; £10,000 from bank borrowing (at 15 per cent interest) and £10,000 out of cash flow. Simple profit planning calculations had been carried out to support the viability of this level of investment, these are detailed in Figure 6.5 as taken from the proprietor's own schedules.

Assumptions:

1.

	Sittings	Covers
Mon	1	10
Tues	1	10
Wed	1.5	15
Thur	2	20
Fri	2	20
Sat	2.5	25
Weekly extra covers		100

Average spend	£13

Weekly additional revenue	£1,300

Net of VAT	£1,106

2.

Additional staff 2
Shifts per week 6
Wage per shift £20
Weekly wage £240

Additional annual profit calculation

Annual increased revenue		£57,532
Gross profit (64.5%)		£37,108
Less		
Wages	12,480	
Rent	12,000	
Depreciation	2,000	
Interest	1,500	£27,980
Additional annual operating profit		£9,128

Figure 6.5 An example of profit planning undertaken by a small restaurant

- *Operational details.* All the operational details of the proposed expansion could easily be furnished as the proprietor was actively working on the preparations for the expansion: architect's plans, additional equipment and facilities, costings, staffing requirements.

- *Marketing*. The proprietor had carried out informal market research on his customers over a long period of time. This research had established that there was a group of potential customers who were deterred by a large queue outside the restaurant. It was also clear that the owner had a detailed knowledge of the past and the product, and a full understanding of the strengths and weaknesses of the business. Using this detailed knowledge, he had developed a 'feel' for the situation. In his opinion, the key to success was not to change a winning formula significantly – instead to improve the experience for customers so that they and their friends would come more often and spend more on each visit.

To summarize, this restaurant and its proposed expansion offer an opportunity to see an example of a business planning exercise in the hospitality industry. The example illustrates informal planning in action in a small, single proprietor business.

BUSINESS PLANNING AND SMALL FIRM SUCCESS

This section reviews the empirical studies that have attempted to find a relationship between business planning and small firm success. The use of the word 'success' presents problems of definition. This is because it is not clear that all businesses use similar measures of success. In fact, a recent survey of small tourism and hospitality firms (Thomas *et al.*, 1997) suggests that traditional motivators such as profitability and growth should be seriously questioned as success measures in these industries. Further, Quinn *et al.* (1992, p. 12) note that: 'many small catering businesses do not grow and this is often due to the owners' decision rather than market forces which have dictated otherwise'. Perhaps the best way to judge success is to consider whether the goals of the particular business have been achieved. This would allow a wide range of different goals to be taken into account (see Chapter 2 for development of this theme).

There are two strands to the research reviewed here, based on the two main types of business plans: investment plans and working plans.

Investment plans

Investment plans form part of the information normally made available to banks in applications for loan finance. Hughes and Storey (1994, p. 9) suggest that banks' risk assessment hinges on information flows available to them as lenders, but they also comment that 'a common response of bankers charged with creating debt gaps through credit rationing is that the proposals inhabiting the gap are not particularly well thought out or documented' (see Chapter 4).

For investment plans to be prepared, it can be argued that, as they contain a high proportion of financial information, small businesses must have adequate financial management practices. This implies that those small firms without good financial management will always be in a weak position when seeking to obtain loan finance. Nayak and Greenfield (1994) and Peel and Wilson (1996) have attempted to gather empirical data on small business financial management practices. These studies, although limited in scope, enable a more realistic picture of small business financial management practices to be gained.

Nayak and Greenfield (1994) concentrate on very small businesses with fewer than ten employees. Included in their sample of 200 West Midland businesses are caterers and a holiday company (among 21 types of business in total from manufacturing, services and retailing). In terms of financial accounting, their questions relate to transactions with the outside world and detailed record keeping. Their findings in the first area suggest that firms doing 'well' are more likely to keep accounting books up to date and to keep records of debtors and creditors. They also examine day-to-day monitoring of the business and find that smaller firms and those doing only 'adequately' or 'not well' were less likely to use budgets. Some service firms appear to lack the ability to calculate weekly profits, and Nayak and Greenfield recommend that they perhaps need advice on this. The implication is that small firms which are successful also have good financial management.

Whether at start-up, or after a period of trading, businesses usually have to spend money on items which will benefit the business for several years and will require a relatively large investment. In such a situation, a business has to be able to make decisions about the type of finance and the viability of the expenditure. This will involve investment planning to show the effect of the decision being considered. By doing this the business manager will, whether consciously or not, be carrying out a form of investment appraisal. Peel and Wilson (1996) obtained 84 responses from the sample of 250 manufacturing and service firms with 50 or fewer employees. They asked each firm to say which techniques[1] it used for 'capital budgeting' (if any). They found that 21 per cent of their respondents used no formal techniques at all, and that 22.3 per cent of those who used a technique considered only a one-year time horizon when capital budgeting. This suggests that a high proportion of small businesses do not use formal capital budgeting techniques when making capital expenditure decisions.

Nayak and Greenfield's findings support the previous study's findings about the lack of formal investment appraisal techniques in use by small firms, but they state that:

> The responses showed a very real understanding of the issues involved because in most cases the capital would have to be provided by the proprietors [and] the owners' involvement in the business makes the decision procedure informal. (Nayak and Greenfield, 1994, p. 215)

Further, they argue that the lack of formal paper analysis appears to be more a function of not having to justify the expenditure to anyone else, than a lack of analytical thought. This suggests that the use of sophisticated, formal techniques is not always necessary for small businesses, and that informal methods may still allow sensible decisions to be made.

Recent publications in the hospitality literature (Harris, 1992; Pannell Kerr Forster, 1992; Reich, 1993; Arnold, 1994; Phillips, 1994) appear to support the view that good financial management and financial planning are essential to business success in the industry. However, these publications are not based on empirical research into methods in use in practice. Although they provide insights as to the current position in the tourism and hospitality industries, there is a clear need for further empirical research into the efficacy of business planning in those industries.

To summarize, it appears that investment plans require good financial management on the part of the business owner in order to produce a credible financial plan as part of the loan application process. The evidence suggests that for some small business owners the production of financial plans is a very difficult operation. This could mean that in some cases inadequate financial plans will lead to a lack of success in obtaining external funding. There is a need for research to focus on this and, in particular, on the tourism and hospitality industries.

Working plans

Research by Ackelsberg and Arlow (1985) examined the relationship between business planning and success measured in terms of increases in sales and profits. Their research was based on a questionnaire on planning sent to 732 small business firms listed in the chambers of commerce in a six-county area in the eastern part of the United States. A total of 135 usable questionnaires were received, with answers to 70 questions that assessed the frequency of various small business planning activities. Nearly one-third of the responses were from service industry businesses, which were likely to have included tourism and hospitality firms.

Most respondent businesses in the sample did plan. However, from this result it would be dangerous to conclude that most small businesses *per se* plan. The low response rate could be because businesses which plan are more likely to respond to a questionnaire on planning. From the sample it was also found that respondent planning firms had greater increases in both sales and profits over a three-year period than respondent non-planners, with very large differences between planners and non-planners in sales and profits. As many commentators now recognize, the authors note that the relationship between planning and economic performance will never be unambiguous, because of other factors, such as the stage of the firm's life cycle and the external environment.

The methodological weaknesses of the Ackelsberg and Arlow study are overcome to an extent in the study by Sexton and Van Auken (1985). They carried out a longitudinal study based on over 300 small companies in Texas using an interview method, with companies being asked the same set of questions in 1981 and again two years later. This study may be considered more robust because of its inclusion of a longitudinal element and because the sample was not skewed towards planning firms.

From the results of the interviews they graded firms into five categories of planning, ranging from zero to four. Zero represented a firm with no knowledge of next year's sales, profitability or profit implementation plans. Four represented a firm with knowledge of next year's company and industry sales, anticipated company profits and profit implementation plans. Only the final category included profit implementation plans, and this category accounted for only 18 per cent of the original sample and 14 per cent of the second sample two years later. This suggests that across a broad range of small firms there is very little planning taking place.

Sexton and van Auken's results show the findings for industrial classifications, including those relating to tourism and hospitality, which are reproduced in Table 6.1. It can be seen that, of the 28 firms in these three groups, 17 were in the two lowest planning categories. Although as a sample Table 6.1 does not show findings which are statistically significant, the findings for tourism and hospitality firms are consistent with those across the whole sample.

In terms of business performance, Sexton and Van Auken's (1985) results showed very little relationship between changes in planning levels and levels of sales or numbers of employees. However, interesting results were obtained by looking at the 1981 planning levels of the 47 firms which went out of business before the follow-up in 1983. These showed that 20 per cent of the zero planners went out of business, as opposed to only 7.9 per cent of the firms with the highest levels of planning. Although the sample is too small to be representative, there seems to be some relationship between planning and business survival.

More recently, Shrader *et al.* (1989) surveyed 115 small businesses in central Iowa, USA, in terms of strategic and operational planning. They defined a small business as

Table 6.1 Planning levels of tourism and hospitality firms

	Total number of firms	Planning level				
		0 Low	*1*	*2*	*3*	*4* High
Retailing – eating and drinking	22	10	4	0	3	5
Hotels and lodging	2	2	0	0	0	0
Amusement and recreation	4	1	0	1	1	1

Source: Extract from table in Sexton and Van Auken (1985, p. 10).

having at least ten but no more than 100 employees. The benefit of this study is that it distinguished between a strategic plan – a written long-range plan – and an operational plan – setting short-term objectives for specific functional areas such as finance, marketing and personnel. Both plans fit into the definition of a working plan discussed earlier in the chapter, as there is no implication that either type of plan is made with the sole purpose of obtaining financing.

Of the 97 firms that responded to the request for an interview, 65 indicated that they had no form of plan covering one year or more. However, all the firms in the sample engaged in some form of operational planning. This supported the hypothesis that operational planning was more common than strategic planning in small firms. Beyond this point, the findings and the analysis are inconclusive – particularly when the very small size of the sample is considered. The most significant correlations were between operational planning and measures of performance such as sales, numbers of employees and after-tax profits. Levels of strategic planning showed little relationship with performance across all sectors covered in the sample. Overall, the results are not convincing, as the analysis was not multivariate, in that it considered only the correlations between one pair of variables at a time and ignored more complex relationships between all variables.

Shrader (in Schwenk and Shrader, 1993) followed up on his earlier study by carrying out a comprehensive meta-analysis[2] on the effects of formal strategic planning on financial performance in small firms. Their findings are illuminating, in that they are able to provide support for the general assertion that strategic planning does have a significant, positive association with performance across studies. However, they do go on to say that the small improvement in performance as a result of planning may not be worth the effort involved. Having drawn from 26 previous studies examining the link between strategic planning and performance and carried out a meta-analysis, they concede that their analysis merely confirmed the association between planning and performance and did not demonstrate causality.

Storey (1994, p. 148), considering the factors influencing the growth of small firms, identifies planning as a factor and makes the following comments:

> Formal planning procedures and their monitoring appears to be more characteristic of larger businesses. It may also be the case that faster-growing firms are more likely to be devising and implementing formal planning procedures. The evidence is less clear as to whether this is a factor which encourages growth, or whether it is merely associated with a movement towards greater size and diversity.

These comments suggest that the existing research has failed to provide conclusive evidence of a link between planning and growth.

Schrader *et al.* (1989), looking at the aggregate nature of planning, suggest that planning might be a proxy for a number of organizational activities and characteristics, such as management competence, managerial involvement, leadership style and employee involvement. This issue is complex, as it requires more sophisticated analytical techniques, and in many cases the organizational activities suggested are not measurable in quantifiable terms. Jarvis *et al.* (1995) offer a potential approach to this issue in a study of financial management strategies of small business owners. This study uses a 'grounded theory' approach involving the unstructured examination of a small sample of businesses in depth. This methodology may be a way of gaining better insight into factors influencing small businesses success – such as business planning.

CONCLUSIONS

Recent government pronouncements see business planning as a vital task for small firms, but one which may be neglected owing to lack of time on the part of business owners. The government is not alone in its view, as business planning appears to be one of those management techniques which most commentators agree is vital to the survival and success of small firms. However, the evidence available from empirical studies of planning by small firms and its contribution to business success is very mixed.

A key feature of business plans is the production of financial forecasts. The literature suggests that a significant proportion of small businesses lack the expertise to operate relatively simple financial and accounting systems. This calls into question the likelihood of small businesses being able to produce useful business plans. If good business plans are an important feature of applications for bank and external finance, it may be that small firms are disadvantaged. However, there is apparently a dearth of research which has examined this link between business planning and successful applications for finance.

A problem highlighted by this review is that business planning is not a technique with a clear definition. It can mean different things to different people. For example, in some cases business owners may not recognize that they are engaging in the process simply because it is not formalized. When one considers the link between business planning and small firm success, the studies reviewed in this chapter do not provide a clear causal link. The key problem is that there are many other factors potentially influencing the performance of a small firm. With this multitude of factors at play in any given situation, it will be very difficult to prove causality between planning and success.

It is not clear from the literature what measures of success small tourism and hospitality firms use. Success measures, such as increased sales, profits and numbers of employees (Ackelsberg and Arlow, 1985; Sexton and Van Auken, 1985), may be inappropriate to small tourism and hospitality firms where evidence suggests that many firms have no desire to grow.

Finally, the point should be made that research into small firm business planning in the tourism and hospitality industries is, as yet, very limited. The generic research carried out to date has perhaps tended towards relatively large samples and has proved to be inconclusive. Perhaps more detailed studies of a smaller number of businesses would be appropriate. Although these may not easily enable a causal relationship to be determined, they may offer clearer insights in terms of understanding the dynamics of the planning process and its role in the management of small tourism and hospitality firms.

NOTES

1. Techniques include payback, accounting rate of return and discounted cash flow (for details of these techniques see Samuels *et al.*, 1990).
2. By meta-analysis is meant an analysis of previous studies so as to transform the information from the statistical tests in each study into a common measure for effect size for these studies (Schwenk and Shrader, 1993, p. 57).

REFERENCES

Ackelsberg, R. and Arlow, P. (1985) 'Small businesses do plan and it pays off', *Long Range Planning*, **18(5)**, 61–7.

Arnold, D. (1994) 'Profits and prices: a lodging analysis', *The Cornell HRA Quarterly*, February, 30–3.

Atkinson, H., Berry, A. and Jarvis, R. (1995) *Business Accounting for Hospitality and Tourism*. London: Chapman and Hall.

Baker, W.H., Addams, H.L. and Davis, B. (1993) 'Business planning in successful small firms', *Long Range Planning*, **26(6)**, 82–8.

Brush, S.W. (1993) 'Developing a hotel business plan: a how-to manual', *The Cornell HRA Quarterly*, June, 72–82.

Cabinet Office (1996) *Competitiveness – Creating the Enterprise Centre of Europe. A Summary*. London: HMSO.

Cosh, A. and Hughes, A. (1994) 'Size, financial structure and profitability: UK companies in the 1980s', in Hughes, A. and Storey, D.J. (eds) *Finance and the Small Firm*. London: Routledge.

English Tourist Board (1991) *Funding a Tourism Business – A Development Guide*. London: ETB.

Fry, F.L. and Stoner, C.R. (1985) 'Business plans: two major types', *Journal of Small Business Management*, January, 1–6.

Harris, P.J. (1991) 'An approach to financial planning using computer spreadsheets', *International Journal of Hospitality Management*, **10(1)**, 95–106.

Harris, P.J. (1992) 'Hospitality profit planning in the practical environment: integrating cost – volume – profit analysis with spreadsheet management', *International Journal of Contemporary Hospitality Management*, **4(4)**, 24–32.

Hodgetts, R. and Kuratko, D. (1995) *Effective Small Business Management*, 5th edn. Fort Worth, TX: Dryden Press.

Hughes, A. and Storey, D.J. (eds) (1994) *Finance and the Small Firm*. London: Routledge.

Jarvis, R., Kitching, J., Curran, J. and Lightfoot, G. (1995) 'Financial management strategies of small business owners: the case of cash flow management', paper presented at the 18th ISBA National Conference, Paisley.

Lightfoot, G. (1993) 'Review of Dickey, T. (1992) Budgeting: a practical guide for better business planning. London: Kogan Page', *International Small Business Journal*, **11(3)**, 100.

Martin, N. and Smith, C. (1993) *Planning for the Future – An Introduction to Business*

Planning for Voluntary Organisations. London: NCVO (incorporating Bedford Square Press).

Mason, C. and Harrison, R. (1994) 'Informal venture capital in the UK', in Hughes, A. and Storey, D.J. (eds) *Finance and the Small Firm*. London: Routledge.

Nayak, A. and Greenfield, S. (1994) 'The use of management accounting information for managing micro businesses', in Hughes, A. and Storey, D. J. (eds) *Finance and the Small Firm*. London: Routledge.

Pannell Kerr Forster Associates' Column (1992) 'Towards success and greater profits', *International Journal of Contemporary Hospitality Management*, **4(2)**, i–iii.

Peacock, M., Reeve, R. and Shaw, H. (1994) '"Spend money on that?" Investment appraisal in the hospitality industry', *International Journal of Contemporary Hospitality Management*, **6(6)**, i–iii.

Peel, M.J. and Wilson, N. (1996) 'Working capital and financial management practices in the small firm sector', *International Small Business Journal*, **14(2)**, 52–68.

Phillips, P.A. (1994) 'Welsh hotel: cost–volume–profit analysis and uncertainty', *International Journal of Contemporary Hospitality Management*, **6(3)**, 31–6.

Quinn, U., Larmour, R. and McQuillan, N. (1992) 'The small firm in the hospitality industry', *International Journal of Contemporary Hospitality Management*, **4(1)**, 11–14.

Reich, A.Z. (1993) 'Applied economics of hospitality production: reducing costs and improving the quality of decisions through economic analysis', *International Journal of Hospitality Management*, **12(4)**, 337–52.

Samuels, J.M., Wilkes, F.M. and Brayshaw, R.E. (1990) *Management of Company Finance*, 5th edn. London: Chapman and Hall.

Schrader, C.B., Mulford, C.L. and Blackburn, V.L. (1989) 'Strategic and operational planning, uncertainty, and performance in small firms', *Journal of Small Business Management*, October, 45–60.

Schwenk, C.R. and Schrader, C.B. (1993) 'Effects of formal strategic planning on financial performance in small firms: a meta-analysis', *Entrepreneurship Theory and Practice*, **17(3)**, 53–64.

Sexton, D.L. and Van Auken, P. (1985) 'A longitudinal study of small business strategic planning', *Journal of Small Business Management*, January, 7–15.

Small, J. (1988) 'Financial control in the smaller business', in Pocock, M.A. and Taylor, A.H. (eds) *Financial Planning and Control*, 2nd edn. London: Gower, 341–62.

Storey, D.J. (1994) *Understanding the Small Business Sector*. London: Routledge.

Thomas, R., Friel, M., Jameson, S. and Parsons, D. (1997) *The National Survey of Small Tourism and Hospitality Firms, Annual Report 1996–97*. Leeds: Centre for the Study of Small Tourism and Hospitality Firms, Leeds Metropolitan University.

Whitehouse, J. and Tilley, C. (1992) *Finance and Leisure*. London: Pitman.

Williams, S. (1994) *Lloyds Bank Small Business Guide*. Harmondsworth: Penguin.

SEVEN

Marketing

Martin Friel

Small firms make up the majority of enterprises in the tourism and hospitality industries, yet little is known about their marketing approaches or activities. Although there has been a steady growth in interest in small tourism and hospitality firms over the past five to ten years, there has not been a concomitant growth in marketing-related studies. Until recently, small tourism and hospitality firms were thought to mimic the marketing activities of their larger competitors. Indeed, much of the small firms literature in general and the tourism and hospitality literature in particular took the view that small firms were miniature versions of larger firms. The small firms literature in many cases regurgitates the tenets underpinning large firm marketing practice and applies them almost unchanged to the case of small firm marketing (see Dewhurst and Burns, 1993; Scarborough and Zimmerer, 1996; and Ahmed and Krohn, 1994; Witt and Moutinho, 1994; Morrison, 1996b, for sector-specific commentaries). As a consequence, much of the literature glosses over those characteristics that help to define small firm marketing. But it is becoming increasingly clear that small tourism and hospitality firms, while having much in common with larger tourism and hospitality firms, operate according to often quite different marketing imperatives. In short, there is more that differentiates small firms from large firms in terms of their marketing than size alone. Differences may be found, for example, in business objectives and management style (see Chapters 1 and 2), both of which influence small firm marketing.

This chapter examines the small firm marketing debates in the context of the tourism and hospitality industries. In order to present as up-to-date a picture of small tourism and hospitality firm marketing as possible, and in order to provide a treatment that offers insights that are both judicious and well-founded, the chapter draws on recent primary research. Much of this is taken from the National Survey of Small Tourism and Hospitality Firms (Thomas *et al.*, 1997) the first comprehensive survey of small tourism and hospitality firms ever undertaken in the UK. The chapter also attempts to provide some indication of the relative strengths and weaknesses of the marketing practices of small tourism and hospitality firms.

THE IMPORTANCE OF MARKETING TO SMALL TOURISM AND HOSPITALITY FIRMS

In a marketing context, a small tourism and hospitality firm may be said to be a business entity operating within the tourism and hospitality industry that has neither the resources to have its own discrete marketing department with specialised job roles nor the funds to hire the services of an external marketing agency. While resources dedicated to marketing in such firms may be limited, this does not necessarily imply that they cannot or should not undertake marketing activities; nor does it imply that they are any less effective in these undertakings than larger firms.

Marketing is a valuable tool in managing change, and managing change is crucial to a firm's survival, particularly in such rapidly evolving and intensely competitive industries as tourism and hospitality (Quinn *et al.*, 1992). Carson *et al.* (1995) argue that all firms must grow in order to survive. Thus, some products or markets will decline or die, and in order to fill the gap that they leave new ones must experience growth. This growth is fuelled by new sales and these will generally result from some form of marketing activity. Hence, marketing activity may need to account for possible new markets, new products and services, more customers, new equipment, new employees and so on. In addition to this, the small tourism and hospitality firm has to contend with limited funds and limited marketing expertise. The complexity of the small firm's world may require a different approach to marketing or an added emphasis on marketing; as the business environment becomes increasingly complex, the small firm's marketing needs to reflect this by becoming increasingly sophisticated to allow it to compete successfully in this complex environment.

Many small firms already recognize the benefits that may accrue as a result of marketing activity. Cox (1993), for example, contends that over 50 per cent of small firms view marketing as a guiding philosophy for doing business, and Barkham *et al.* (1996) found that the 37 per cent of small firms in which marketing was viewed as a very important strategy grew more quickly than those in which it was not viewed as such. Cohn and Lindbore (1995), however, argue that small firm owner/managers differ from professional marketing managers in that they have negative attitudes towards marketing, they perceive marketing as a cost, they treat distribution and selling as uncontrollable problems and they believe each case to be so specific that it cannot be treated with general marketing rules. The evidence at this stage, then, is contradictory and, in the case of tourism and hospitality, flimsy.

Knowledge of customers' needs is vital to the survival of all firms, large and small alike (Berkowitz *et al.*, 1992), and while it is acknowledged that small firms in tourism and hospitality may have intimate knowledge of customers' needs and wants, this can be distorted through subjectivity. Regular and formal reassessment of these needs and of the business environment against established criteria is important to small tourism and hospitality operators (Allen, 1985). If it is accepted that an understanding of and a receptivity towards customers and their needs are crucial to success in tourism and hospitality businesses, the importance of marketing to large firms and small firms alike is unequivocal.

CHARACTERISTICS OF SMALL FIRM MARKETING IN TOURISM AND HOSPITALITY

Schollhammer and Kuriloff (1979) posit a number of qualitative characteristics of small firm marketing that may be categorised as follows.

- *Scope of operations*. This relates to whether firms choose to focus their resources on a local or regional/national market. Many small firms in the tourism and hospitality industries tend to serve local markets with limited or specialized offerings where there is often not enough profit for larger operators (Morrison, 1996a). This is particularly so in the case of guest houses, visitor attractions, travel agents, transport providers, restaurants, public houses and fast food operators, who are more reliant on physical location for trade. It may be less applicable to small tour operators and hotels, which owing to the nature of their products, can and need to target markets beyond the local area. As there may not be great financial resources available to the small firm, this will severely limit its ability to extend its scope of operations.
- *Scale of operations*. Although small firms in the hospitality industry, for instance, account for more than 90 per cent of all hospitality businesses (Chapter 1), the actual share of a given market for each operator is limited. Consequently, turnover and number of employees are equally limited. This impacts negatively on the marketing aspect of the business, as the resource base upon which marketing can draw is low.
- *Ownership*. Small firms are owned by one person or a small group of people, and they are generally managed directly by this person/group. In some respects, this confers benefits on the small firm that are difficult for the larger firm to enjoy. For example, the decision-making process is considerably shorter in small firms, as it does not have to pass through several layers of management, thus allowing small firms to respond more quickly to the changing business environment and emerging opportunities. Quality can more readily be established and maintained, as the owner may have more direct contact with customers and more control and influence over employees and their standards of performance (Moutinho, 1990). On the other hand, ownership by one person or at most a few people brings with it disadvantages. For example, there is limited access to capital and business expertise, as the small firm generally relies on the funds provided by the owner/s, friends and family, and on the skills of a limited number of people. Marketing skills may not necessarily count among those possessed by the firm, and this in turn will affect how, if at all, the small firm makes use of marketing (Gaedeke and Tootelian, 1992).
- *Independence*. The small firm is not part of a greater entity from which it can draw funds, resources and skills, but an independent operation reliant solely on its owner/manager(s) and its limited pool of employees. Access to marketing skills may, therefore, be impeded, though small firms in the tourism and hospitality industries may seek to circumvent this obstacle by becoming members of marketing consortia.
- *Management style*. The small firm tends to be managed in a personalized way, i.e. the owner/manager knows the employees, is involved in all aspects of the business and rarely shares decision-making. This may have two main impacts on marketing. First, the owner/manager may not be a marketing specialist but may undertake

marketing tasks for which he or she might not be equipped, or marketing may be accorded a low priority or not undertaken at all. Second, such regular direct contact with customers and staff may influence customer service quality and procedures through enhanced knowledge of needs.

Each of these characteristics impacts not only on the business in general but on the marketing aspects of the business in particular, and they are compounded by the particular features of the tourism and hospitality industries: high fixed costs, seasonality, interdependence of the products, perishability of the products, high customer contact levels, inability to sample the products before purchase and so on. These highlight, *inter alia*, the primacy of appropriate demand management, as espoused by Middleton (1994).

Many small firms occupy niches where they may be able to maintain higher prices and profits than the industry norm (Storey, 1994), although the evidence for this assertion in the context of the tourism and hospitality industries is weak. Small firms often find a gap in the market that would be difficult or costly for larger businesses to target (Hooley and Brooksbank, 1986; Morrison, 1996b), tending to use focus strategies and the provision of better service in more limited segments. Cox (1993), however, found that small firms did not generally focus their activities, so there is some disagreement in the literature. But as technology improves and mass customization takes root in larger companies, these larger companies can also provide high levels of service to specified segments (Hooley and Brooksbank, 1986).

The focus in many small firms is on survival: that is, sales and the shorter-term view take precedence (Cox, 1993). Robinson and Pearce (1984) conclude that the small firm's view of marketing is essentially operational and has little strategic focus. There is some evidence to support this in the tourism and hospitality context. Thomas *et al.* (1997) found that 58 per cent of small firms in their survey formulated a marketing plan of some sort in the previous twelve months, but 73 per cent of these planned only one year ahead at most. Those that planned up to five years ahead accounted for only 5 per cent of the sample. While some caution is to be exercised, in that survey respondents may have had varying interpretations as to what constituted a marketing plan, it is evident that small firms in the tourism and hospitality industries were giving some thought, whatever its form, to the future.

This is at odds with a number of authors (Scase and Goffee, 1980; Carson *et al.*, 1995) who contend that marketing in small firms is largely intuitive, unplanned and with a limited strategic focus. Carson *et al.* (1995) argue that marketing activities in small and medium-sized enterprises (SMEs) may be characterized as follows.

- *Stage of development.* Younger firms show less sophistication in their marketing than older, more mature firms. The Thomas *et al.* (1997) data provide little support for this assertion, suggesting perhaps that small tourism and hospitality firms are becoming more familiar with marketing and adventurous in their application of it. The data also show that there was a more marked emphasis on customer needs and quality issues, the business environment in general, new product/service development, awareness of local competition and assessment of marketing effectiveness among those respondents who had attended a marketing course of some sort in the previous 12 months. Stage of development of a firm may thus play a less significant part than stage of development or expertise of the owner/manager(s).
- *Restricted in marketing scope and activity.* Carson *et al.* (1995) suggest that, because

of their small size, their stage of development and limited resources, small firms undertake a limited number of marketing activities. Again, there is little evidence to support this in the tourism and hospitality industries. Thomas *et al.*'s (1997) work suggests that small firms engage in a wide variety of marketing activities, with only merchandising, sponsorship and competitions underrepresented in relation to other marketing activities. The extent to which the firms surveyed actually engaged in each activity, in terms of resources committed, was not measured, however.

- *Simplistic and haphazard.* Carson *et al.* (1995) contend that much small firm marketing is *ad hoc* in nature, responding as it does to external factors under the influence of the owner/manager(s), with limited resources. Scase and Goffee (1980) suggest that marketing in small firms is largely intuitive, as does Cox (1993), who argues that small firms seem to exist more on a day-to-day basis. Dunn *et al.* (1985) report that most small firms do not plan. Again, the Thomas *et al.* (1997) study does not wholly concur, suggesting that a majority of small tourism and hospitality firms undertake some form of marketing planning, although no measure of the sophistication of this planning or of the firms' adherence to plans or targets was made.
- *Responsive and reactive to the competition.* This assertion is given some support in the Thomas *et al.* (1997) survey, certainly with regard to pricing policy. Over one-fifth of firms followed the prices set by their local competitors, and 45 per cent of firms conducted formal marketing research into their competitors. Generally, upwards of 45 per cent of all firms surveyed conducted formal marketing research into aspects of their business, their competitors, their customers and, to a limited extent, their business environment. However, apart from research into customer needs and customer service and quality issues, this does mean that a majority of firms did not conduct such research, with as few as one in five firms examining their business environment. Given the generally intense and competitive nature of the business environment for tourism and hospitality firms and the necessity to adapt quickly to factors in this environment, this lack of research on the part of the small tourism and hospitality firms surveyed is a source of concern. As Allen (1985) argues in the context of small tour operators, constant reassessment of the environment is important to both small and large operators in a rapidly-changing industry. Indeed, the greater uncertainty of the external environment is, according to Storey (1994), one of the central distinctions between small and large firms, and thus it would benefit small tourism and hospitality firms to take greater cognizance of it.
- *Inherently informal.* Few, if any, formalized structures for marketing decision-making tend to exist in the smaller firm. Much, if not all, decision-making is undertaken by the owner/manager(s), but their decisions can be readily influenced through informal and usually daily contact with employees (see Chapters 9 and 10).
- *Opportunistic.* Since there are few formalized structures for marketing decision-making, the smaller firm has the advantage of being able to react quickly to external events and to customer needs, and can quickly introduce new concepts and activities, thus capitalizing on opportunities.
- *Short term.* A combination of the above characteristics engenders a short-term approach to marketing planning and marketing activity. This short-term, operational view of small firm marketing is shared by Mendelson (1991) and Robinson and Pearce (1984) among others. There is some evidence to support this from the Thomas *et al.* (1997) survey, with over 73 per cent of firms planning no more than

one year ahead, although a short-term approach is by no means universal and varies from one sector to another.

OTHER SALIENT CHARACTERISTICS OF SMALL TOURISM AND HOSPITALITY FIRMS

Other characteristics of small firms include niching as a strategy (Wilson *et al.*, 1992), cooperative marketing approaches (De Kadt, 1979; Dicken, 1992; Buttle, 1994; Morrison, 1996b), limited customer base (Morrison, 1996b), innovative approaches (Allen, 1985, Carson *et al.*, 1995), intense rivalry and minimal information exchange between industry players (Clarke, 1995).

Niching

Small tourism and hospitality firms can more readily marshal their resources to make an impact on small, more focused segments that value high levels of specialization and customization. Market niching is typically associated with small companies (Wilson *et al.*, 1992; Storey, 1994). Small businesses can niche in a number of ways:

- geographically (e.g. in their early days, Sunmed with Greece-only holidays or Sunvil with Cyprus-only holidays);
- by type of end-user (e.g. canal enthusiasts or history lovers);
- on a quality/price spectrum (e.g. country house hotels, cottages overseas);
- level and standards of service (e.g. local travel agent customizing travel arrangements);
- by product feature (e.g. 'cycling for softies').

Cooperative marketing approaches

Small firms on their own cannot hope to achieve the marketing economies of scale of their larger competitors, and must thus seek some of the advantages that large size confers by other means. De Kadt (1979) was one of the earliest proponents of cooperative marketing arrangements as a means of offsetting the disadvantages, in marketing terms, that are inherent in small size. Independent small firms in the tourism and hospitality industries can work together by pooling resources in order to achieve marketing economies of scale, or by establishing a reciprocal business referral arrangement between two or more companies. In this way, small firms stand to reap many of the benefits that a larger business enjoys, while still maintaining the advantages of being small (Buttle, 1994).

Dicken (1992) points out that not only is there now a substantial number of cooperative marketing arrangements for small tourism and hospitality firms, but their scale, proliferation and the centrality of the role they play in small firm marketing are growing considerably.

There are many potential benefits that may accrue to small firms as a result of membership of a marketing cooperative. These include: access to professional expertise and training; jointly-funded brochures; marketing research; increased purchasing power; regular exchange of information and research findings; a more extensive and effective distribution system; and a stronger lobbying voice (Middleton, 1994).

Limited customer base

As a consequence of smaller size, smaller 'production' capacity and more limited access to resources in terms of funds and expertise, small firms can generally service fewer customers and fewer types of customer. On the one hand, this leaves them open to the vagaries of changes in customer needs, and should these change suddenly, the small firm may find itself with a reduced customer base. On the other hand, such a narrow focus on customers can pave the way to greater understanding of their market and may allow the small firm to anticipate better and satisfy customer needs (Cannon, 1991; Morrison, 1996).

Innovative approaches

Carson *et al.* (1995) suggest that small firms tinker with existing products, often in response to needs identified by their customers, and that these incremental developments can be interpreted as evidence of the small firm's market orientation. Some suggest, however, that this does not constitute real innovation, which is characterized by devoting scarce resources over a longer period of time to developing new ideas and taking risks with these new ideas in bringing them to market. Given their putative limited research and development function and their limited resources, it is argued that small firms are therefore unlikely to generate truly innovative products, but are more likely to engage in continuous incremental and short-term tinkering. This is supported by Cox (1993), who found that, contrary to expectations, small firms were not more active in emerging markets. In opposition to this stance, Pavitt *et al.* (1987) contend that small firms are more likely to introduce fundamentally new innovations than larger firms, a view which Allen (1985) supports. Rothwell (1983) argues that small firms are great innovators, and Wynarczyk *et al.* (1993) assert that innovation is one of the key areas in which small firms differ from large firms. Cannon (1991) attributes greater innovative and creative marketing in small firms to top management's (usually the owner's) commitment and ability to influence staff at all levels, and thus to marshal the firm's resources behind its marketing efforts. This draws tentative support from Thomas *et al.* (1997). Their work found that 40 per cent of small tourism and hospitality firms had conducted research into possible new products or services. By staying close to their customers and their customers' needs and wants, small firms may unwittingly inhibit innovation by catering predominantly for these needs.

Lack of cooperation among industry players

Clarke (1995), in her examination of farm accommodation providers, suggests that, as a consequence of their small size, firms in the tourism and hospitality industries tend to be isolated from main tourism flows, which results in attitudes of rivalry and minimal information exchange between industry players. This finding is supported by Friel (1991) in his examination of small-scale tourism firms in rural areas of Ireland.

STRENGTHS AND WEAKNESSES OF SMALL TOURISM AND HOSPITALITY FIRMS' MARKETING

Some of the previously mentioned characteristics of small firms can work to their advantage, allowing them to compete effectively and to be successful where larger firms might struggle. Equally, some characteristics may be regarded as weaknesses in the marketing task.

Strengths
- Quality of service may be controlled better as management is more closely linked to labour.
- Closer contact with customers allows small firms to track changes in customers' needs and wants.
- Smaller scale allows management to adjust service offerings more rapidly to these changes in customers' needs and wants.
- Small firms may therefore be in a position to offer more specialized and individualized products.
- Small firms may be more likely to be able to assess price elasticity at the individual customer level.
- Some customers have a perception of smaller firms as providing higher levels of service.
- The press and media may be more sympathetic to the needs and achievements of smaller businesses, and may thus provide publicity and coverage at little cost.
- Good knowledge of local markets or regional markets.
- Limited share of market may engender a more focused, more informed approach.
- Ability to act quickly in response to external opportunities and developments, as only one person or a small group of people takes all the key decisions.
- Greater internal consistency of the small firm's motivations and actions, as it is managed exclusively by one person or a small group of persons.
- Many small firms occupy niches where they may be able to maintain higher prices and profits.
- Small firms can offer appropriate and successful products in these niches that larger firms would find difficult or costly to copy.
- Small firms are often very innovative.
- Small firms serve the needs of the local community.
- Many small firms service specialist needs or the needs of particular user groups (e.g. customized business travel services, small museums).
- Top management's commitment and ability to influence staff at all levels is not easily matched by the larger firm.

Weaknesses
- Difficult to enjoy economies of scale, although this can be partially addressed through membership of marketing consortia.
- Perception on the part of some customers that small firms may be less reliable, may have fewer suitable products, may charge higher prices and possess less expertise, etc.
- Lack of specialist marketing expertise.
- Small firms can be more product-oriented than the larger firms: that is, the marketing effort is organized around products more than markets.

- Greater external uncertainty of the small firm business environment.
- Staying close to customers and their needs and wants can tie the firm in to its current customer base and may thus inhibit innovation.
- Limited customer base, where small firms may have all their eggs in one or two baskets.
- Knowledge of customers may be distorted by subjectivity and selectivity.
- Resources are limited so it may be difficult to establish fully a comprehensive and adequate range of marketing activities and to compete effectively with larger firms.
- Limited resources may also restrict the small firm's ability to capitalize fully on its marketing strengths.

It is useful to remember that not all of the above strengths and weaknesses will apply to all small tourism and hospitality firms in all circumstances, and that some strengths will be outweighed or neutralized by some weaknesses, and vice versa.

KEY CONSIDERATIONS IN SMALL TOURISM AND HOSPITALITY FIRMS' MARKETING

Middleton (1994) states that the marketing mix consists of the four Ps of product formulation, pricing, promotion and place (distribution). Middleton argues against subdividing the mix further, as proposed by Booms and Bitner (1981) and many subsequent authors (Cowell, 1984; Morrison, 1989; Payne, 1993; Dibb *et al.*, 1994), stating that 'it helps the understanding of a central marketing concept to focus on an unambiguous, easy to understand four Ps' (Middleton, 1994, p. 66). Given that the four Ps are in general use even in the tourism and hospitality industries, they provide a useful framework for the following discussion, together with an examination of marketing research and marketing planning.

Product formulation

Davis *et al.* (1985) have proposed that small firms may be more successful in offering perishable products or those requiring substantial levels of service. In other words, small firms may be at an advantage as regards superior customization of products and personalization of service (Morrison, 1996b). This is the case for most tourism and hospitality products, where there is generally high customer contact, and where management, in the words of Davis *et al.*, is better able to control the quality of service and adjust service levels as required, in that it is often more closely linked to labour.

Davis *et al.* (1988) also argue that, for large firms, standardization is important, as they can thereby enjoy economies of scale, but for small firms offering unique or distinctive products, standardization is not always possible or desirable. While it may be true that economies of scale in production may be difficult for small firms to achieve, through cooperative arrangements or consortia small firms can achieve marketing economies of scale and a certain increase in purchasing leverage. Although the number of small firms in the Thomas *et al.* (1997) survey that are members of a consortium is low at 6 per cent, almost one-third were members of a national trade/professional association, regional tourist board or local tourism association (see Table 7.1). This provides some, albeit crude, indication of the importance of cooperative arrangements amongst small tourism and hospitality firms.

Table 7.1 Membership of associations and other professional bodies

Association or body	No. of members (%)
Consortium	6.1
Local general business association	14.1
Local industry-specific association	6.5
Local TEC	3.6
National trade/professional association	27.7
Regional tourist board	27.4
Local tourist association	27.5

Source: Data from Thomas *et al.* (1997).

Pricing

Price is one of the key tools in the marketing 'toolbox' and is particularly important in helping to manage demand and sales. Many tourism and hospitality firms are price followers, responding to the dictates of the market place (Middleton, 1994). Small firms cannot compete on price with larger competitors, and non-price competition is safer and often more successful for small firms (Scarborough and Zimmerer, 1996). It is suggested that small firms in the tourism and hospitality industries use the tools of pricing much as larger firms do (Morrison, 1996b). However, one-third of respondents in the Thomas *et al.* (1997) study used variable pricing approaches, and although almost half of all firms used cost-plus pricing, when the figures are adjusted to account for large numbers within particular sectors which distort the mean, the most used pricing technique across the tourism and hospitality sectors surveyed was a variable pricing approach. This provides some tentative support for Curran *et al.*'s (1995) contention that the price-setting approach of small business owners is not the simplistic, mechanistic process that it is frequently depicted. Indeed, Davis *et al.* (1985) have suggested that small firms may be more likely than larger firms to assess price elasticity at the individual customer level by negotiating prices. Increasingly nowadays, however, larger companies seem to be allowing their employees some latitude in this area.

It is suggested (Storey, 1994) that small firms can maintain higher prices and profits than the industry norm, as many small firms occupy niches by providing highly specialized services (possibly in a geographically isolated area) and often do not perceive themselves to have clear competitors. In many cases, higher prices are often equated with higher levels of service and better quality levels of service (Carson *et al.* 1995). Carson *et al.* also argue that perhaps as a result of feeling vulnerable on price, particularly in relation to larger competitors, small firms' marketing is oriented around price. This may inhibit innovation in other areas of the marketing mix and may ultimately be detrimental as a result of retaliatory actions by competitors.

Promotion

Promotion constitutes another key area of marketing activity. It usually comprises a variety of activities and objectives, which include creating awareness of the firm's products and values, reinforcing current customer buying habits and encouraging customers and non-customers to try the firm's products. The ultimate objective of promotional activity is to help to achieve a certain level of demand for tourism and hospitality products. It could be argued that the main objective of promotion for larger firms is to reinforce buying habits among their current customer base (Seaton and Bennett, 1996). For smaller firms, promotion often serves to act in the role of creating awareness. It must be remembered that smaller enterprises usually operate within quite severe resource constraints: their promotion budget cannot match that of their larger competitors and they are therefore limited in the scope, scale and often sophistication of their promotional efforts. In that the bulk of sales of small firms is to highly localized markets (Storey, 1994), it is to be expected that local advertising will feature prominently in small firm promotional activities.

Some evidence for this can be found in the Thomas *et al.* (1997) study, where over two-thirds of firms sampled used local advertising (see Table 7.2). Interestingly, however, it also found that national advertising was the third most used form of promotion, and in the accommodation sectors it constituted the most used form of promotion. This may be partly ascribed to many small hospitality firms availing themselves of national registers, guidebooks and directories.

Table 7.2 Use of promotion methods by sector (percentages)

	Mean % for all sectors	Visitor attractions	Travel agents	Hotels	Bed and breakfasts	Self-catering	Public houses	Fast food/ take-aways	Restaurants/ cafes
Local advertising	63	75	61	60	53	53	76	63	72
Sales literature	48	66	44	82	68	89	29	30	34
Price promotions	48	60	46	64	43	55	55	30	41
National advertising	37	50	34	73	75	93	16	6	14
Personal selling	23	21	49	34	12	18	26	15	20
Competitions	20	19	17	16	5	15	41	10	12
Merchandising	14	15	12	9	3	0	35	4	8
Sponsorship	13	11	15	12	4	9	19	13	14
Internet	11	28	5	28	26	15	2	0	3

Source: Thomas *et al.* (1997, p. 45).

Perhaps unsurprisingly, the joint second most used forms of promotion by small tourism and hospitality firms were price promotions and sales literature. Price promotions are a common competitive tool in the tourism and hospitality industries as a result of the ready substitutability of many of their products. Just under half the firms used this form of promotion. The same number of firms used sales literature as a form of promotion, which may be partly explained by the pivotal role that timely and appropriate information provision plays in tourism and hospitality.

The least used form of promotion was advertising on the Internet, closely followed by sponsorship and merchandising (see Table 7.2). While advertising on the Internet was the least used form of promotion, overall it ranked much higher in certain sectors, particularly the accommodation sectors (see Table 7.3), where many firms have made their brochures available for browsing on the Internet. It is noteworthy that over 10 per cent of small tourism and hospitality firms advertised on the Internet, and this in itself constitutes a sizable number of firms. This figure is likely to increase over the next few years, as small firms recognize the potential of the Internet, particularly as a competitive tool and a booking medium.

Table 7.3 Promotion methods ranked within each sector

	Visitor attractions	Travel agents	Hotels	Bed and breakfasts	Self-catering	Public houses	Fast food/ take-aways	Restaurants/cafes
1	Local advertising	Local advertising	Sales literature	National advertising	National advertising	Local advertising	Local advertising	Local advertising
2	Sales literature	Personal selling	National advertising	Sales literature	Sales literature	Price promotions	Price promotions	Price promotions
3	Price promotions	Price promotions	Price promotions	Local advertising	Price promotions	Competitions	Sales literature	Sales literature
4	National advertising	Sales literature	Local advertising	Price promotions	Local advertising	Merchandising	Personal selling	Personal selling
5	Internet	National advertising	Personal selling	Internet	Personal selling	Sales literature	Sponsorship	National advertising
6	Personal selling	Competitions	Internet	Personal selling	Competitions	Personal selling	Competitions	Sponsorship
7	Competitions	Sponsorship	Competitions	Competitions	Internet	Sponsorship	National advertising	Competitions
8	Merchandising	Merchandising	Sponsorship	Sponsorship	Sponsorship	National advertising	Merchandising	Merchandising
9	Sponsorship	Internet	Merchandising	Merchandising	Merchandising	Internet	Internet	Internet

Source: Thomas et al. (1997, p. 46).

Interestingly, merchandising was cited by only one in seven firms in the Thomas *et al.* (1997) research, which would would seem to indicate a failure on the part of most firms to capitalize fully on the presence in-house of visitors or guests by maximizing customer spend. Caution in interpreting this result is opposite, however, as the term 'merchandising' may have been misunderstood.

The picture is broadly similar for growth firms in the sample, with local advertising being the most used form of promotion, followed by sales literature and discounted prices. The major difference in terms of promotion between those firms identified from the survey as growth firms and the sample as a whole lies in the greater proportion of growth firms using the above three forms of promotion, with figures at least 10 per cent higher than for the sample as a whole. Other differences of note include a lower incidence of national advertising (though still a form of promotion used by a third of growth firms) and double the use of merchandising, which points perhaps to a greater exploitation of in-house selling opportunities.

There is little to suggest that there are significant differences in use of promotion methods between small tourism and hospitality firms of different sizes, although firms at either extreme of the size spectrum were marginally more likely to engage in national advertising, which may point towards over-ambitiousness and lack of experience on the part of smaller firms and greater confidence and/or experience and resources on the part of the larger firms.

As firms get older, however, they tend to do more national advertising, although local advertising is still the dominant promotion method. Significantly, perhaps, half of the small tourism and hospitality firms who had made particular use of local advertising saw an increase in turnover and three-quarters of firms had either the same turnover as the previous year or a higher turnover. This does mean that a quarter of all firms making particular use of local advertising saw a decrease in turnover, although it must be remembered that no causal link can be shown. As regards both national advertising and discounted prices, three-quarters of firms had either the same turnover as the previous year or saw an increase in turnover. This rises to almost nine in ten of those firms making particular use of the Internet. It is of note that two-thirds of firms who had attended a marketing course in the previous 12 months reported a rise in turnover.

Research

While it is generally acknowledged that small firms can have a more intimate knowledge of their customers, as many serve the needs of a local community or a specialist market and the owner/manager(s) may know many of the firm's customers personally, this knowledge of customers can be distorted by subjectivity or selectivity (Cannon, 1991). Research into customer needs on a regular basis is a key activity, informing other elements of the small tourism and hospitality firm's business activities. These activities cannot, however, take place in a vacuum, without reference to key influencing factors in the external environment which may impact on the growth and development of the small firm. Ahmed and Krohn (1994) argue that it is to the benefit of small tourism firms to undertake marketing research, in that it will provide them with information that will help them to make better, more informed decisions, and to select more wisely from a range of marketing alternatives. They further state that some small firms incorrectly consider marketing research to be an activity only for larger companies and therefore not applicable to them. Coltman (1989) insists that marketing research is *more* important for the small firm because it does not have the size and, therefore, the resources to rely on if major marketing errors are made.

Cox (1993) posits the view that many small firm managers may see marketing research as a waste of precious resources, in that they already know their customers well. Undoubtedly many do, but regular updating in a structured way – that is, via a marketing research programme – can do much to offset some of the failings of a more intuitive, judgement-based approach.

Recent research (Thomas *et al.*, 1997) has shown that, for a majority of small tourism and hospitality firms, customer needs are the main area of their marketing research activities, and that this focus on customer needs is consistent across the sectors surveyed (see Table 7.4). This provides some tentative and perhaps unsurprising indications of the degree to which the marketing concept is practised in small tourism and hospitality firms. This focus on customer issues is consistent across the sectors. The results are similar for those firms identified as tourism and hospitality growth firms.

Table 7.4 Areas of marketing research on a sectoral basis

	Mean % for all sectors	Visitor attractions	Travel agents	Hotels	Bed and breakfasts	Self-catering	Public houses	Fast food/ take-aways	Restaurants/ cafes
Customer needs	55	58	47	52	44	60	60	50	49
Customer service/quality	51	52	44	48	40	57	56	44	49
Local competition	46	18	36	42	33	28	62	42	43
Marketing effectiveness	40	39	25	48	53	66	34	19	29
New products/ services	39	24	33	28	26	21	52	46	40
Business environment	21	6	14	21	13	11	26	19	23

Source: Thomas *et al.* (1997, p. 42).

Understandably, given the nature of the intensely competitive environment within which tourism and hospitality firms operate, and the importance of physical proximity to their main markets, there is significant research effort focused on the local competition, although there is considerable variation across the sectors, with public houses most likely to undertake such research and visitor attractions least likely.

The other main area of marketing research in small tourism and hospitality firms is marketing effectiveness, i.e. research into how successful the firm's marketing actions had been over the previous 12 months. Over 40 per cent of firms had undertaken such research, although again there were considerable variations across the sectors, with travel agents, fast food/take-aways and restaurants/cafes conducting much less research into marketing effectiveness than the other sectors (see Table 7.4).

Interestingly, the least researched area among the Thomas *et al.* (1997) sample was the external business environment, with just one-fifth of firms conducting such research, and only 6 per cent of visitor attractions. This has obvious implications for the efficacy of long-term planning, where, oddly, small-scale visitor attractions was the most represented sector. However, the number of growth firms conducting such research is only marginally up on the sample as a whole, so perhaps taking cognizance of the external business environment may not be a prerequisite for growth. It is often assumed that it is vital in such intensely competitive and rapidly changing industries for small firms to monitor their business environment in order better to respond to and manage change and exploit opportunities. Thomas *et al.* (1997) provide some evidence of an apparent myopia in the marketing research activities of small tourism and hospitality firms.

Ahmed and Krohn (1994) contend that few small tourism firms have ever conducted a comprehensive marketing research study, i.e. one that includes an assessment of marketing advantages, an analysis of market needs, an examination of competitive threats and a review of environmental factors. While there may be some validity in this, the data from the Thomas *et al.* (1997) project seem to suggest that research is undertaken into market needs and into the competition by small tourism and hospitality firms, even if research in many cases might be restricted to keeping track of how customers and guests had sought or found information on the firm. One area of concurrence between that study and the evidence proffered by Ahmed and Krohn is the relative dearth of research conducted by small firms into environmental factors pertinent to their business.

It is surprising that relatively few small tourism and hospitality firms conducted research into developing new products or services. This contrasts somewhat with small firms in other research studies, where they have manifested consistently high levels of innovation with regard to new services and products (see Storey, 1994; Barkham *et al.* 1996).

Growth firms do not appear to be very much more innovative by way of introducing new products or services, although it is in this area that there is the greatest difference between the growth firms and the sample as a whole.

The Thomas *et al.* (1997) study provides further insight into marketing research related issues. In relation to firm size, almost half of all research into customer needs and customer service was undertaken by small tourism and hospitality firms with fewer than ten employees, lending weight to Coltman's (1989) argument that smaller firms stand to lose more by not doing research (see above). It is also of note that approximately half of all research into the effectiveness of marketing actions of small tourism and hospitality firms was conducted by firms employing fewer than ten employees, again probably as a result of needing to optimize limited resources. In each of these three areas – customer needs, customer service and marketing effectiveness – the tendency to conduct research increased as the firm size increased, an indication perhaps of firms using marketing as a way of maintaining close links with the customer as communication lines get longer, and having the resources available to do so. The growth firms followed roughly the same pattern as the sample as a whole, except for the area of marketing effectiveness, where a much greater percentage of growth firms conducted such research.

There is little variation in terms of marketing research undertaken according to the age of the firm, although firms aged between five and nine years old were slightly more likely to undertake research into customer needs and customer service. Generally, age seemed to be a poor indicator of a firm's propensity to conduct research, particularly in the area of marketing effectiveness. If anything, size is a more reliable indicator.

One particularly interesting finding from the survey was that small tourism and hospitality firms who had attended a marketing course tended to do more research in each of the six areas surveyed than the sample as a whole. This will be encouraging for those agencies which advocate the value of marketing courses to small firms, particularly the tourist boards and the HtF. For the growth firms, the increases are much more marked, with increases of between 10 and 23 per cent. It must be stressed, however, that these increases may not be attributable in part or in whole to attendance at a marketing course.

Planning

The prescriptive literature takes as its starting point the assumption that most small firms do not undertake formal marketing planning. There is some evidence from the Thomas *et al.* (1997) study that this is not the case generally in the tourism and hospitality industries, where just over half of all firms surveyed had formulated a marketing plan over the previous 12 months. It must be pointed out, however, that the number of firms attesting to having a formal marketing plan was low, at 14 per cent of the sample, while the majority of those who indicated that they had a marketing plan in fact formulated an informal plan (see Table 7.5). The fact that those drawing up a formal marketing plan constituted such a low percentage of Thomas *et al.*'s (1997) respondents may lend support to the assumption that most small firms do not plan. Problems arise, however, in trying to determine the extent to which a plan may be interpreted as formal, as this was likely to have varied across respondents. It is perhaps more appropriate to count both formal and informal planning as evidence of recognition on the part of small tourism and hospitality firms of the importance of planning.

Table 7.5   Type of marketing plan formulated

Type of marketing plan	Firms (%)
Formal	14
Informal	44.5
None	41.5

Source: Thomas *et al.* (1997).

This recognition seems to extend mainly to considering the short term, as the vast majority of small tourism and hospitality firms planned no more than one year ahead. This is in line with the short-run, operational imperatives of the tourism and hospitality industries, and with small firms in other industries. (see Chell, 1985). It seems that a minority of small tourism and hospitality firms plan on a long-term basis:

Devised a plan (formal or informal)	58%
Of which:	
Planned up to one year ahead	73%
Planned up to three years ahead	22%
Planned up to five years ahead	5%

It is interesting to note that the visitor attraction sector differed markedly from the other sectors in this respect, being three times more likely to undertake marketing planning up to five years ahead. This may be partly explained by the relatively small numbers of visitor attractions represented in the survey, proportionate to other sectors. The finding needs to be treated with some caution, although it may point to a genuine difference in marketing planning practice in small tourism and hospitality firms (see Table 7.6). Those sectors with the greatest number of firms formulating marketing plans are visitor attractions and the self-catering sectors, with fast food/take-away establishments posting numbers well below the mean for all sectors. Further research into the reasons behind such wide variation in values is needed, although one explanation for low numbers among fast food/take-away establishments may be that they take a more operation-oriented, short-term perspective, exacerbated by intense local competition and the urgency for a speedy response to competitor marketing actions. It is interesting to note that most of the marketing planning of public houses, fast food/take-away establishments and restaurant/cafes tended to be of a mostly short-term nature, more so than other sectors. It is useful here to recall March's (1994) insight that marketing within different tourism sectors is not necessarily homogeneous, and that it might be more beneficial to consider products that show similar marketing practices and exigencies as opposed to firms grouped together according to business category or sector.

Table 7.6 Extent of marketing planning by sector

	Mean % for all sectors	Visitor attractions	Travel agents	Hotels	Bed and breakfasts	Self-catering	Public houses	Fast food/ take-aways	Restaurants/ cafes
Plan in general	58	72	61	61	52	72	58	45	52
Up to one year	73	60	69	54	63	60	85	83	82
Up to three years	22	26	28	29	32	36	11	11	16
Up to five years	5	14	3	4	5	4	4	6	2

Source: Thomas *et al.* (1997, p. 39).

Cox (1993) argues that small firms' marketing input to strategic planning is limited to a support role or little input at all, and that strategic planning is conducted by top management. Again, there is some evidence that this is the case in tourism and hospitality firms.

On balance, however, the Thomas *et al.* (1997) survey would seem to have provided some evidence of a substantial degree of marketing planning among small tourism and hospitality firms, certainly in the short term, where a majority undertook such planning, and to some extent in the medium term, where between one-fifth and one-third of firms undertook marketing planning. It must be borne in mind, however, that the survey did not attempt to gauge the extent of marketing planning other than to determine how far ahead firms planned, or whether the plans were largely adhered to. Nor was any measure taken of the effectiveness of the firm's marketing planning.

Leppard and McDonald (1987) state that the acceptance of marketing planning is determined in the main by the stage of development of the firm. It is acknowledged that, in determining which stage of development a small firm has reached, factors other than age need to considered. However, age of firm is here examined on the basis of providing some indication of stage of development. In this regard, the younger the small tourism and hospitality firm, the more likely it was to produce a marketing plan. There may be several explanations for this. One is that many small tourism and hospitality firms have availed themselves of start-up courses and may have been required to include a marketing element in their business plan. Another is that relative inexperience and a tendency towards risk minimization on the part of the small firm's owner/manager(s) may encourage firms to be more thoroughgoing and methodical at the outset in their desire to do the right thing and not to slip up. Possibly, as firms get older, more experienced and more pressured, less value is accorded the role of the formal marketing plan. Another explanation may be that older firms have become set in their ways and may be unwilling to try a new approach, whereas younger firms may more readily buy into the much vaunted benefits of marketing. It is not clear how this finding squares with the fact that the bigger the firm, the greater the likelihood of it producing a marketing plan. This may more than likely be attributed to increased job specialization as the firm grows and more time and resources being made available to the marketing function. However, the findings for age of firm and size of firm and the likelihood of producing a marketing plan must be regarded as somewhat tentative and inconclusive.

CONCLUSIONS

Much of the evidence concerning the marketing practices and approaches of small firms in general and of small tourism and hospitality firms in particular is contradictory. There is still much research to be conducted into small tourism and hospitality firms' marketing before conclusive observations can be made.

However, it would seem that small tourism and hospitality firms do not by and large conform to the traditional image of the small firm as a business entity relatively unversed in the art of marketing and given to scepticism of marketing. A majority of small tourism and hospitality firms conduct research into key aspects of their business, notably customer needs and customer service issues; a majority of small tourism and hospitality firms formulate a marketing plan, of which three-quarters plan up to one year ahead; a majority use a cost-plus pricing method, but other, more market-oriented, methods are also used; a wide variety of promotional activity is undertaken and one-quarter of firms attended a marketing course. Whether these are reliable indicators of the nature of small tourism and hospitality firm marketing or are an aberration remains to be seen.

REFERENCES

Ahmed, Z.U. and Krohn, F.B. (1994) 'Developing a strategic marketing plan for a small tourism firm', *Journal of Professional Services Marketing*, **10(2)**, 111–27.

Allen, T. (1985) 'Marketing by a small tour operator in a market dominated by big operators', *European Journal of Marketing*, **19(5)**, 83–90.

Barkham, R., Gudgin, G., Hart, M. and Hanvey, E. (1996) *The Determinants of Small Firm Growth – An Interregional Study in the United Kingdom 1986–1990*. London: Jessica Kingsley Publishers.

Batchelor, R. (1996) 'Overseas marketing – guidelines for small operators', *Insights*, **7**, A149–58.

Berkowitz, E., Kerin, R.A., Hartley, S.W. and Rudelius, W. (1992) *Marketing*. Chicago: Irwin.

Booms, B.H. and Bitner, M.J. (1981) 'Marketing strategies and organization structures for service firms', in Donnelly, J. and George, W.R. (eds) *Marketing of Services*. Chicago: American Marketing Association.

Bramsgrove, C.E. and King, B.E.M. (1996) 'Strategic marketing practice amongst small tourism and hospitality businesses', in *Proceedings of IAHMS spring symposium*, Leeds Metropolitan University.

Buttle, F. (1994) *Hotel and Foodservice Marketing*. London: Cassell.

Cannon, T. (1991) 'Marketing for small businesses', in Baker, M.J. (ed.) *The Marketing Book*. Oxford: Butterworth-Heinemann.

Carson, D.J. (1985) 'The evolution of marketing in small firms', *European Journal of Marketing*, **19(5)**, 7–16.

Carson, D., Cromie, S., McGowan, P. and Hill, J. (1995) *Marketing and Entrepreneurship in SMEs: An Innovative Approach*. Hemel Hempstead: Prentice Hall.

Chell, E. (1985) 'The entrepreneurial personality: a few ghosts laid to rest', *International Small Business Journal*, **3(3)**, 43–54.

Clarke, J.R. (1995) 'Sustainable tourism: marketing of farm tourist accommodation', PhD thesis, School of Hotel and Catering Management, Oxford Brookes University.

Cohn, T. and Lindbore, R.A. (1972) 'How management is different in small companies: an AMA management briefing', in Carson, D. *et al.* (eds, 1995) *Marketing and Entrepreneurship in SMEs: An Innovative Approach*. Hemel Hempstead: Prentice Hall.

Colleran, J.F. (1985) 'Strategic marketing considerations for the small firm', *European Journal of Marketing*, **19(5)**, 17–31.

Coltman, M.M. (1989) *Tourism Marketing*. London: Van Nostrand Reinhold.

Cowell, D. (1984) *The Marketing of Services*. Oxford: Butterworth-Heinemann.

Cox, T. (1993) '*Marketing differences between small, medium and large companies*', in Proceedings of the MEG annual conference, Loughborough Business School.

Curran, J., Jarvis, R., Kitching, J. and Lightfoot, G. (1995) '*The pricing decision in small firms: complexities and the deprioritising of economic determinants supporting entrepreneurship and policy*', in Proceedings of the eighteenth IBSA National Conference, Paisley.

Davis, C.D., Hills, G.E. and LaForge, R.W. (1985) 'The marketing/small enterprise paradox: a research agenda', *International Small Business Journal*, **3(3)**, 31–42.

De Kadt, E. (1979) *Tourism: Passport to Development*. Oxford: Oxford University Press.

Dewhurst, J. and Burns, P. (1993) *Small Business Management*. Basingstoke: Macmillan.

Dibb, S., Simkin, L., Pride, W.M. and Ferrell, O.C. (1994) *Marketing Concepts and Strategies*. London: Houghton Mifflin.

Dicken, P. (1992) *Global Shift*. London: Paul Chapman Publishing.

Dunn, M., Birley, S. and Norburn, D. (1985) 'The marketing concept and the smaller firm', *Marketing Intelligence and Planning*, **4(3)**, 3–11.

Friel, M. (1991) '*The development of rural tourism in Ireland with particular reference to the organisations involved and their marketing activities*', MSc dissertation, Department of Management Studies, University of Surrey, Guildford.

Gaedeke, R.M. and Tootelian, D.H. (1992) *Small Business Management*, 3rd edn. Hemel Hempstead: Prentice Hall.

Greenbank, P. (1995) 'Small businesses: from growth to decline?', *Economics and Business Education*, **3(4)**, 148–52.

Hooley, G.J. and Brooksbank, R. (1986) 'Marketing strategies in medium-sized UK companies', *Contemporary Research in Marketing*, **1**, 143–58.

Horner, S. and Swarbrooke, J. (1996) *Marketing Tourism, Hospitality and Leisure in Europe*. London: International Thomson Business Press.

Leppard, J. and McDonald, M. (1987) 'A re-appraisal of the role of marketing planning', *Journal of Marketing Management*, **3(2)**, 159–71.

March, R. (1994) 'Tourism marketing myopia', *Tourism Management*, **15(6)**, 411–15.

Mendelson, J. (1991) 'Small firms and the marketing mission', *Accounting*, **107**.

Middleton, V.T.C. (1994) *Marketing in Travel and Tourism*. Oxford: Butterworth-Heinemann.

Moller, K. and Antilla, M. (1987) 'Marketing capability – a key success factor in small business?', *Journal of Marketing Management*, **3(2)**, 185–203.

Morrison, A.J. (1994) 'Marketing strategic alliances: the small hotel firm', *International Journal of Contemporary Hospitality Management*, **6(3)**, 25–30.

Morrison, A.J. (1995) *'Small firm strategic alliances: the UK hotel industry'*, PhD thesis, Scottish Hotel School, University of Strathclyde, Glasgow.

Morrison, A. (1996a) 'Guesthouses and small hotels', in Jones, P. (ed.) *Introduction to Hospitality Operations*. London: Cassell.

Morrison, A.J. (1996b) 'Marketing the small tourism business', in Seaton, A.V. and Bennett, M.M. (eds) *Marketing Tourism Products, Concepts, Issues, Cases*. London: International Thomson Business Press.

Morrison, A.M. (1989) *Hospitality and Travel Marketing*. Albany, NY: Delmar.

Moutinho, L. (1990) 'Strategies for tourism destination development: an investigation of the role of small businesses', in Ashworth, G. and Goodall, B. (eds) *Marketing Tourism Places*. London: Routledge.

Pavitt, K., Robson, M. and Townsend, J. (1987) 'The size distribution of innovating firms in the UK: 1945–1983', *Journal of Industrial Economics*, **45**, 297–306.

Payne, A. (1993) *The Essence of Services Marketing*. Hemel Hempstead: Prentice Hall.

Quinn, U., Larmour, R. and McQuillan, N. (1992) 'The small firm in the hospitality industry', *International Journal of Contemporary Hospitality Management*, **4(1)**, 11–14.

Robinson, R.D. and Pearce, J.A. (1984) 'Research thrusts in small firm strategic marketing', *Academy of Management Journal*, **25**, 128–37.

Romano, C. and Ratnatunga, J. (1995) 'The role of marketing: its impact on small enterprise research', *European Journal of Marketing*, **29(7)**, 9–30.

Rothwell, R. (1983) 'Innovation and firm size: a case for dynamic complementarity', *Journal of General Management*, **8(3)**.

Scarborough, N.M. and Zimmerer, T.W. (1996) *Effective Small Business Management*. Hemel Hempstead: Prentice Hall.

Scase, R. and Goffee, R. (1980) *The Real World of the Small Business Owner*. London: Croom Helm.

Schollhammer, H. and Kuriloff, A. (1979) *Entrepreneurship and Small Business Management*. Chichester: John Wiley and Sons.

Seaton, A.V. and Bennett, M.M. (eds) (1996) *Marketing Tourism Products, Concepts, Issues, Cases*. London: International Thomson Business Press.

Storey, D., Watson, R. and Wynarczyk, P. (1989) 'Fast growth small businesses. Case studies of 40 small firms in North East England', *Department of Employment Research Paper* no. 67.

Storey, D.J. (1994) *Understanding the Small Business Sector*. London: Routledge.

Thomas, R., Friel, M., Jameson, S. and Parsons, D. (1997) *The National Survey of Small Tourism and Hospitality Firms Annual Report 1996–97*. Leeds: Centre for the Study of Small Tourism and Hospitality Firms, Leeds Metropolitan University.

Wilson, R.M.S., Gilligan, C. and Pearson, D.J. (1992) *Strategic Marketing Management*. Oxford: Butterworth-Heinemann.

Witt, S.F. and Moutinho, L. (1994) *Tourism Marketing and Management Handbook*.

Hemel Hempstead: Prentice Hall.

Wynarczyk, P., Watson, R., Storey, D.J., Short, H. and Keasey, K. (1993) *The Managerial Labour Market in Small and Medium-sized Enterprises*. London: Routledge.

EIGHT

Quality management

Ivor Church and Guy Lincoln

INTRODUCTION

Quality, in the business context, is generally defined as 'fitness for purpose' (Juran, 1979, p. 2.2), although it is often paraphrased as 'meeting the customers' needs'.

The management of quality has changed significantly in recent years, as the traditional organization-led, product-based, mechanistic approach has been superseded – in some areas at least – by a customer-led, process-based, humanistic alternative. This 'new' approach is characterized by a holistic philosophy by which a number of elements together comprise a 'quality system'. For the most part, this change has been led by and been successful in larger manufacturing organizations, although an increasing number of service organizations are now adapting and using the approach (see, for example, Watson *et al.*, 1992; Messenger and Atkins, 1994). The validity of this approach to the tourism and hospitality industries has been widely discussed (Johns, 1992a,b,c). However, the debate has been primarily focused not upon practical management, but upon issues such as the elements that determine perceived quality and the effects of and challenges posed by the intangible, perishable nature of the service elements of the tourism and hospitality product (Lockwood *et al.*, 1992). In consequence, there appears to be little consensus as to the most appropriate approach to managing the quality of the tourism and hospitality product.

This chapter will discuss the importance of quality in small tourism and hospitality firms and review the available literature and empirical evidence in an attempt to identify the most appropriate approach to quality management in these firms.

QUALITY IN THE SMALL TOURISM AND HOSPITALITY CONTEXT

There is little if any published material available that is specific to quality management in small tourism and hospitality firms. However, the need for such firms to have some approach to quality management is self-evident. What is needed, therefore, is to determine the approach that is most appropriate. We will begin to do this by looking in more detail at the importance and role of quality management in these firms. The benefits offered by quality have been well documented in both the small firms literature (e.g. Bemowski, 1992; Reeves and Hoy, 1993; Boon, 1995; British Standards Institution, 1995) and that concerning the tourism and hospitality industries (e.g. Hillier, 1992a, b; Gilbert and Joshi, 1993; Witt and Muhlemann, 1994). To a large extent these benefits are similar, and include:

- improved financial performance through reduced waste, improved efficiency and increased turnover;
- marketing advantage through a better focus on customer needs and the development of competitive strategy;
- operating improvements giving greater control and end-product quality, increased morale, better communication and improved performance from staff. These ultimately lead to business survival and growth.

The importance of any aspect of business management can be determined by how it contributes to the success of that business. A study presented in Barrow (1993) shows that quality of the product or service is identified by small businesses as the single most important indicator of the success of that business. It is important to understand this relationship between quality and prosperity for small tourism and hospitality firms in more depth, as they are operating in an increasingly competitive market (Crawford-Welch, 1992; Sinclair and Arthur, 1994; Lee and Hing, 1995), in which more than 90 per cent of the businesses are classed as small (Manchester Business School, 1995). The nature of the tourism and hospitality product is such that, if a firm does not offer a quality product, the customer can easily switch, at negligible cost, to one that does. This situation raises two possibilities: first, that quality products are required to retain existing customers (Lee and Hing, 1995; Yasin and Zimmerer, 1995); second, that they may be used to establish competitive advantage and thus attract new customers (Haywood, 1983; Gilbert and Joshi, 1993). It is our contention that, in the current tourism and hospitality market, the first of these possibilities is most likely (i.e. a quality product is a minimum requirement to stay in business). This is not to argue that the element of quality cannot provide a small tourism and hospitality firm with a competitive advantage, but this would necessitate a progression from 'quality', as defined here, to 'excellence'. Simply put, excellence can be said to be exceeding the expectations of customers. The flexibility and innovative nature of small firms makes this strategy a real possibility. However, the sustainability of this advantage is more debatable, as other firms can see the success of any initiative and copy it with relative ease. This results, over time, in it becoming a requirement if the customers are to perceive the product as possessing quality. This development in the expectations customers have of the products of small tourism and hospitality firms make it more difficult for them to use quality to competitive advantage.

LARGE VERSUS SMALL FIRMS

There is general agreement that the techniques of quality management were defined in the large firm context and have become devolved down to the small firm level (North *et al.*, 1995). The response of small firms to this is summed up by a quotation from the report from the Institute of Directors (IOD, 1996, p. 25): 'The rules were made by big business, for big business, then inflicted on small business.' Barrier (1992, p. 25) proposes an interesting argument as to why this should be the case when he states that large firms adopt formal quality management approaches in an attempt to 'recapture the spark which made them big in the first place'. This pattern is repeated within the small business sector itself: a survey reported by Bemowski (1992) showed that larger small firms (in that case defined as 100 to 500 employees) were twice as likely to focus on quality improvement as smaller small firms (fewer than 20 employees).

Some writers argue that although large firms may adopt quality management approaches more often, there is actually little difference in the type of approach appropriate in small or large firms (Barrier, 1992; Bemowski, 1992). However, others propose that larger firms do, in fact, adopt more formal and structured approaches to quality management (Chittenden *et al.*, 1995; North *et al.*, 1995). These more formal approaches have certain elements in common:

- the use of specific quality management and processes;
- they are more likely to be systematic, with well-developed administrative support;
- they are more likely to be bureaucratic and involve some form of accreditation or quality standard (e.g. BS EN ISO 9000).

It was suggested earlier that all companies need and possess some form of approach to ensure the quality of their goods and services. This seems to contradict the findings of Bemowski (1992) that only 27 per cent of the smallest firms are considering quality improvement. This can perhaps be explained by the findings of Cranswick (1995) that a number of small firms were actually using the techniques of a formal approach, but were either unaware of this or were using them in isolation, rather than as a part of a structured quality management system.

Chittenden *et al.* (1995) support the argument that most small firms use some form of informal approach to quality management. These were found to be largely satisfactory for the small firms involved and did not present any problems for the market acceptance of their products and services. The success or otherwise of the formal approach is found to depend on a number of criteria. These include the management strategies, the attitudes and motivations of management and employees, the size of the firm and the operating environment (North *et al.*, 1995). The management style of the business owner or operator may also play a part here. The Small Business Research Trust (SBRT, 1994) suggests that because of the 'hands on' approach of small business operators, it is possible to adopt successfully the less formal approach to quality.

MANUFACTURING VERSUS SERVICES

We have already identified that the majority of the formal approaches to quality are derived from larger companies. It is also widely accepted that these approaches were developed in and for manufacturing firms. Much recent discussion has focused on the differing requirements for quality assurance and enhancement in services and manufacturing. This debate does not suggest that service industries should ignore formal approaches to quality, but that such approaches have to be modified. Heymann (1992) sums up this argument when he says that, in the area of quality management, the hospitality industry can no longer seek guidance from manufacturing industries. This does not appear to be a lesson that the industry has been quick to learn – eight years previously, Wyckoff (1984) stated that manufacturing approaches were inappropriate for the tourism and hospitality industries, as they tended to remove the personal touch and treated staff like unthinking 'cogs' in the process. Despite this, the mechanistic approach has been widely used (Coyle and Dale, 1993). There is still some belief in the value of the mechanistic approaches in considerations of food quality. In respect of the service element of the tourism and hospitality product, however, this approach is beginning to be considered inappropriate in all but the most structured, systematized and impersonal operations. This debate about the differing needs of tourism and hospitality firms is still found in more recent considerations of quality issues in the industry (Lockwood *et al.*, 1992; Gilbert and Joshi, 1993; Witt and Muhlemann, 1994; Sinclair and Arthur, 1994; Zetie *et al.*, 1994a). A consensus has yet to emerge, and a number of authors on quality management in tourism and hospitality propose approaches which have a lot of elements similar to the formal approaches used in manufacturing (Heymann, 1992; Johns, 1992a,b,c; Hubrecht and Teare, 1993).

The elements that are common include the need for:

- a detailed and comprehensive knowledge of the product to be delivered to customers, which should be used to develop a precise definition of the product and service as an objective for the firm;
- a holistic approach where the importance of all the elements of quality is understood and managed;
- recognition of the importance of people within the quality system, (i.e. having a culture which supports the achievement of quality and recognizes the value of teams in supporting this culture, motivating the workforce and training people to be able to contribute effectively to the achievement of quality objectives);
- measurement and auditing of the quality/customer satisfaction achieved.

So we have a situation where it is recognized that for small firms the less formal approach to quality is more appropriate. Yet, in the tourism and hospitality literature, the recommended approach seems to contain most of the elements of a formal system. At this stage it is not possible to see how this theory articulates with practice, as most accounts of quality management practices adopted in the tourism and hospitality industries are largely anecdotal and case based. This is a situation which has been unchanged since Gilbert and Joshi (1993, p. 158) identified that, 'although a range of quality control models have been proposed, there lacks a body of empirical research undertaken specifically with regard the hospitality product'. That which is available is almost exclusively based on firms adopting formal approaches, and is largely concerned with one of three areas:

- the use of certification (Hillier, 1992a,b; Samuel, 1995);
- the application of total quality management (TQM) (Hubrecht and Teare, 1993; Baldacchino, 1995; Breiter *et al.*, 1995; Camison, 1996).
- the use of measurement/audit models (Fick and Ritchie, 1991; Barsky, 1992; Newton and van der Merwe, 1992; Lee and Hing, 1995).

Although there are examples of authors recommending the use of statistical and other mechanistic techniques in specific situations (Wyckoff, 1984; Records and Glennie, 1991), there is agreement in general that the extremely mechanistic approaches are not appropriate for either small firms or tourism and hospitality businesses. A lot of the criticisms of these formal approaches are the same for both small businesses and tourism and hospitality firms. Thus, for small tourism and hospitality firms, the difficulties are compounded. Formal approaches, it has been claimed, tend to stifle the creative and innovative nature of small tourism and hospitality firms. Peacock (1996) proposes that innovation is one means by which customers perceive the quality of these firms, and that they are inherently more innovative and creative than large organizations. This creativity offers a major marketing edge for the small tourism and hospitality firm. Thus, approaches to quality which are too formal can be argued to have a negative effect on the performance of these businesses. Specifically, the approaches of larger firms which are geared to standardization are not just inappropriate: they can actually be harmful.

The difficulty of specifically defining the tourism and hospitality product is well documented (Haywood, 1983; Johns, 1992a,b; Coyle and Dale, 1993). If this is true for the larger companies, with all their resources and specific marketing and operations expertise, then the problem must be compounded in small firms which do not have these attributes. This specification is the first stage of a formal approach to quality management and the difficulties inherent, therefore, make the use of formal systems in small tourism and hospitality management firms more difficult and unlikely. However, this can be mitigated by the closeness of small firms to the customer (Zetie *et al.*, 1994b). This closeness reduces the need for the more formal methods of establishing customer needs such as detailed market research. Finally, as identified earlier, the large amount of time and effort devoted to the human resource element of formal quality control systems is not necessary in smaller firms. The smaller a firm, the easier it is to communicate the vision, to motivate the workforce and to ensure a belief in and commitment to quality without the large-scale culture change and training exercises of larger firms. In short, the people elements of a quality system should come more naturally to a small firm, and consequently they do not need formal elements to develop these.

We have argued that small tourism and hospitality firms should adopt an approach to the management of quality which is less formal but still recognizes the importance of a quality product and all the elements that influence this. It is now necessary to examine the possible strategies and techniques that could make up this approach to determine what is most appropriate in the small tourism and hospitality business context.

RETROSPECTIVE AND PREVENTATIVE QUALITY CONTROL

Traditionally, manufacturing organizations have attempted to control product quality in an informal, retrospective manner, based upon standards against which samples of product are inspected, usually by specialist quality control staff. Many hospitality and tourism firms have used a similar approach, although a number of drawbacks have been identified. These may be categorized as being generic or specific to the nature of the tourism and hospitality product.

The generic drawbacks are that failure both incurs expensive reprocessing or discard and provides little information regarding the reasons for failure. This information is necessary if similar failures are to be avoided in the future.

The drawbacks specific to the food product relate to the time requirement for, and the reliability of, end-product testing. As the hot holding of food detrimentally affects its quality, chefs aim to minimize the period between production and service. Thus, inadequate time for detailed, objective, inspection exists. This is of particular importance with the microbiological safety of food, as this cannot be reliably assessed sensorially. The major drawback relating to the retrospective control of service quality is that inspection is highly intrusive in the service encounter.

These drawbacks have resulted in the increasing acceptance of an alternative approach, namely preventative quality control. This differs from its predecessor in that the process (of producing the food or delivering the service) is controlled much more tightly using process standards and procedures. This increased level of control reduces the probability of failure and thus enables end-product testing to be reduced or eliminated. This has been shown to produce significant cost savings.

The design and implementation of preventative quality control systems is aided by two tools, namely hazard analysis critical control points (HACCP) and failure modes and effects analysis (FMEA). These are almost identical, in that they both identify potential failures that may occur within a system in order for them to be controlled (usually by the setting and monitoring of process standards). The only difference of note between the two tools is in application: HACCP is used primarily for food safety (although it can be readily adapted to include sensory and nutritional aspects of food quality), whereas FMEA may be applied to all service delivery systems. The former has been widely discussed (e.g. Sprenger, 1993), whereas the latter is perhaps less familiar and thus merits more detailed discussion here.

Hazard analysis critical control points

HACCP is a tool that enables the systematic design and implementation of a preventative food safety control system. It involves the examination of the ingredients, processes and environment involved in the production of a single product (e.g. steak and kidney pie) or related group of products (e.g. meat-based pies) in order to identify where a physical, chemical or microbiological risk to consumers exists. These points are referred to as 'risk inputs'. Each risk input has one or a number of corresponding control points – factors that, if controlled, will reduce the risk to an acceptable level. The risk inputs (and thus corresponding control points) present different levels of risk in terms of probability and severity. Those which present the greatest risk (i.e. where a loss of control would result in an unacceptable risk to the consumer) are designated as critical control points. These are controlled by the application of (primarily process) standards and procedures. The documentation of such a system (primarily by designated staff confirming conformance or otherwise by signature) is potentially of great value in establishing the defence of 'due diligence' under food safety legislation (Sprenger, 1993, p. 208).

Little work has been undertaken regarding the use of HACCP in small catering firms. However, anecdotal evidence indicates that many consider it to be unnecessary, unduly complex and expensive to implement.

Failure modes and effects analysis

FMEA is a tool designed to identify potential failures within a production or service delivery system in order that they may either be eliminated or controlled. It is well established in manufacturing industries (Gevirtz, 1994) but may be readily adapted to other contexts, including small tourism and hospitality firms. It has five stages, as follows.

1. Define the product or service to be examined. In the case of food products, this involves the preparation of a detailed definition of the product in terms of its sensory (and, where relevant, nutritional) quality attributes. The sensory quality attributes should provide a highly detailed description of the product in terms of factors such as appearance, texture, flavour, service temperature and portion size. In the case of service delivery systems, this stage involves preparing a process flow diagram to represent the passage of the customer through the system. The customer requirements at each of the external interfaces (i.e. the points at which the customer comes into contact with the system) should be defined in terms of quality attributes (e.g. when ordering either a meal in a restaurant or a holiday in a travel agent, a customer would expect the staff to be friendly, tidy, competent and possess some product knowledge).

2. List all possible failure modes. These are the ways in which the product or service could fail to achieve the intended quality in a manner noticeable to the customer. A food product, for example, could be overseasoned or undercooked; in a service delivery system, staff could be unfriendly or untidy.

3. Set down the effects that each failure mode is likely to have upon both the customer and the organization. Effects upon the customer should include factors such as 'annoyance' or 'health risk'; effects upon the organization should include factors such as the impact upon operational efficiency and the risk of legal action.

4. List all possible causes of each failure mode (e.g. overcooking of food may be the result of a failure to follow the recipe, the incorrect operation of equipment or equipment malfunction; untidy staff may be the result of poor recruitment, inadequate training or laundry shortages).

5. Use experience, reliability data (if available) and professional judgement to assess numerically the failure modes on a scale from one to ten for the following categories. *Probability* of occurrence (P), where 1 = unlikely to occur, 10 = almost certain to occur. *Severity* of the failure on the customer (S), where 1 = minor nuisance, 10 = very severe effect, safety hazard. Difficulty of *detecting* the failure before the product or service is used by the customer (D), where 1 = easily detected, 10 = unlikely to be detected.

The allocation of scores is made easier and more objective if they are defined in some detail. Although a number of generic guidelines have been published (e.g. Gevirtz, 1994), they should – ideally – be situation-specific.

- Calculate the product of the ratings (i.e. $P \times S \times D$) for each failure mode. This is the risk priority number (RPN) or criticality index (CI). This indicates the relative importance of each failure mode in terms of failure prevention and control.
- Rank the failure modes according to their RPN.
- Beginning at the top of the ranked list, identify suitable preventative measures for each failure mode. These generally involve the formulation of standards and monitoring procedures as previously discussed.
- Once the preventative control system is in place, FMEA may be used to support continuous improvement. In this context, FMEA is undertaken periodically, and on each occasion the highest ranking failure modes are addressed – either by redesign of the process to eliminate the problem or by the revision of the preventative measures.

The use of tools such as HACCP and FMEA can undoubtedly produce an effective preventative quality control system. They do not, however, necessarily produce the holistic approach to quality management that should be the aim of most organizations, large and small. This, however, may be encouraged by the utilization of other standards, methods and strategies, namely Investors in People, benchmarking, BS EN ISO 9000, TQM and quality costing. These will now be discussed in the context of small tourism and hospitality firms.

INVESTORS IN PEOPLE

Investors in People (IiP) is an award achieved by organizations who attain a national standard relating to the continuous training and development of their management and staff – this being strategically planned and linked to the business objectives. This improved education and training is said to result in or be accompanied by increased levels of staff motivation, communication and involvement. Moreover, it is claimed by Investors in People UK that this in turn, improves business performance and ultimately 'creates a culture of continuous improvement' (IiP UK, 1995a, p. 1). The practical difficulties involved in creating cultural change are well documented, and the efficacy of IiP in addressing them alone is disputable. The claim that IiP forms a step on the way to TQM (IiP UK, 1995b, p. 9) is however, less contentious.

Another benefit claimed for IiP is that it enhances the image of the organization in the eyes of both customers and potential recruits, thus providing both marketing and recruitment benefits.

Of the little work that is available to support or deny these claims in the small business context, that of Moore (1995) is probably the most comprehensive. This reported the results of a postal survey sent to the first 236 small (employing fewer them 25 employees) firms to achieve the award. In all 167 (i.e. 70.2 per cent) firms responded, of which 82.2 per cent offered either financial or 'other' services. Tourism and hospitality businesses were not specifically identified. The most frequently cited benefit of IiP was a general improvement in staff motivation, commitment and morale (41.9 per cent of responses), followed by the formalization of training and development procedures and systems (28.1 per cent). It would perhaps be expected – particularly in such a 'service'-oriented sample – that these benefits would be accompanied by a significant improvement in quality output. This, however, was not the case: only 15 per cent of respondents claimed a 'major' improvement in quality as a direct result of IiP. This would appear to indicate that IiP alone is not a total solution to quality problems, even in the so-called 'people industries'. Other benefits identified were that IiP increased recognition and credibility, improved business planning and, in some cases (37 per cent of respondents) led either directly or indirectly to improved financial performance.

The promotional material produced by Investors in People UK (IiP UK, 1995b, p. xiii) includes one hospitality SME, namely the (81-bed) Cumberland Hotel in London. It is claimed that over a three-year period (1991 to 1993), during which it gained the standard, a number of benefits were obtained. These included increased productivity (and consequent reduced real wage costs) and a reduction in labour turnover from 20 to 7 per cent. Although IiP was undoubtedly a contributory factor, little real evidence was provided that it was directly or primarily the cause of the improvements.

Little attention has been paid to the disadvantages of IiP. However, Wood (1995) reported that many small firms are concerned about both bureaucracy and the time and potential costs of achieving the standard. Some attempt has been made to address these concerns by minimizing the amount of documentation necessary. It should be noted, however, that with such standards a certain level of documentation is an absolute requirement.

In the tourism and hospitality context, IiP appears to address several issues of importance. First (and despite the data of Moore, 1995, discussed previously), any improvements in staff skill and attitude must logically produce some improvement in quality. In addition, it could, in part, enhance the industry's image as a poor employer. Finally, IiP would also appear to address the fact that many small firms seem to regard training as the responsibility of larger organizations.

BENCHMARKING

Benchmarking is a strategic tool by which organizations continually evaluate and improve their processes and/or performance by learning from and comparing themselves with other organizations. The process involves a formalized partnership between two organizations for the specific purpose of addressing an issue or problem. The most powerful use of the technique involves the identification and investigation of different approaches to process problems. However, a simpler use, namely the comparison of performance indicators (e.g. gross profit), has proven useful in highlighting areas of potential improvement. Three options exist regarding benchmarking partners: they may be internal (i.e. within the same organization), external (i.e. a different organization, usually within the same industrial sector) or 'best practice' (i.e. an organization representing the highest standards, regardless of industrial sector). Each of these types has particular advantages and disadvantages. Internal benchmarking is relatively simple to arrange and undertake, but is unlikely to produce any significantly different approaches or solutions. Its major function, therefore, is to allow the technique to be practiced in a low-risk situation. External benchmarking is rather more difficult to arrange (as the partners are, by definition, potential competitors), but the chances of producing significantly different approaches or solutions are greater. Best practice benchmarking is the most challenging (as the mutual understanding arising from similar interests and experiences is removed), but is most likely to produce radical approaches or solutions.

Small firms are excluded from internal benchmarking by definition, although the other options are available. As small firms are qualitatively different (Storey, 1994) from and may have difficulty establishing credibility with larger firms, it may be advisable – initially at least – for small firms to benchmark against each other. The various small business and/or trade associations have a potentially important role in this respect, particularly in terms of effecting introductions between interested parties (IOD, 1996). An extension of this role would allow some of the potential problems of external benchmarking to be addressed – for example, the endemic fear of 'helping the competition' could be eliminated by linking geographically separate firms.

Little has been published specific to tourism and hospitality firms and that which is available is anecdotal in nature (e.g. Tutcher, 1995). The Department of National Heritage (DNH, 1996) has published a booklet entitled *Benchmarking for Smaller*

Hotels, but its content is primarily composed of (survey-derived) criteria against which hoteliers may evaluate their own performance, and would perhaps have been more accurately entitled *Benchmarks for Smaller Hotels*.

BS EN ISO 9000

BS EN ISO 9000 (commonly referred to as ISO 9000) is an international standard that aims to ensure consistency of production/delivery, principally by means of documented procedures. In order to attain the standard, an organization must conform to approximately 20 requirements relating to the quality management system and be successfully audited by a third-party certification body. The auditing process is repeated at regular intervals to ensure that conformance is maintained. An organization may achieve certification under one of three parts. (ISO 9001, 9002 or 9003). This is dependent upon the nature of the business. ISO 9002 (BSI, 1994) is considered to be the most appropriate for tourism and hospitality firms. Specific guidelines exist to aid the application of the standard to both small businesses (DTI, 1995a; Institute of Quality Assurance (IQA), 1995) and the hotel and catering industry (BSI, 1991). A number of general (e.g. Oakland, 1993; Dalfonso, 1995) and specific (e.g. Stebbing and Pengelly, 1994) texts discuss ISO 9000 in the small business context. Collyer (1996) offers guidance for small firms contemplating the implementation of ISO 9000, including some selection criteria for consultants and certification bodies. These imply that previous experience of small firms is the primary requirement.

Considerable debate has taken place regarding the value of ISO 9000 to small businesses, and although much of this is anecdotal in nature, several objective investigations have been undertaken. Perhaps the most exhaustive investigation undertaken to date is that of the Small Business Research Trust (SBRT, 1994; Chittenden *et al.*, 1995). Data collection was by postal questionnaire sent to 31,000 small firms. The results were based upon 4091 responses (a response rate of 13.2 per cent). The respondents were claimed to be representative of the sample population and the sample 'broadly representative' of the small firms sector. The categorizations used do not allow tourism and hospitality firms to be specifically identified.

Two primary motives for certification were identified, namely a need or desire either to 'improve quality' to or 'win new customers' (cited by 88 and 84 per cent of respondents respectively). The relative importance of these two factors was reversed, however, in the data concerning the benefits of certification: 'new markets', 'increased sales' and 'retained business' all having scores equal to or higher than those for any statement relating to quality improvement. From this and other data, it was concluded that ISO 9000 offers some (mainly marketing) benefits to some small businesses, particularly larger small manufacturing firms that sell to larger customers on a national basis. It was stated, however, that more widespread certification is discouraged by a number of practical barriers, particularly the cost and time requirements to obtain and maintain the standard. These, it was suggested, should be minimized.

The other major conclusion was that the close personal involvement and 'hands on' management style of many owner/managers is in conflict with the formalized approach of ISO 9000. In addition, it was stated that: 'there is no evidence that informal quality systems based upon the personal involvement of business owners and employees with detailed knowledge of customer requirements, are in any way inferior to more detailed systems' (SBRT, 1994, p. 2).

These conclusions are similar to those of other investigations (e.g. Rayner and Porter, 1991; North *et al.*, 1993; Campbell, 1994; IOD, 1996) and thus merit further discussion.

Marketing benefit will, of course, only arise if the award is recognized by the customer. Whereas ISO 9000 is widely recognized in the business community, recognition levels among domestic consumers are low. The reason for this is that ISO 9000 was originally designed to tell one company about another, not (as is the case with Michelin stars) to imply quality to the customer. The low recognition is probably the reason why certification levels among tourism and hospitality firms are negligible, except among operations whose business is primarily dependent upon tendering (such as hospital cook-chill units and contract caterers and cleaners). In manufacturing, there is evidence that some small firms have been forced into certification by the demands or expectations of larger customers. This is rarely an issue for small tourism and hospitality firms.

The effectiveness of ISO 9000 in ensuring or improving quality in small tourism and hospitality firms has been a source of some debate. Traditionally, formalized quality systems have been subservient to personal and professional skill and pride. The claim that the standard eliminates necessary factors such as empathy and creativity is based upon the assumption that it is prescriptive and inflexible. This is, however, not the case: the procedures can (and should) be written to allow those to occur. Similarly, the claim that it necessitates a restrictive amount of paperwork (Vallely, 1993) is misleading. The level of documentation required can, to some extent, be adjusted to the needs of the firm in terms of the probability and potential consequences of failure. Food providers, and others with a significant risk of litigation in the case of failure, require the highest level of documentation. In all cases, however, considerable care is required to ensure that the documentation is effective yet causes minimum disruption to staff. This is usually achievable by the careful definition of standards and document design.

SBRT (1994) recommended that effective informal systems should be recognized as being of equal value. Although this proposal appears superficially attractive, it should be noted that any reduction in formality that compromised the effective documentation of the system would be undesirable, particularly where statutory requirements and/or the risk of litigation exist.

The costs of ISO 9000 are often mentioned in the context of small firms (e.g. Campbell, 1994). Two categories of cost exist: those associated with implementing and maintaining the quality system (e.g. management time, consultancy charges) and those associated with obtaining and retaining certification (e.g. certification body, or auditing, charges). These costs are undoubtedly significant. However, the improvements in organizational performance arising from the resulting system should, in most cases, recoup the costs in a relatively short period of time.

Waller *et al.* (1993) note that it is possible for 'very small operations' to implement a system to the ISO 9000 standards, but not undergo the rigours and expense of certification. In some situations this may be a sensible strategy. However, the small firm focus upon marketing benefits will render it inapplicable in most cases.

TOTAL QUALITY MANAGEMENT

Total quality management (TQM) is a strategy designed to control quality (i.e. meet the customer's requirements consistently and cost-effectively) and improve both quality and operational efficiency, primarily by team empowerment.

A vast amount has been written about TQM in recent years, although relatively little of this has been specific to small firms. Disagreement is evident: for example, Huxtable (1995) proposes the TQM model as being appropriate to small businesses in their attempts to manage quality, whereas Davies (1990) suggests that the size of small firms makes TQM an irrelevance. A problem exists regarding the definition of TQM that causes usage estimates to be inflated. For example, Cranswick (1995) reported that 'almost every' respondent to a postal survey of over 1000 small firms had undertaken at least two of nine techniques of TQM. This was taken to indicate an increased awareness and use of TQM among small firms. This conclusion appears questionable for two reasons: first, some of the techniques used (e.g. 'documented quality system') are not exclusive to TQM; second, the inherently holistic nature of TQM was not addressed.

Two stages exist in the implementation of TQM: the decision to implement and the actual implementation itself. The decision to implement TQM is often discouraged by two factors: risk and inertia (Zetie *et al.*, 1994b). Both, it is argued, are lessened in small firms. The risk is less as small firms are generally more 'manoeuvrable' and thus more able to backtrack if and when wrong decisions are made. Inertia tends to be overcome by the awareness of either need or effect, and – in theory at least – this is more likely in small firms in which the management tends to be closer to both the process and the customers. Despite this, the majority of TQM users appear to be larger firms. This may well be due to the existence of a number of hurdles to small firm use: Zetie *et al.* (1994b) note that many small firms (especially those with owner/managers) have little if any desire to develop, and suggest that whereas managers in small firms are confident in making risky decisions about commercial matters, they are less so when the decisions have organizational implications.

Implementing TQM necessitates a change in culture (i.e. management style and employee attitudes). The relative ease with which this is brought about is determined by a number of factors, including owner/management commitment, organizational structure, staff attitude and resourcing.

Owner/management commitment is essential, and where this exists small firms have, in theory at least, an advantage in that, owing to the smaller numbers of both people and levels of hierarchy, it is less likely to become diluted as it cascades down the organization.

Both MacDonald and Piggott (1990) and Zetie *et al.* (1994b) state that the informal, open structure and flat management pyramid usually found in small firms are more amenable to cultural change than the formalized departmental structure generally found in larger organizations. It should be noted, however, that the attitudes of the individuals within the organization are perhaps of greater influence, and there is no reason to assume that the employees of small firms are necessarily more open to such ideas. That said, it does seem likely that, in small firms, the implementation of empowered teams would be somewhat easier and the relative closeness of the employees to their customers may result in them being more immediately aware of any improvements which may, in turn, motivate them further.

TQM requires significant resourcing, and although no hard evidence is available, it is probable that small firms are generally less able to provide this. The major hurdle in this respect is management time, although specialist knowledge will also be a factor in many cases. These hurdles may be addressed by the use of consultants or cooperative ventures.

Zetie *et al.* (1994b) discussed the implementation of TQM in a small (25 employee) service firm specializing in the assembly, sale and maintenance of hydraulic hoses. As is typical, their first step was to attempt to establish quality circles and cross-functional Teams. However, the traditional size (i.e. 10 to 12 members) and formality (especially the recording and evaluation of decisions) of the former caused unacceptable disruption, and in consequence an alternative approach was devised. This utilized smaller than usual (i.e. two to four member) quality circles (designated 'quality bubbles') that operated in a similar way to traditional quality circles (i.e. identification and solution of actual and potential problems within the department), but the formalized recording and evaluation was discarded and replaced by an informal (and admittedly somewhat subjective) system by which 'self-evidently' good proposals were implemented. Problems that were interdepartmental in nature were addressed by the coalescence of the individual bubbles for the duration of the project – similar to cross-functional teams. These initiatives were supported by five others: flash meetings, a suggestion box, action teams, a staff appraisal scheme and a customer feedback programme.

Flash meetings are short, spontaneous and highly informal (i.e. unrecorded) meetings designed to solve problems as they arise. The suggestion box is an attempt to encourage staff comments (by financial reward). The initial fear that employees would hold back their better ideas in the bubbles in the hope of financial gain was not realized, and it is unclear as to the purpose of the box, other than to give an extra opportunity for ideas that are rejected or for those employees (if any – this is not made clear) not involved in the 'bubbles'.

Action teams are temporary and formed to address specific problems. No clear differentiation was made between action teams and the interdisciplinary teams mentioned previously.

The staff appraisal scheme is aimed at encouraging participation and idea generation. The staff are rewarded financially for any aspect of their work that contributes to the TQM ideal. The customer feedback programme exists in recognition of the fact that, although small firms tend to be closer to their customers, it would be unwise to rely totally upon informal feedback. This approach would be applicable to small tourism and hospitality firms.

QUALITY COSTING

The BSI defines the cost of quality as the: 'cost of ensuring and assuring quality as well as the loss incurred when quality is not achieved' (BSI, 1990). It is widely accepted that the cost of quality is invariably large (i.e. typically ranging from 5 to 25 per cent of sales turnover) and is often unmonitored (i.e. fewer than 40 per cent of companies record quality costs) and, therefore, uncontrolled. The costs associated with failure to achieve quality can exceed 79 per cent of the total (BSI, 1990), and are avoidable. No data specific to small firms are available, but it is probable that their performance in this respect is similar to, if not worse than, that of larger organizations. As margins tend to be lower in small firms, this is a matter of some concern.

Two fundamental approaches to quality costing exist: the prevention, appraisal and failure (PAF) model (BSI, 1990) and the process cost model (BSI, 1992). The former is the traditional approach, and involves the classification of quality costs under three main headings: prevention, appraisal and failure. The basic function of the model is to balance prevention and appraisal (i.e. quality control) costs against those of failure, in order to produce the highest quality at the lowest cost. Thus, failures are accepted if the cost of their control is greater than the cost of the failure itself. The PAF model has been criticized for two reasons: first, its acceptance of failure is in conflict with the TQM ideal of 'right first time' or 'zero defects'; second, the required cost information is not easily available within conventional accounting systems (Dale and Plunkett, 1995).

The process cost model addresses these criticism of the PAF model and, in addition, enables the TQM principle of 'continuous improvement' to be implemented by means of business process re-engineering (see Weiss, 1994). This model considers the cost of quality to be the cost of the process by which the product is produced or the service delivered. Specifically, it categorizes costs as either cost of conformance (COC) or cost of non-conformance (CONC). BSI (1992, p. 3) defines these as follows:

COC: 'The intrinsic cost of providing products or services to declared standards by a given, specific process in a fully effective manner.'
CONC: 'The cost of wasted time, materials and capacity (resources) associated with a process in the receipt, production, despatch and correction of unsatisfactory goods and services.'

In the service industry context, the identification of these costs primarily involves the recording of time. The identification of these costs, in conjunction with product and/or service quality data, allows the cost of quality to be both controlled and continuously improved. This is achieved by the manipulation and/or enhanced control of the process: the CONCs are minimised or eliminated and the COCs are reduced if this can be achieved without detrimentally affecting the product or service quality. Bowdin *et al.* (1995) provide a practical example of process cost modelling that may be readily be applied to small tourism and hospitality firms.

CONCLUSIONS

It is evident that small firms and those who represent them regard themselves as being significantly different from their larger counterparts in terms of quality management needs. The major difference in this respect is seen to be the level of formality required in the quality management system. Although it is undoubtedly true that some small firms use highly informal approaches to great effect, it must be recognized that in many situations they are likely to prove inadequate. Such situations include growth and the consequent loss, by the owner-manager, of close 'hands on' control, high staff turnover and the production and delivery of products or services which are inherently variable or require customization. Because of these factors, tourism and hospitality firms are unlikely to be adequately served by completely informal approaches.

The available evidence suggests that a preventative quality control system based upon FMEA would be more pragmatic and cost-effective than the more traditional retrospective approach. Although few small tourism and hospitality firms currently utilize such systems, they appear to merit serious consideration. Similarly, quality costing, particularly if introduced alongside a preventative system, would appear to offer significant benefits, both financial and operational. With both preventative quality control and quality costing, the major challenge for small users will be ensuring that they are, in terms of documentation, effective yet practical. Despite concerns, there is no conclusive evidence to indicate that such a balance is unattainable in small tourism and hospitality firms.

Investors in People appears to be potentially useful, given the people-oriented nature of the tourism and hospitality industries. The applicability of the remaining elements discussed (benchmarking, ISO 9000 and TQM) is less certain. ISO 9000 accreditation appears to have little value except a direct marketing benefit – something that is unlikely except in firms that primarily deal with a corporate or local government clientele. Benchmarking and TQM, the evidence would suggest, may be desirable in the longer term, but only merit consideration once effective preventative quality control is in place and a basic quality culture in operation.

Overall, many small firms appear to reject many of the techniques, systems and initiatives for no other reason than they were designed by, or for use in, larger firms. The effect of this is that many potentially useful ideas are lost to the small business community. Consequently, small businesses should be more receptive: not to the degree of slavishly following their larger counterparts, but by selecting and adapting techniques for their own needs.

REFERENCES

Baldacchino, G. (1995) 'Total quality management in a luxury hotel: a critique of practice', *International Journal of Hospitality Management*, **14(1)**, 67–78.

Barrier, M. (1992) 'Doing well what comes naturally', *Nation's Business*, **80(9)**, 25–6.

Barrow, C. (1993) *The Essence of Small Business*. Hemel Hempstead: Prentice Hall.

Barsky, J. (1992) 'Customer satisfaction in the hotel industry: meaning and measurement', *Hospitality Research Journal*, **16(1)**, 51–69.

Bemowski, K. (1992) 'Small in size but not in stature', *Quality Progress*, **25(11)**, 23–7.

Boon, S.J. (1995) 'Implementing quality – an action research perspective', in *Proceedings of the 18th ISBA National Conference*, Paisley, November.

Bowdin, G.A.J., Church, I.J. and Margerison, J.P. (1995) 'Towards a pragmatic approach: quality costing for the tendering process', in Teare, R. and Armistead, C. (eds) *Services Management: New Directions, New Perspectives*, London: Cassell, 45–8.

Breiter, D., Tyink, S. and Tuckwell, S. (1995) 'Bergstrom Hotels: a case study in quality', *International Journal of Contemporary Hospitality Management*, **7(6)**, 14–18.

BSI (1990) *BS 6143 Part 2. Guide to the Economics of Quality: Prevention, Appraisal and Failure Model*. Milton Keynes: BSI.

BSI (1991) *Guidance Notes for the Application of ISO 9002/EN29002/BS 5750: Part 2. The Hotel and Catering Industry*. Milton Keynes: BSI.

BSI (1992) *BS 6142 Part 1. Guide to the Economics of Quality: Process Cost Model*. Milton Keynes: BSI.

BSI (1994) *BS EN ISO 9002. Quality Systems. Model for Quality Assurance in Production, Installation and Servicing*. Milton Keynes: BSI.

BSI (1995) *Quality Systems for Small Business; Quality Assurance in Small Business Service*. Milton Keynes: BSI.

Camison, C. (1996) 'Total quality management in hospitality: an application of the EFQM model', *Tourism Management*, **17(3)**, 191–201.

Campbell, L. (1994) 'BS 5750 – what's in it for small firms?', *Quality World*, June, 377–9.

Chittenden, F., Mukhtar, S.M. and Poutziouris, P. (1995) 'BS 5750 and quality management in SMSs', in *Proceedings of the 18th ISBA National Conference*, Paisley, November.

Collyer, R. (1996) 'Small firms and ISO 9000', *Training for Quality*, **4(1)**, 37–9.

Coyle, M.P. and Dale, B.G. (1993) 'Quality in the hospitality industry: a study', *International Journal of Hospitality Management*, **12(2)**, 141–53.

Cranswick, D. (1995) 'Entrepeneurs and quality. Are small firms utilising the techniques of total quality management?', in *Proceedings of the 18th ISBA National Conference*, Paisley, November.

Crawford-Welch, S. (1992) 'Competitive marketing strategies', in Teare, R. and Olsen, M. (eds) *International Hospitality Management*. London: Pitman, 95–105.

Dale, B.G. and Plunkett, J.J. (1995) *Quality Costing*. London: Chapman and Hall.

Dalfonso, M.A. (1995) *ISO 9000. Achieving Compliance and Certification*. Chichester: John Wiley and Sons.

Davies, P. (1990) 'TQM in small firms', *Total Quality Management*, **2(5)**, 251–2.

DNH (1996) *Tourism: Competing with the Best 2. Benchmarking for Smaller Hotels*. London: DNH.

DTI (1995a) *Implementing BS EN ISO 9000. A Guide for Small Firms*. London: HMSO.

DTI (1995b). *TQM and Effective Leadership*. London: HMSO.

Fick, G. and Ritchie, J. (1991) 'Measuring service quality in the travel and tourism industry', *Journal of Travel Research*, **2(9)**.

Gevirtz, C. (1994) *Developing New Products with TQM*. New York: McGraw-Hill.

Gilbert, D.C. and Joshi, I. (1993) 'Quality management and the tourism and hospitality industry', in Cooper, C.P. and Lockwood, A. (eds) *Progress in Tourism, Recreation and Hospitality Management, Vol. 4*. London: Bellhaven Press, 149–67.

Haywood, K.M. (1983) 'Assessing the quality of hospitality services', *International Journal of Hospitality Management*, **2(4)**, 165–77.

Heymann, K. (1992) 'Quality management: a ten point model', *Cornell Hotel and Restaurant Administration Quarterly*, October, 51–60.

Hillier, C. (1992a) 'Challenge of the 90s. Part 1', *Caterer and Hotelkeeper*, 5 March, 44–6.

Hillier, C. (1992b) 'Challenge of the 90s. Part 2', *Caterer and Hotelkeeper*, 12 March, 42–3.

Hubrecht, J. and Teare, R. (1993) 'A strategy for partnership in total quality service', *International Journal of Contemporary Hospitality Management*, **5(3)**, i–v.

Huxtable, N. (1995) *Small Business Total Quality*. London: Chapman and Hall.

IiP UK (1995a) *Investing in People. How to Get Started*. London: Investors in People UK.

IiP UK (1995b) *Investing in People. The Benefits of Being an Investor in People*. London: Investors in People UK.

IOD (1996) *Your Business Matters*. London: IOD.

IQA (1995) *Quality Systems in the Small Firm. A Guide to the Use of the ISO9000 Series.* London: Institute of Quality Assurance.

Johns, N. (1992a) 'Quality management in the hospitality industry. Part 1. Definition and Specification', *International Journal of Contemporary Hospitality Management*, **4(3)**, 14–20.

Johns, N. (1992b) 'Quality management in the hospitality industry. Part 2. Applications, systems and techniques', *International Journal of Contemporary Hospitality Management*, **4(4)**, 3–7.

Johns, N. (1992c) 'Quality management in the hospitality industry. Part 3. Recent developments', *International Journal of Contemporary Hospitality Management*, **5(1)**, 10–15.

Juran, J.M. (1979) *Quality Control Handbook.* New York: McGraw-Hill.

King, C.A. (1984) 'Service oriented quality control', *Cornell Hotel and Restaurant Administration Quarterly*, November, 92–8.

Lee, Y.L. and Hing, N. (1995) 'Managing quality in restaurant operations: an application of the SERVQUAL instrument', *International Journal of Hospitality Management*, **14(3)**, 293–310.

Lockwood, A., Gummesson, E., Hubrecht, J. and Senior, M. (1992) 'Developing and maintaining a strategy for service quality', in Teare, R. and Olsen, M. (eds) *International Hospitality Management: Corporate Strategy in Practice.* London: Pitman, 312–38.

MacDonald, J. and Piggott, J. (1990) *Global Quality. The New Management Culture.* London: Mercury.

Manchester Business School (1995) *Small Business Briefings – Hotels and Catering.* Manchester: Gee.

Messenger, S. and Atkins, T. (1994) 'The Prudential experience of total quality management', *International Journal of Contemporary Hospitality Management*, **6(1/2)**, 37–41.

Moore, J. (1995) *Investors in People – A Framework for Improving Small Business Performance?* Leicester: Leicester University, The Centre for Labour Market Studies.

Newton, S. and van der Merwe, C. (1992) 'Quality assurance and the mystery guest programme in Harvester restaurants', in Cooper, C. and Lockwood. A. (eds) *Progress in Tourism, Recreation and Hospitality Management, Vol. 4.* London: Bellhaven Press, 169–74.

North, J., Curran, J. and Blackburn, R. (1993) 'Small firms and BS 5750: a preliminary investigation', *National Small Firms Policy and Research Conference*, **16**, 141–51.

North, J., Curran, J. and Blackburn, R. (1995) 'Quality and small firms. A policy mismatch and its impact on small enterprise. Entrepreneurship and education/quality in SME's', in *Proceedings of the 18th ISBA National Conference*, Paisley, November.

Oakland, J. (1993) *Total Quality Management.* London: Butterworth Heinemann.

Peacock, M. (1996) 'In defence of the hospitality business independent: a personal view', *International Journal of Contemporary Management*, **8(2)**, 31–3.

Rayner, P. and Porter, L.J. (1991) 'BS 5750/ISO 9000 – the experience of small and medium-sized firms', *International Journal of Quality and Reliability Management*, **8(6)**, 16–28.

Records, H.A. and Glennie, M.F. (1991) 'Service management and quality assurance: a systems approach', *Cornell Hotel and Restaurant Administration Quarterly*, May, 26–35.

Reeves, C. and Hoy, F. (1993) 'Employee perceptions of management commitment and customer evaluations of quality service in independent firms', *Journal of Small Business Management*, **31(4)**, 52–9.

Samuel, S. (1995) 'This quality thing is here to stay', *The Hospitality Yearbook*. Reading: HCIMA.

SBRT (1994) *Small Businesses and BS 5750. Executive Summary*. Milton Keynes: SBRT.

Sinclair, J. and Arthur, A. (1994) 'Inhospitable culture and continuous improvement', *International Journal of Contemporary Hospitality Management*, **6(1/2)**, 30–6.

Smith, S. (1988) 'How to quantify quality', *Management Today*, May, 44–8.

Sprenger, R. (1993) *Hygiene for Management*. Doncaster: Highfield Publications.

Stebbing, L. and Pengelly, R.J. (1994) *Quality Management for the Small Business*. London: Ellis Horwood.

Storey, D. (1994) *Understanding the Small Business Sector*. London: Routledge.

Tutcher, G. (1995) 'Benchmark for success', *Food Service Management*, July, 68–9.

Vallely, I. (1993) 'Should you jump on the BS 5750 bandwagon?', *Works Management*, March, 25–9.

Waller, J., Allen, D. and Burns, A. (1993) *The Quality Management Manual*. London: Kogan Page.

Watson, H., McKenna, M. and McLean, G. (1992) 'TQM and services: implementing change in the NHS', *International Journal of Contemporary Hospitality Management*, **4(2)**, 17–20.

Weiss, J. (1994) 'Reengineering small business', *Small Business Reports*, **19(5)**, 37–42.

Witt, C. and Muhlemann, A. (1994) 'The implementation of TQM in tourism: some guidelines', *Tourism Management*, **15(6)**, 416–24.

Wood, L. (1995) 'Transformed by training – a standard that can change corporate cultures', *Financial Times*, 4 October, 16.

Wyckoff, D. (1984) 'New tools for achieving service quality', *Cornell Hotel and Restaurant Administration Quarterly*, November, 78–91.

Yasin, M.M. and Zimmerer, T.W. (1995) 'The role of benchmarking in achieving continuous service quality', *International Journal of Contemporary Hospitality Management*, **7(4)**, 27–32.

Zetie, S., Sparrow, J., Woodfield, A. and Kilmartin, T. (1994a) 'The tyrannical chef: a barrier to TQM?', *International Journal of Contemporary Hospitality Management*, **6(1–2)**, 42–5.

Zetie, S., Sparrow, J., Woodfield, A. and Kilmartin, T. (1994b) 'Hydrapower dynamics: service delivery in a small organisation', in Teare, R., Atkinson, C. and Westwood, C. (eds) *Achieving Quality Performance: Lessons from British Industry*. London: Cassell, 55–78.

NINE

Management development

Graham Beaver, Conrad Lashley and Jim Stewart

INTRODUCTION

The significance of small firms in delivering a substantial part of the total output of tourism and hospitality goods and services is a long established feature of these industries. That said, the growth of a small number of huge national and international organizations which control disproportionately large sections of lodging, restaurant, public house and holiday markets is a remarkable feature of the current landscape.

In theory, the small tourism of hospitality enterprise, located close to its market and in personal contact with its customers, has a considerable advantage, being able to respond to customer needs and demands. While there are many small tourism and hospitality firms that do successfully compete in their local market, small firms in general are losing market share to the bigger firms. Some commentators (Slattery, 1992) go as far as to dismiss the future existence of the small firm in hospitality provision. While the economic might of large firms to establish brands and operate at lower costs because of scale advantages goes some way to explain the loss of market share by small firms, the level of skills and talents together with the limited aims and objectives of those who own and manage small tourism and hospitality firms are also significant factors.

This chapter examines the nature of management in small firms, and shows that there are significant differences in the managerial tasks in small and large firms. Even among small firm owner/managers, there are clearly different aims and objectives and reasons for running small enterprises. Small firm management in the tourism and hospitality industries, in particular, takes place in an industrial setting where there is a general tendency for low levels of employee development and a lack of systematic training. Management development in small tourism and hospitality firms is also at a low level, and the chapter provides some explanations as to why owners/managers in 'micro' firms do not give priority to their own development. The chapter also provides a framework for establishing a development plan for those entrepreneurs who have commercial, growth-oriented objectives, and who see their own development as key to future success.

MANAGEMENT IN THE SMALL FIRM

The management process in the small firm is unique. It bears little or no resemblance to management processes found in larger organizations, which have been the subject of substantial academic research, resulting in numerous models, prescriptions and constructs.

In the larger organization, management is seen primarily as a *predictive* process concerned with the clarification of long-term objectives, the formulation of appropriate policies to meet such objectives and the feedback of information to indicate successful or unsuccessful achievement of the goals established (see, for example, Faulkner and Johnson, 1992). In contrast, management in the smaller firm is primarily an *adaptive* process, concerned with adjusting a usually limited amount of resources in order to gain the maximum immediate and short-term advantage. In the small firm, efforts are concentrated not on predicting but on controlling the operating environment, adapting as quickly as possible to the changing demands of that environment and devising suitable tactics for mitigating the consequences of any changes which occur.

In the smaller enterprise, the management process is characterized by the highly personalized preferences, prejudices and attitudes of the firm's entrepreneur, owner and/or owner-manager. The nature of managerial activity expands or contracts with the characteristics of the person fulfilling the role(s). Such expansion or contraction is partly conditioned by the adaptive needs of the context in which the business operates, and is partly dependent upon the personality and needs of the owner, manager or entrepreneur. Consequently, the management process in the small enterprise cannot be viewed in isolation from the skills demanded of the three key roles of entrepreneur, owner and manager, together with technical skills relevant to hospitality operations. However, in the smallest firms all these roles may be enacted by one individual. It is only following a period of business growth and expansion that each role may become enacted by separate individuals. The small firm management process cannot be separated from the personality set and experience of the key role-player(s).

Another characteristic of the small firm management process is the closeness of the key role-players to the operating personnel and activities being undertaken. This provides the key role-players with extraordinary opportunities to influence these operatives and activities directly. However, these relationships are often informal, there being no precise definition of rights and obligations, duties and responsibilities. Appointment and promotion are often made on the basis of birth or personal friendship rather than on the basis of educational and technical qualifications.

Organization structures, in so far as they exist, are likely to develop around the interests and abilities of the key role-players. Such organization structures are likely to be organic and loosely structured rather than mechanistic and highly formalized. Thus the management process in the small firm is seldom a readily visible process. It often has an abstract rather than concrete form. However, the key role-players must fulfil a number of basic managerial functions, duties and roles if the organization is to succeed. Logically, it follows that the lack of attention to these fundamental managerial activities and tasks will, at best, lead to sub-optimal performance and may even threaten the survival of the firm. These essential managerial activities have been defined and refined throughout a long history of management research.

Applying these principles specifically to the small firm management process suggests that the key skills and abilities outlined in Figure 9.1 need to be utilized. While it may be argued that these skills and abilities are generic to all management situations, the complexity of the small business environment demands a unique blending of skills to succeed in exploiting competitive advantage to achieve superior performance. Naturally, inherent dynamism will demand fluidity, flexibility and adaptability. Thus, the lone small business practitioner may be asked to enact any one of the multiplicity of roles implied by the above at any one time.

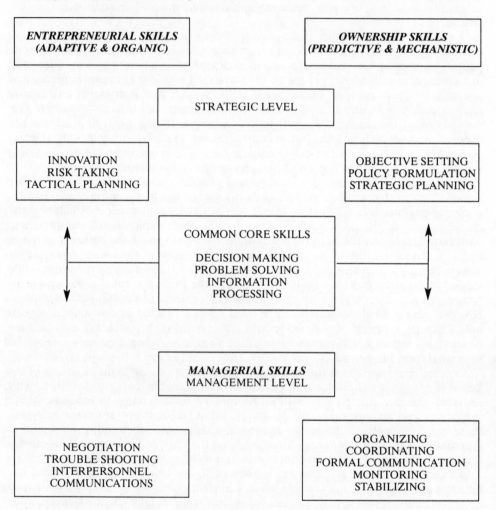

Figure 9.1 The small firm management process
Source: Beaver and Jennings, 1995.

In any given small business management situation, these roles can be considered to be akin to different stakeholders, each demanding the possession and application of specific skills and abilities. As Mitroff (1983, p. 250) points out, 'different stakeholders do not generally share the same definition of an organisation's *problems*, and hence, do not in general share the same *solutions*'. Each stakeholder approaches the organization's problems from a unique perspective and demands a unique solution. Traditional concepts of decision-making would emphasize the need to achieve consensus and agreement between alternative stakeholders in order to lead to effective outcomes. However, Mitroff (1983) goes on to argue that in fact the individual human psyche or personality contains a *'plurality of selves'* – alternative and sometimes conflicting perceptions of self – which constitute stakeholders, thus influencing behaviour. The small business practitioner is, therefore, subject to a number of competing and conflicting influences which may cause dissonance, leading to erratic, unpredictable and unacceptable behaviour, which is in complete contrast with the rational, professional and acceptable management behaviour portrayed by Mintzberg (1973) and others. Frequently, as Osborne (1991) points out, the power which accompanies majority ownership cannot be challenged by other stakeholders in the smaller enterprise situation, and therefore the ability of the key role-player(s) to cope with absolute power and leadership responsibility has a significant impact upon the survival and growth potential of the enterprise.

For any firm to remain successful over a sustained period, there must be a capability to adapt to changing circumstances. Greiner (1972) shows that failure to adapt to a series of 'crises' caused by growth is one of the principal causes of failure for all organizations. Hence, one of the primary ingredients in small firm success must be the managerial competence of the owner-manager.

What are these managerial competencies which underpin the successful small business? A useful guide may be to examine the usual contents of small business training and development programmes. There is a need to distinguish between training and development which might be necessary for employees within a small business training, and development which is focused upon the specific needs of the owner-managers themselves. The small firm owner-manager requires specific, transferable, managerial skills directly related to entrepreneurship and professional management within the operating environment of the business, as shown in Figure 9.1. He or she needs to be able to initiate and implement change and improvement in services, products and systems.

It is very easy to note the obvious: that providing all the necessary skills and competencies are found across the whole team which makes up the small enterprise, the business should be capable of achieving success. However, adept management is still required to blend and bring out these abilities and, as Jennings and Beaver (1995) illustrate, the personality and positional power of the entrepreneur often mean that latent talent within the team goes unrecognized or underutilized. This raises the question of whether small businesses fail through lack of managerial skills, which let down otherwise good skill and competence in providing the product or service, or through lack of competence in providing the product or service demanded by the customer, despite otherwise competent management in the organization.

Ineffective management cannot simply be identified as the primary cause of small business failure without recognition of several factors which are peculiar to the small business operating context. The study by Grieve-Smith and Fleck (1987), using a case study approach to examining business strategies in small high-technology firms in Cambridge, raises several interesting managerial issues. They point out that small enterprises can experience real difficulties in developing or obtaining appropriate managerial skills, since they cannot provide the salaries and benefits that managers could expect from larger organizations. Furthermore, their case studies highlight several other important issues. For example, they refer to the founders of certain companies being conscious, at the start, of the need to recruit external managers and to appoint these individuals from larger companies, presumably to facilitate business growth and development. Finally, they refer to the need to attract managers with additional skills to those already in the firm, to complement the expertise on which the company was based. This would suggest that the business founder had the desire to 'construct a balanced managerial team' as one of the prime drivers to sustained business expansion and performance. It is also a factor that many well dramatically reduce the risk of business failure.

It must be emphasized, however, that there are many types and categories of small business, each with its own particular operating context. Equally, there are many different ways of organizing and managing in the search for competitive advantage and continued survival, and an even greater diversity of small business owners and managers with varying motivations, expectations and abilities. It would, therefore, be unwise simply to focus on small high-technology firms as a basis upon which to make generalizations about management strategies for business growth and failure prevention. The analysis of the managerial contribution to small business failure must acknowledge the factor of disadvantage, owing not only to the size of the firm but also to the nature of the operating context and the relatively ineffective support infrastructure (Beaver and Harrison, 1994). This is particularly relevant to the hospitality industry, where the barriers to entry are relatively low and many would-be entrepreneurs feel that they have the technical competence for success because of the link between hospitality and domestic activities. For some entrants, the attractions of cooking and entertaining friends can be misguiding. Successful hospitality business management requires an array of competencies which extend beyond being merely hospitable.

Nicholson and West (1988) illustrate the many significant differences between managers in small and large firms, confirming both the presence and nature of disadvantage. Furthermore, there is some evidence provided by Handy (1988) in his international review of the education, development and training of managers that: 'Small companies are different. In no country do they take the same long term view of management development, nor are they prepared to spend time and money on any form of training which does not have an almost immediate pay-off.'

Management processes in small firms are unique. Much of the contemporary management theory is founded upon the empirical analysis of managerial action in large organizations. These principles, no matter how refined, cannot be applied directly to the small enterprise. While common managerial skills need to be in evidence in many organizational situations, the contextualization of these skills to meet the requirements of the small business operating context is distinctive. Competitive advantage in small firms is an elusive concept. It is fashioned by the actions and abilities of the principal role players, and owes much to their personal perception of satisfactory performance and business direction. Growth and development of the smaller enterprise brings with it many challenges, especially in terms of the separation of ownership and control. Delegation and professionalization of management activities invariably demand a less personalized and consequently more formal management process.

HUMAN RESOURCE DEVELOPMENT IN HOSPITALITY ENTERPRISES[1]

The development of managers in small hospitality firms is shaped by important and interrelated factors, namely the link with the hospitality industry and the small size of the firms under consideration. As industries, tourism and hospitality tend not to have a robust history of training and employee development. The 1992 NEDO report registered concern that the industry had a poor training record and was not making the most of the resource it employs. More recently, an HtF (1996) report on training across the hospitality industry suggested that 43 per cent of employers in the industry do not train employees, and that only 25 per cent of firms trained all employees. Even those who did provide training were mostly training to meet a 'legislative or perceived inspection threat', and when these are accounted for, 'a lamentably low level of training is actually carried out' (HtF, 1996, p. 64).

The situation is worse in small hotels, cafes, restaurants and public houses. The report concludes: 'In these establishments, a training culture does not exist, neither is there an acceptance on the part of employers to take responsibility for training and developing their staff' (HtF, 1996, p. 63). Interestingly the picture painted by this recent national survey reveals much in common with our earlier work (Lashley, 1993). Semi-structured interviews with local owners of small firms revealed that only 19 of the 55 firms that took part in the survey had any formal training policy, and only a small proportion of establishments (approximately 20 per cent) made any budgetary provision for staff training. The situation was more stark when organization size and form of ownership were taken into account. Thus, firms employing fewer than ten employees, and which were owner-managed, rarely undertook systematic training of staff. These two factors were also related to the limited perception of training needs in cafes and bed and breakfast establishments. Owner-managers in these types of business registered the lowest perception of training needs for either themselves or their staff.

Commenting on the low participation rate of small firms in employee training, the HtF report points to some problems faced by small firms. Training programmes are costly and time consuming to implement. Supply side difficulties can present barriers to participation where programmes are inappropriately structured, timetabled at busy period for the owner/manager or too expensive. The report makes some suggestions about the delivery of programmes, which suggest that flexible delivery, mixed mode delivery and the use of training consortia could help to overcome some barriers. The Nottingham Business School survey (Lashley, 1993) confirmed that half-day modular programmes were the most popular, particularly where they allowed participants to mix and match the modules to suit their particular needs. That said, the report suggests that while the mismatch between supply and demand for training causes some problems, the difficulties are more fundamental. 'Employers generally demonstrate a lack of interest in, or ability to seize upon training initiatives and they certainly do not appear to accept responsibility to invest in training to improve in business performance' (HtF, 1996, p. 64). At the same time, the industry is experiencing a skills shortage. Over 40 per cent of employers registered recruitment difficulties in the previous 12 months, and many identified an inability to recruit the appropriately trained staff as the key difficulty.

As further confirmation of the low level of training activity, the general awareness of training provision and training institutions was low among hospitality employers. While the take-up and use of National Vocational Qualifications and Scottish Vocational Qualifications is low in the industry, the general understanding and use of Investors in People (IiP) is even worse. Only one-quarter of employers were aware of IiP, and a mere 3 per cent of the employers in the HtF survey were certificated. Even more worrying was the situation with Training and Enterprise Councils (LECs in Scotland). Only half of the employers had heard of them, and just 18 per cent had any idea of what they did; only 1 per cent claimed to have used them. However, this might be distorted by the respondents' lack of awareness of links back to services which they are using: for example, by attending short courses funded by TECs but not perceived to be provided by them.

An examination of management training provision reveals similar shortages of trained managers and a low level of management development provision in the industry in general, and within small hospitality firms in particular. The recent HtF survey has altered the analysis and presentation of the statistics by bringing together needs for managers and supervisors, so direct comparison of trends is difficult. The earlier report, 'Meeting competence needs in the hotel and catering industry' (HCTC, 1992), suggested that some 29,000 managers were needed to replace managers who had left the industry (including retirement) and for growth. At that point, the annual output from colleges and universities was just 2000 per year – a shortfall of some 93 per cent. The HCTC (1992) report detected some improvements in the levels of trained managers in the industry, but said that there was still a long way to go when compared with the economy as a whole. At that time, some 30 per cent of hospitality managers had no formal qualifications, compared with 12 per cent across all UK industries.

The combined manager and supervisor figures in the 1996 HtF report estimated that the industry would need some 25,000 managers and supervisors to cover losses to the industry, and growth, with an annual output from colleges of 5000. The report, therefore, suggests that current college and university outputs of newly qualified employees represent 22 per cent of the annual need for managers and supervisors. In addition to these estimates of shortfalls in replacement needs, the report suggests that only 18 per cent of hospitality managers had a higher education, and that just under 30 per cent had no qualifications whatsoever. While these figures make it difficult to show precise trends, and the picture is confused by both a reduction in management needed through delayering and some increase in education provision, it is fair to conclude that the industry still has a large shortage of appropriately trained and qualified managers.

Current management development practices show that middle and supervisory managers were more likely to have been trained in their present job than operatives or senior managers. The HtF research showed that 81 per cent of middle and junior managers had received training in their current jobs. That said, much of the training appeared to relate to legislative responsibilities, and this has to be set against the key sources of training identified. Of the establishments where training took place, just under half reported that environmental health officers and equipment suppliers had been the source of training. Interestingly, in the HtF survey, more senior managers than middle managers and supervisors registered that they were dissatisfied, or very dissatisfied, with the current levels of training they received.

There are examples of firms who have a systematic approach to human resource development in their organizations. Organizations like TGI Friday's, which trains all employees, and only allows trained employees to serve customers or take over a kitchen position, place a high priority on employee development. McDonald's Restaurants Limited makes a significant investment in both employee and management development. In the main, these businesses are untypical of many hospitality operations. More typically, the industry as a whole makes a low investment in training and employee development, and has a lower proportion of managers with a higher education and a higher proportion of managers with no educational qualifications at all. The picture that emerges from the recent HtF research seems to suggest that where management training is taking place, much of it appears to be aimed at improving technical competence and an understanding of legislation.

Apart from the general impression that the picture of management development, as with all forms of employee training, is lower in small firms, there is little systematic research into training activities within small firms. The following section reports on some insights which have been gained through research carried out at Nottingham Business School.

MANAGEMENT DEVELOPMENT IN SMALL HOSPITALITY FIRMS

There are two problems for potential providers of management development pro-grammes to small firms in the hospitality industry. Much of the research which might aid providers focuses on employee development in the hospitality industry as a whole, and thereby includes large organizations, which, as was argued above, have an array of different realities to face. The second problem is that all small hospitality firms are treated as being similar, and there is little recognition of the potential differences in objectives for, and constraints on, those managing different types of hospitality busi-ness. The research project undertaken by staff at Nottingham Business School attempted to build a picture of management development needs which overcame these two shortcomings.

The project started with assumptions that appear to validated by the HtF's (1996) findings that a reason for owner-managers not participating is that there are barriers to entry for small firms. It was the team's view that provision was inappropriate, too expensive and being delivered in the wrong way for many owners of small firms to participate. The research project aimed to build a picture of the management develop-ment needs in terms of both content and delivery, and to identify general needs of small firms across the sector as a whole and within specific types of hospitality operation.

Fifty-five semi-structured interviews were conducted with employers in ten different categories of hospitality business: hotels (large, medium, small), bed and breakfast establishments, restaurants, cafes, pubs and bars, (freehold, tenanted, managed) and clubs. The key theme of the research was to identify the perceived training needs of those taking part. The research instrument asked respondents to identify skill areas where they might have a training need. The skill areas were arranged under a number of largely functional headings: finance, marketing, communicating, management (of people), legal aspects, quality, staff deficiencies, computer skills, maintenance and general management. Although there was a relatively small sample in any one cate-gory, the research did provide some rich data on managerial perceptions of training needs across the sector's small firms.

Table 9.1 provides an overview of the findings of the interviews. Bearing in mind the tentative nature of the findings (Lashley, 1993), there are some interesting outcomes in both the nature of the training needs identified and owner/manager responses in different establishments. Concern to improve financial performance and a variety of marketing, human resource management and information technology skills, together with concern about understanding legal responsibilities, particularly in relation to staff, comes across quite strongly. More importantly, however, these findings suggest that some hospitality owners managers appear to be more aware of, and concerned by, their perceived management deficiencies than others.

Owners managers in small hotels and tenanted pubs registered the most perceived skill deficiencies. In both cases, the respondents running these businesses registered higher levels of perceived skill deficiencies across the range than respondents in other

Table 9.1 Perceived managerial skill deficiencies in different categories of hospitality establishment

Establishment		Registered skill deficiencies by skill area										
	No.	Fin.	Mkt.	Com.	Man.	Law	Qua.	Sta.	Comp.	Mai.	Gen.	Total
Hotels												
Small	6	8	12	4	14	9	–	5	1	2	–	55
Medium	5	5	1	1	4	1	–	6	–	–	–	18
Large	5	2	0	1	3	7	–	5	–	2	–	20
Bed/bkfast	6	5	–	–	–	–	–	–	–	–	–	5
Public houses												
Managed	5	–	–	–	–	–	–	–	–	–	–	0
Tenanted	6	20	15	7	16	12	1	11	4	3	–	89
Free houses	6	3	1	1	–	–	–	–	–	–	–	5
Clubs	5	11	6	3	5	4	–	3	4	–	–	36
Restaurants	5	6	6	2	–	1	–	–	–	–	–	15
Cafes	6	1	4	–	–	–	–	–	–	–	–	5
Total	55	61	45	19	42	34	1	30	9	7	0	248

Source: Lashley (1993).

categories. Similarly, respondents running cafes, free houses and bed and breakfast establishments registered significantly lower levels of concern for skill deficiencies.

Given the small sample of establishments in this survey, caution needs to be applied in generalizing the findings, but the general thrust of the findings does need some further discussion because they do raise issues relevant to the provision and take-up of management development in small firms. The generic term 'small firm manager' covers a wide variety of individuals with different motives and aims for the organization. This is discussed in more detail below, but the findings do suggest that these variations in motives and material experiences present different possibilities for training providers.

Owners/managers of tenanted pubs and small hotels appeared to be the most aware of their own training needs, and both may reflect a sense of vulnerability because of their position in relation to the market. Those running tenanted pubs, for example, will have required limited capital to invest in the tenancy, and may have limited additional resources to invest in the business. Often the properties offered by the breweries for tenancy were marginal in business terms. The best houses were generally kept under the direct managerial control of the brewery. Releasing a pub for a tenancy, or more recently for leasing, retained the units as an outlet for the brewery's sales, but simplified the managerial task. In many cases, the breweries received rents from these units, and made profits on goods supplied, but provided little assistance for the tenant. It is possible to recognize that owners/managers running pub tenancies would feel isolated and lack the skills needed to make the business a success, and this might heighten awareness of training needs.

Owners/managers of small hotels (5 to 16 bed spaces) may well have committed more capital to the venture than pub tenants, but they feel equally vulnerable. The entry barriers to running a small hotel are still quite low, most requiring capital investment within the realms of domestic property investment. In many cities, this type of business is located in former Victorian and Edwardian domestic properties. The source of vulnerability might also stem from a limited ability to invest, so as to compete with larger firms. The demand for accommodation has, at almost every level of the market, shifted to a requirement for *en suite* facilities. The very nature of the properties limits the ability to locate full bathroom facilities in every room without a loss of capacity. On the supply side, system-built budget accommodation is being provided by the large brands, such as Travel Inns and Travel Lodge. Again, these individuals perceive the threat, or business difficulty, and develop a heightened awareness of their skill deficiencies.

These findings are entirely consistent with general trends in small firm management development, in that it is important to look to business triggers which stimulate awareness of the need for training. Business start-up, growth and decline are traditionally periods in a business's life cycle which create such stimuli. The HtF (1996) report similarly concludes that few firms have ongoing development plans, and much training and development is sporadic and triggered by some immediate short-term problem.

The second issue to emerge from these interviews with owners/managers is that it may be a mistake to assume that all small business owners/managers are motivated by the same drives. The responses from bed and breakfast, cafes and public houses which are freehold (independent from any one brewery) is interesting, in that all three categories of establishment registered the lowest interest in training and development. Owners/managers in all 18 establishments expressed a low concern for their skill development. Across the whole array of possibilities, the respondents registered few skills in which they were deficient for current business needs, or likely to need the skill in the future. Common sense would say that the individuals managing these organizations must objectively have some skill deficiencies, but they did not register that they perceived the deficiency as a problem.

Although this might seem to be common sense to the outsider, the individuals running these businesses see things differently and clearly have different motives and reasons for their business ventures. In part, the confusion experienced by commentators is located in the use of generic terms which mask a variety of motives. Terms like 'small business', and 'entrepreneur' reflect generalizations which can have the impact of suggesting homogeneity when heterogeneity is the case. Each term represents an organizational metaphor through which to describe these firms. 'Small business' implies that the key focus is in relation to the size of resources available to it. The Bolton Report (1971) suggested an economic definition of small firm which pointed to the firm's relatively small market share, its owner/management structure and independence from a large enterprise. More recently, the European Union has defined 'small and medium-sized enterprises' as employing fewer than 250 employees. Using numbers of people employed, they identify three categories *micro* (< 10), *small* (10 < 49) and *medium* (50 < 250). 'Entrepreneur' suggests that the focus is the motives and nature of the management. The first metaphor suggests that these firms are handicapped, or limited, by their size, while the second suggests that those running these businesses are guided by entrepreneurial drives. Those shaping public policy towards these business have often been overconcerned with the 'small business' metaphor and have intervened in a way to compensate for their lack of resources through the provision of management training and an array of courses designed to provide the training which the organization itself does not yet have the resources to provide.

The entrepreneurial metaphor has potential to be of assistance, because it suggests that the focus should be concerned with the individual in the business leadership role. However, we need to exercise caution, because the metaphor does suggest meanings that have an image of growth, of individualism and of profit maximization which may, or may not, describe the intentions and motives of those running small firms. The entrepreneurial metaphor can also suggest more homogeneity than is the case. Recent literature on entrepreneurs and entrepreneurship suggests that there are a range of types of entrepreneurs, and it is possible to identify some of these within the hospitality context.

- The *entrepreneurial venture* provides a most powerful metaphor for small firms. It suggests that these are firms dedicated to growth and the grasping of opportunities as they emerge. While the image is powerful and widely held, only a minority of firms can be said to be 'entrepreneurial' (Morrison *et al.*, 1998).
- The *lifestyle enterprise* is a firm which provides the owner/manager with a means of economic survival within a desired style of living. In the hospitality industry this might include businesses set within the countryside, say in rural hotels or public houses. In other cases, the business may be set a round a leisure activity, say in water sports or rock climbing. The key motive for running the business is to create sufficient resources to live within the manner and setting desired by the owners.
- The *family enterprise* is common within the hospitality industry. Many independent hotels, restaurants and freehold and tenanted public houses represent family concerns, with different individuals performing different roles within the business. In some cases, the family venture represents just one of several sources of income to the family. A bed and breakfast venture which provides the family home and a source of income in addition to wage income from family members is an example.
- The *female enterprise* has witnessed some increasing growth over the past decade. Female self-employment grew from 20 per cent in 1981 to 26 per cent in 1994. Given women's traditional domestic roles in the UK, it is not surprising that hospitality industry ventures have provided some attractive business ventures for women. Bed and breakfast establishments, for example, have provided opportunities for some women to meet domestic role expectations and earn income.
- The *ethnic minority enterprise* provides members of various ethnic minority groups with an opportunity to promote their economic well-being and protection against disadvantage within the host community. The restaurant sector in the UK has several examples where ethnic minority restaurants have successfully developed niche markets for specialist segments of the eating out market.
- *Self-employment and control* are important motives for some owner-managers. Self-employment can provide a chance to exercise skills and talents which are personally satisfying to the owners, and, given the right market segmentation, can help the individuals to maintain self-employment with a reasonable degree of personal control over their working lives. Again, the restaurant sector includes examples of individuals who enjoy the skills of food production and service, and who are not particularly motivated by desires to increase revenue, profits or the scale of the business.

While this is not an exhaustive list of different entrepreneurial types, it is sufficient to show that the motives of those setting up and maintaining small hospitality firms are not always compatible with 'rational' economic calculations. Motives associated with personal preferences or which relate to self-image do not automatically lead to levels of self-analysis which suggest that a lack of business skills presents a major threat to their business goals. In many cases, entrepreneurs are commercially satisficing. Providing the business meets immediate survival needs, pays the bills and delivers an appropriate level of security, there is limited awareness of, or interest in, the development of skills through which to build the business. In these circumstances, owner-manager interests and concerns are focused on commercial issues in a secondary manner, and only become important if the venture is under particular threat or difficulty.

On another level, it may be that the characteristics and personalities of those who start up a business are by their very nature more 'inner directed' than 'outer directed'

(Goffee and Scase, 1995). Attempts to establish a social psychology of the entrepreneur have produced some contradictory findings, but common features are an ability to work independently, limited need for the structure, support systems and prescribed roles found in large organizations and a self-image independent from others' opinions. The National Westminster Bank's Survey of Small Businesses (1990) shows that in firms with one to four employees, 55 per cent of small business proprietors stated 'independence' as a key motive for starting the venture, while only 16 per cent claimed that 'making money' was the important factor. Similarly, a Leeds Metropolitan University study of over 1000 small firms showed that 11 per cent of respondents stated that 'making more money' was the most important reason for starting the business. Almost 74 per cent stated 'to do what I enjoy' or 'to be my own boss' as the key reasons (Thomas *et al.*, 1997). In these circumstances, the nature of the self-image and importance of personal independence are likely to create a situation where the business owner's attentions and perceptions are so 'inner directed' as to preclude consideration of skills and talents which might be developed externally.

Given these variations in business aims and motives for starting a business, it is possible to identify the variations in interest in management development, outlined in Table 9.1, as being associated with differences in reasons for start-up and perceptions of threat on the owner. People who start up many of the small firms outlined in the survey have aims and ambitions for the business which are not related to the immediate commercial gain. For some, the aims are for the maintenance of a desired lifestyle; for others the aim is to create a family opportunity; and for others the aim is to create opportunities not available because of disadvantage on the grounds of gender, or ethnicity, experienced in the wider society. Some entrepreneurs, while still desiring these things as primary goals, may feel under threat because of their specific market position. Thus, the owners of small hotels and tenanted pub businesses interviewed in the study are in a position of threat because of their limited resources and market power. Their perception of the need for an increased array of skills is heightened.

These differences in business aims and objectives are also a factor when one attempts to show the impact of management development and small firm performance. Westhead and Storey (1996) maintain that links between the development of managers in small firms and improved business performance are somewhat weak. Some studies do show improvements in performance relating to management training, while others do not. In part, the problems are owing to difficulties with research methodologies which attempt to link performance to a mono-causal factor. In part, the problem is that attempts to measure business performance are often commercially defined. Success is frequently identified in terms of universal economic indicators, when many of these firms are being run by people who have other motives for running the enterprise.

That said, Westhead and Storey do suggest a range of reasons why management development in small firms is less frequently undertaken than in large firms. They suggest that the 'price' paid by small firms is greater. The market price may be the same, but the opportunity cost of having managers and supervisors away on courses will be greater for the small firm. The second factor which they suggest impacts on the small firm is the reduced 'income' through which to spread the cost of management development. The third factor they identify is 'taste'. Here the assumption is that managers in small firms do not purchase development programmes for a number of non-price reasons. These firms are frequently concerned with short-termism. They do not have an internal labour market, and thereby a need to develop manager progression, and the presentation of programmes may be inappropriate in content and mode of delivery. Finally, the size of small firms often means that managers have to span a wide range of management functions and do not have detailed information about training available.

A FRAMEWORK FOR DEVELOPMENT

The foregoing has shown that much management development activity may be inappropriate to the needs and aspirations of those managing small enterprises, because their motives and ambitions do not always include enhanced management competence and improved business performance. We now turn our attention to small firms that do have ambitions for growth and commercial success which might require management development. Our concern here is with the question of how to initiate and practise management development.

There are a number of factors which need to be examined in response to this question, since they will have an influence on the answers sought and provided. These concern what Jones and Woodcock (1985) refer to as 'organization readiness'. This general term can encompass a number of organizational variables which will affect decisions on approaches and methods. The following list is indicative:

* top management commitment;
* organization/business priorities;
* intended future strategies;
* resource availability allocation;
* understanding of managerial role and needs;
* size of organization/numbers of managers.

Many of these variables are self-explanatory, and they are of course connected and interrelated. For example, top management commitment will be influenced by business priorities and how they can be supported or achieved by management development. This in turn will have an impact on resource availability and allocation. A second example links the final two variables. More formalized and individual career-focused approaches and methods may only be relevant in a period of expansion with numbers of managers increasing, and the content in terms of knowledge and skills will be influenced by the level of understanding of the requirements of managing in different roles.

These variables will in their totality affect the particular approach of management development applied in any particular context. John Burgoyne (Mumford, 1993) provides a typology of six approaches which, to a greater or lesser extent, are influenced by the variables. Burgoyne's approaches are as follows.

* no systematic management development;
* isolated tactical management development;
* integrated and coordinated structural and development tactics;
* a management development strategy to implement corporate policy;
* management development strategy input to corporate policy formation;
* strategic development of the management of corporate policy.

The key factor influencing adoption of these approaches is what Burgoyne refers to as 'organizational maturity' (see Mumford, 1993). However, the variables listed earlier can be associated with the idea of 'maturity', and will also have independent influence. Mumford (1993) provides a simpler typology of three types of, or approaches to, management development.

1.   Informal managerial: accidental processes.
2.   Integrated managerial: opportunistic processes.
3.   Formal management development: planned processes.

Each of these types has different characteristics which have implications for effectiveness. The first type has the merit of focusing on 'real work', but has the drawback of being undirected. Type 3 works in reverse, in that it has the merit of being directed but the drawbacks of being distant from 'real work' and/or missing opportunities that arise in the conduct of normal work. Type 2 is intended to maximize the strengths and minimize the weaknesses of the other two types. Thus, the argument is that type 2 represents the most effective approach to management development (Mumford, 1993). This would seem, in part at least, to be relevant to the small business sector, since, as we argued earlier, the more formalized and systematized approaches are less likely to be viable options. However, as Mumford himself argues, type 2 does not negate the need for planning and some degree of formalization. Many small organizations probably apply type 1 approaches by default and, therefore, experience ineffective management development.

One commonly applied concept within management development which has the potential of supporting type 2 approaches is that of management competence. This concept is not a simple one to explain or describe, and it is not without controversy or criticism (Mumford, 1993; Tate, 1995). It is, though, at the heart of national policy on vocational qualifications and has been applied by the Management Charter Initiative (MCI) to produce 'occupational standards' for management (Harrison, 1992; Reid and Barrington, 1994). These standards provide a national specification of competencies, or abilities, required by managers in different roles and at different levels, and can therefore provide a starting point in raising understanding of management roles and development needs. However, the MCI initiative is criticized on a number of grounds of relevance to this chapter. Mabey and Salaman (1995) highlight research which suggests that progress in implementing the best practice model of MCI has been achieved at the expense of the small business sector. Other writers have criticized the generalist nature of the MCI model, which can ignore the specific contextual factors of particular managerial roles (see Mumford, 1993, and Tate, 1995, for a discussion of these and other criticisms). There do now exist national standards for managers working in small businesses, and therefore it could be argued that the problem of relevance has been solved. However, since they are also national standards, and therefore by definition generic, the problem of relevance to specific and particular contexts remains. In addition, application of occupational standards normally requires fairly sophisticated systems and therefore leads into type 3 approaches. This argument is confirmed by the research mentioned earlier and quoted in Mabey and Salaman (1995).

There are alternative specifications of competence to that provided by MCI. Jones and Woodcock (1995), for example, base their prescription for management development on a specification produced by their own research. Many large organizations have produced their own, in-house specifications. Mumford (1993), while criticizing the MCI national standards, acknowledges the value of some framework or model of competence. He further argues that any model needs to focus on effectiveness and to take account of the ambiguity of managerial work. He also provides a list of methods which meet those criteria by focusing on the job processes. The methods are as follows (Mumford, 1993).

- Changes in job: promotion; job rotation; secondments.
- Changes in job content: additional responsibility and tasks; specific projects; membership of committees or task groups; junior boards.
- Within the job: coaching; counselling; monitoring and feedback from boss; mentoring.

These methods exclude many of the more formalized methods which occur off the job. Alternative classifications are offered by Reid and Barrington (1994) and by Jones and Woodcock (1995). These classifications add the following methods:

- group-based methods, e.g. managerial grid;
- in-house courses;
- planned experience outside the organization;
- external course;
- role analysis;
- seminars;
- exchange consulting;
- performance review;
- career development.

The last two methods have links with succession planning, which is discussed by Harrison (1992) as an approach to and method of management development. The key argument about decisions on methods centres on taking account of the organizational variables listed in this section, and, according to his analysis and arguments, ensuring that the selection and application of methods constructs Mumford's (1993) type 2 approach to management development. The integrative nature of type 2 management development ensures the creation of a 'virtuous learning circle; in which successful outcomes of development in terms of managerial effectiveness lead to enthusiasm for further learning and development, rather than a vicious learning sequence in which generalised learning and problems in application lead to avoidance of further development activities' (Mumford, 1993, pp. 36–7).

Figure 9.2 places some of the methods listed above in the relevant quadrant. The placing of Blake and Mouton's managerial grid (see Stewart, 1996) in the top right quadrant follows the argument that management development is centrally concerned with organization values (Harrison, 1992).

Whatever view is taken on the meaning of management development, and whatever approaches and methods are applied consequent to that view, one thing seems clear from the majority of the research and writing on the subject. This is that management development in practice relies on self-development; or, at least, self-managed development. This view is supported by, among others, Jones and Woodcock (1985), Pedlar *et al.* (1994), Harrison (1992) and Mumford (1993). The merits and value of self-development, and some associated methods, are fully discussed in Stewart (1996). The point here is that self-managed development does not necessarily require formalized systems or allocation of significant resources. Many resources which can and do support development, e.g. other people (Mumford, 1993; Stewart, 1996), do not translate into large sums of money. Taking this argument as a starting point suggests that all

FOCUS

	Individual	Organization
Behaviour	Competence specifications	Managerial grid programme
Career Progression	Career management/ development	Succession planning

PURPOSE

Figure 9.2 Management development approaches and methods

organizations of whatever size have the capability and potential to apply management development as a means of improving prospects for survival and, where desirable, growth.

CONCLUSIONS

This chapter has argued that much of the management development literature is dominated by the concerns of the development needs of large organizations. Managers running small firms have a wider variety of roles than and different priorities from those running larger enterprises. The aims and objectives of the owners of the enterprise are not always neatly consistent with commercial objectives, including business growth and profit maximization. Many owners managers, particularly in the smallest firms, typically found in cafes, bed and breakfast, small hotels, small restaurants, free houses, etc., have objectives motivated by lifestyle and personal control considerations.

In these circumstances, personal development needs will give lower priority to acquiring business growth relevant management skills. Those organizations that have ambitions to provide management development programmes to the owner-managers of small firms need to target their efforts at the owner-managers of small tourism and hospitality firms where there are clear growth-related commercial objectives for the enterprise, or those sectors where owner-managers are experiencing a sense of threat owing to the pressures of the market place.

NOTE

1. Much of this chapter focuses upon small *hospitality* firms. This emphasis reflects the availability of research in this field. There are no *a priori* reasons for expecting significant differences between these and small *tourism* businesses. In any event, the classification of a small business by sector is, in this case, somewhat blurred, since many 'hospitality' establishments are almost entirely dependent upon tourism.

REFERENCES

Beaver, G. and Harrison, Y. (1994) 'TEC support for women entrepreneurs: help or hindrance?', 17th National ISBA Small Firms Policy and Research Conference, Sheffield, November.

Beaver, G. and Jennings, P.L. (1995) 'Picking winners: the art of identifying successful small firms', in D. Hussey (ed.) *Rethinking Strategic Management – Ways to Improve Competitive Performance*. Chichester: Wiley, 91–106.

Beaver, G. and Jennings, P.L. (1996) 'The abuse of entrepreneurial power. An explanation of management failure?', *Journal of Strategic Change*, **5(3)**, 151–64.

Bolton Report (1971) *Report on the Commission of Enquiry on Small Firms*. London: HMSO, Cmnd 4811.

Faulkner, D. and Johnson, G. (1992) *The Challenge of Strategic Management*. London: Kogan Page.

Goffee, R. and Scase, R. (1995) *Corporate Realities: in Large and Small Organisations*. London: Routledge.

Greiner, L. (1972) 'Evolution and Revolution as Organizations Grow', *Harvard Business Review*, July/August, 24–36.

Grieve-Smith, A. and Fleck, V. (1987) 'Business strategies in small high technology companies', Long Range Planning, **20(2)**, 61–8.

Handy, C. (1988) *Making Managers*. London: Pitman.

Harrison, R. (1992) *Employee Development*. London: IPD.

HCTC (1992) *Meeting Competency Needs Now and in the Future*. London: Hotel and Catering Training Company.

HtF (1996) *Training: Who Needs It?* London: Hospitality Training Foundation.

Jennings, P.L. and Beaver, G. (1995) 'The managerial dimension of small business failure', *Journal of Strategic Change*, **4(4)**, 185–200.

Jennings, P.L. Beaver, G. and Banfield, P. (1996) 'Competence-based training for small firms – an Expensive Failure', *Long Range Planning*, **289(1)**, 94–102.

Jones, J.E. and Woodcock, M. (1985) *Manual of Management Development*. Aldershot: Gower.

Kotter, J.P. (1982) *The General Manager*. London: Macmillan.

Lashley, C. (1993) 'Management development needs of small hotel and catering firms', in *Discussion Papers in Hospitality Management*, Paper no. 7. Leeds: Leeds Metropolitan University, Spring.

Lees, S. (1992) 'Ten faces of management development', *Management Education and Development*, **23(2)**.

Mabey, C. and Salaman, G. (1995) *Strategic Human Resource Management*. Oxford: Blackwell Business.

Mintzberg, H. (1973) *The Nature of Managerial Work*. New York: Harper and Row.

Mitroff, I. (1983) *Stakeholders of the Organizational Mind*. San Francisco: Jossey Bass.

Morrison, A., Rimmington, M. and Williams, C. (1998) *Entrepreneurship in the Hospitality, Tourism and Leisure Industries*. London: Butterworth.

Mumford, A. (1993) *Management Development: Strategies for Action*, 2nd edn. London: IPD.

National Westminster Bank (1990) *National Survey of Small Businesses*. London: National Westminster Bank.

NEDO (1992) *UK Tourism: Competing for Growth*. London: HMSO.

Nicholson, N. and West, M. (1988) *Managerial Job Change*. Cambridge: Cambridge University Press.

Osborne, R.L. (1991) 'The dark side of the entrepreneur', Long Range Planning, **24(3)**, 26–31.

Pedlar, M., Burgoyne, J. and Boydell, T. (1994) *A Manager's Guide to Self Development*, 3rd edn. London: McGraw-Hill.

Reid, M.A. and Barrington, H. (1994) *Training Interventions*, 4th edn. London: IPD.

Slattery, P. (1992) 'Unaffiliated hotels in the UK', *ETU Travel and Tourism Analyst*, **1**, 90–102.

Storey, J. (1989) 'Management development: a literature review', *Personnel Review*, **18(6)**, 7–16.

Stewart, J. (1996) *Managing Change through Training and Development*, 2nd edn. London: Kogan Page.

Stewart, R. (1982) *Choices for the Manager*. Maidenhead: McGraw-Hill.

Tate, W. (1995) *Developing Managerial Competence: a critical guide to methods and materials*. Aldershot: Lower.

Thomas, R., Friel, M., Jameson, S. and Parsons, D. (1997) *The National Survey of Small Tourism and Hospitality Firms: Annual Report 1996–97*. Leeds: Centre for the Study of Small Tourism and Hospitality Firms, Leeds Metropolitan University.

Watson, T.J. (1994) *In Search of Management*. London: Routledge.

Westhead, P. and Storey, D. (1996) 'Management training and small firm perfromance: why is the link so weak?', *International Small Business Journal*, **14(4)**, 13–24.

TEN

Employment and employee relations

Stephanie Jameson

INTRODUCTION

This chapter addresses issues which are pertinent to the examination of employment and employee relations in small tourism and hospitality firms. Defining employee relations is a complex procedure, and one author who has attempted to do this within the hotel and catering context is Lucas (1995), who suggests that employee relations is about the management of employment and work relationships between managers and workers. Lucas goes on to argue that these relationships can be individually or collectively based, involving informal or formal arrangements, and will be shaped by a variety of internal and external factors.

Employee relations has not received much attention in the tourism and hospitality literature, and within this literature any analysis of small tourism and hospitality firms is almost non-existent. Small, independently owned firms still predominate in these industries, so research conducted in large corporately owned multinational businesses cannot be said to be representative of employment relationships within these industries.

Research conducted on small firms in the service sector is also almost non-existent, and in any case sector-specific differences can be so great that insights from these firms may not offer much help in understanding small tourism and hospitality firms. This chapter refers to research conducted both in small firms and in larger tourism and hospitality firms, but maintains that small tourism and hospitality firms deserve separate treatment when one examines employment and employee relations.

Throughout the chapter, the terms employee relations and industrial relations are both used. This is a consequence of citing work whose authors have used the term industrial relations. This is not to say that the terms are synonymous or should be used interchangeably. As Lucas (1995) argues, there are fundamental academic differences between them. Employee relations gives greater emphasis to the individual and informal aspects of management–employee relations than to collective bargaining and representative institutions (Marchington and Parker, 1990) and, as Roberts et al. (1992)

suggest, employee relations is seen as more appropriate in the context of small and medium-sized enterprises.

The chapter begins with a discussion of the importance of small firms in the service sector, and goes on to examine some of the issues which are important to an understanding of employment in small tourism and hospitality firms. It is proposed that an understanding of the tourism and hospitality labour market and the way in which it operates is a useful starting point. It is suggested that one important area for consideration is recruitment activity, as this can give some indication of the way in which small firms in tourism and hospitality deal with the local labour market. It is then argued that some understanding of the composition of the labour force is relevant, as this can determine how small firm employers decide to manage. Reliance on the secondary labour market produces particular managerial approaches which result in informal and underdeveloped personnel policies and procedures.

Any meaningful analysis of employment in small tourism and hospitality firms needs to be set in the wider context of some discussion of small firms in the service sector in general, and some insight into employment and employment relations within these firms. Previous research into small service sector firms can help to inform and enlighten tourism and hospitality researchers, as many lessons have been learned and some mistakes can be avoided within the tourism and hospitality context.

It is crucial to examine the service sector when one is studying small firms, as most of the three million small firms in the UK are in the service sector, and two-thirds of jobs in the UK are in services (Storey, 1994, p. 178). Small and medium-sized enterprises (SMEs) have more of a presence in the private service sector than in manufacturing, as they came into focus when manufacturing was shedding labour and the service sector was growing in importance. As the Commission of the European Communities (1989) argues, the shift from an 'industrial society' towards a 'service society' has contributed towards the growing importance of SMEs where larger firms have lost ground in market share and employment.

Small firms are often located in labour-intensive areas of economic activity, such as services. It is crucial to appreciate and understand these major structural changes from manufacturing to services, as these changes have had a massive impact on the structure of employment in the economy.

Although it is clear that small firms predominate in the service sector and are of increasing economic importance, they have, as an area of academic enquiry, historically been neglected. This has led the Commission of the European Communities (1989) to claim that small firms in the service sector have been only very marginally studied, with the focus still remaining on manufacturing industry and larger enterprises. They go on to argue that studies on industrial relations taking size as a dependent variable are rare, and relevant data which consider size as an important factor are hard to collect. They maintain that more research has to be done into specific industrial relations patterns in small-scale firms and stress that the service sector is an unknown field in this regard.

The Bolton Report (see Chapter 1) received severe criticism, as one of its major weaknesses was its lack of analysis of employment. The report comprised 19 chapters, none of which was exclusively on employment. This led Storey (1994, p. 186) to argue that 'there is probably no dimension in which the Bolton Committee report was so seriously in methodological error as in its very brief review of employment relations' He goes on to explain that ignoring employment issues is like '*Hamlet* without the Prince'.

The Commission of the European Communities (1989) believes that this neglect has arisen partly because of research traditions as well as the inherent difficulties associated with research in SMEs. Although they are often referred to as a specific sector, many may have nothing in common except their size. They should not be treated as a homogeneous group of firms, as they present an extremely heterogeneous picture. Scott *et al.* (1989) also warn against the dangers of viewing the small firm sector as homogeneous. Further, Curran *et al.* (1993) argue that a failure to recognize key distinctions between services and manufacturing leads to a highly imperfect understanding of employment and employment relations in small firms. They go on to argue that any meaningful analysis of industrial relations in small firms needs an awareness of the heterogeneity of the small firms sector and an awareness of the industry specific culture of each setting. Storey (1994) elaborates on the fact that there is a huge variety of workplace differences in the service sector and that service sector employment leads to different issues in employment relations.

This notion that managerial styles and organization structures can be quite distinct from those of large firms has been developed by Curran (1986, 1991). Curran maintains that much service employment involves routine direct contact with the customer with production and consumption occurring simultaneously. For him this makes it difficult for the employer to control output quality and employee performance, which is fundamentally different from that of manufacturing. Storey (1994, p. 179) puts it as follows: 'The overall picture which emerges is that the types of jobs and the characteristics of those who fill them do differ between small and larger firms.' This starting point should be expanded and developed to take into account differences between employment in services and manufacturing and sector-specific characteristics within a particular industrial context. Only then can an attempt be made to understand and partially to explain employment and employment relations within small tourism and hospitality firms.

THE LABOUR MARKET

The small business sector is a vital component of the UK labour market. Johnson (1989b) has argued that labour market factors have played a key role in influencing the development of the small firm sector within the UK, and that sectoral trends in employment patterns have favoured services, where small businesses are dominant. It is suggested here that any analysis of employment relations within small tourism and hospitality firms cannot be undertaken without some understanding of the tourism and hospitality labour market.

Much effort has gone into developing theoretical models of labour markets, and one of the most useful theories for the tourism and hospitality industries has been dual labour market theory. Dual labour market theory proposes that the total labour market can be divided into two. The first section is the primary labour market, where jobs tend to be supplied by large, highly profitable firms with a high capital to labour ratio and high productivity. Production is usually large-scale in nature, with a high investment in technology. Employment is normally stable, wage and skill levels are relatively high and there are usually opportunities for training. The secondary labour market is characterized by small firms with low capital to labour ratio, low productivity and small-scale production. Here, wage and skill levels tend to be low, employment is unstable and training opportunities tend to be limited. Clearly, the tourism and hospitality industries tend to operate within the secondary labour market and this view has been supported by Riley (1996) and Goldsmith *et al.* (1997).

It is also argued that one key area which is crucial for any understanding of employment relations is the interaction with the labour market, and more specifically the process of recruitment within the small tourism and hospitality firm. This proposition is also supported in the more general small firms literature, where, for example, Atkinson and Storey (1993) found that interaction with the labour market was one of the key issues for researchers interested in the relationship between small firms and employment.

Interaction with the labour market

A key aspect of labour market interaction is recruitment. Further, the level of recruitment of a firm can illustrate how active a firm is in the labour market. Research by Thomas *et al.* (1997) in small firms in the tourism and hospitality industries indicates that almost 62 per cent of these firms exhibited employment stability over the previous 12 months: that is, the actual number of employees had not changed. However, although the actual number may have remained the same, the people performing in the jobs may have been different, and actual recruitment activity and interaction with the labour market may have been extremely high.

Research examining recruitment activity in small tourism and hospitality firms found that the most dominant method used was word of mouth (Thomas *et al.*, 1997). Small firms research in general illustrates that this mode of recruitment totally dominated for all types of workers (Curran *et al.*, 1993). Likewise, Atkinson and Meager (1994) in their research found that even quite substantial small businesses, such as those with more than 50 employees, continue to use word of mouth as an important tool of recruitment. This was the case even though they also discovered that recruitment methods for virtually all groups of workers became increasingly formalized with increases in firm size. Hospitality and tourism firms are renowned for their reliance on informal recruitment methods, especially word of mouth. Caution must be exercised by employers, as this method of recruitment can prove to be discriminatory, because it relies heavily on the current workforce, which may be composed of a particular gender or race who then 'advertise' the job to individual from the same background. This view has been supported by Jones *et al.* (1994) in their study of ethnic and white businesses in the UK, which found that word of mouth dominated as a method and that Asian firms are more likely to rely on personal recruitment procedures, even when the ten employee threshold has been overcome.

One other characteristic of a primary labour market is that it tends to exhibit a strong internal labour market. Such a labour market usually has precise hiring standards, formalized recruitment, high skill requirements, in-house training and opportunities for promotion. Counter to this, a weak internal labour market normally has vague hiring standards, informal recruitment and low skill requirements, and lacks training and promotion opportunities. As far as the tourism and hospitality industries are concerned, there is heavy reliance on the secondary local labour market. Goldsmith *et al.* (1997, p. 21) go as far as to argue that 'reliance upon secondary, local, labour markets is the defining feature of employment practices in commercial hospitality services.'

It is suggested that, in addition to understanding the labour market within which tourism and hospitality small firms operate, it is crucial to understand the type of labour which makes up the tourism and hospitality labour force. This is important to lay the foundation upon which some understanding of employment relations can be based in the small tourism and hospitality small firms context.

LABOUR FORCE COMPOSITION

It is no longer appropriate to assume that the normal or typical work pattern in the UK economy is full-time and permanent. Nor is it sensible to suggest that the normal or typical worker is male and manual. Contemporary Britain exhibits many varieties and patterns of labour and labourers. Nowhere is this more visible than in the service sector, and especially in tourism and hospitality. It seems highly likely that this trend will continue. Thus, as Lucas (1995, p. 49) argues, 'the hotel and catering industry experience may provide pointers to the way in which the future nature and structure of employment in other sectors may develop'.

One of the most dominant features of the tourism and hospitality labour market is the high incidence of female, part-time, casual, temporary and ethnic minority employees. These type of workers exert an influence on how the tourism and hospitality labour market is managed. An understanding of the predominance of these types of workers is a crucial prerequisite to any understanding of employment relations within small tourism and hospitality firms.

Females

There has been a consistent increase in the participation of women in the labour force throughout most of the post-war period. Women now account for 40 per cent of the workforce, and it is projected that almost half of all jobs will be filled by women by the end of the 1990s (Johnson, 1989b). Women already form the majority of the labour force in the service sector, and their representation has steadily increased since 1980 (Curran et al., 1993). Changes in the sectoral composition of employment and the growth of female labour force participation and changing employment practices among larger employers have also contributed towards the growth of the small business sector in the UK (Johnson, 1989b). Johnson also suggests that smaller businesses tend to rely more heavily on women workers than larger businesses, even allowing for sectoral differences. He goes on to suggest that it is not possible to state conclusively whether small firm growth has caused an increase in female labour force participation by offering employment which is more suited to many women (part-time, flexible hours, located closer to residential areas), or whether the direction of causation runs the other way. Johnson does shed some light on this when he suggests that women are prepared to accept lower wages and lower levels of job security than men, and this increases the attractiveness of women to many small business employers. He also suggests that an increasing female labour force participation may be said to have disproportionately benefited the small business sector by providing a source of labour supply which meets the needs of the small employer.

Others have sought to highlight links between gender preference and sector. In one study, pronounced sectoral differences were apparent in free houses, wine bars and restaurants, where almost half the owner-managers preferred women workers (Curran et al., 1993). Curran et al.'s (1993) research found that the majority of employers who preferred to employ women gave rather mundane reasons for their preference – these included views such as women being more hard-working, reliable and committed than men. Curran *et al.* also noted that several employers mentioned that women had good interpersonal skills and were considered an asset in attracting male customers! Their research also discovered that the kind of jobs on offer tended to attract women, such as kitchen staff and cleaners. They argue that this could be interpreted as women conforming to gender definitions imposed on them historically, and in this way employers were reinforcing these definitions through their recruiting practices.

The tourism and hospitality industries employ high proportions of females. The most up-to-date figures on employment in the industry provided by the Hospitality Training Foundation (HtF) suggest that females dominate the industry, accounting for 73 per cent of its workforce in 1994 (HtF, 1996). According to the HtF, the industry offers good opportunities to earn an income while working flexible hours that suit domestic arrangements. While male and female employment patterns vary across different industry sectors, the HtF found a much higher proportion of females in the catering services sector: 86 per cent, as opposed to 63 per cent in the commercial sectors. They maintain that this is because of the large numbers of housekeeping and domestic staff employed in these sectors, most of whom were females. If gender comparisons are made by occupation, the only occupations where there were more males than females were publicans and hotel porters. (For a more detailed breakdown of employment by occupation and gender, see HtF, 1996). As Purcell (1993, p. 127) has argued, the industry is 'an occupationally sex segmented labour market ... women are horizontally and vertically segregated into particular jobs, grades and areas of operation'.

The differing patterns of employment have also been studied by Curran *et al.* (1993), who, using Dex's (1985) work, suggest that employers' gender preferences are rooted in gender definitions linked to the domestic division of labour and the notion that women's occupations are peripheral or less important than those of men. The result, they argue, is occupational segregation.

Females tend to be highly concentrated in the less skilled or sub-craft occupations. Over two-thirds of all women working in the industry are employed as counter and kitchen hands and domestic staff. As far as management is concerned, women are also proportionately underrepresented, with fewer female managers than males, but more female supervisors than males. Further, the proportion of women managers drops significantly after age 30 (HCIMA and Touche Ross Greene Belfield-Smith Division, 1992).

One further characteristic of the secondary labour market is the high incidence of jobs performed by females. This has implications for the way in which employee relations are managed in small firms. Female workers may accept lower wages and more informal employment policies and procedures, and are much less likely to be organized in a trade union.

Part-time workers

Part-time working is another dominant feature of the service sector. As the primary sector and manufacturing employment continue to decline and the service sector continues to grow, part-time employment will continue to grow rapidly, while full-time will reduce slightly (Department for Education and Employment (DfEE), 1997). The DfEE's (1997) *Labour Market and Skill Trends 1996/97* maintains that the nature of work is changing. It is noted that the proportion who have full-time and permanent work is falling, though full-time employees still form a majority in the employed workforce (61 per cent). It states that more people are self-employed or are moving between part-time and temporary jobs. Between 1981 and 1994 growth in part-time employees accounted for about 1.5 million extra jobs. The number of full-time employees fell by 1.9 million over the same period. The share of all employees who were part-time rose from 21 to 28 per cent.

There is evidence to suggest that it is the smaller firms that are likely to employ a higher proportion of their labour force in a part-time capacity (Storey, 1994). Storey and Johnson (1987) examined employment structure in manufacturing plants, which showed that 22.4 per cent of the labour force in plants with fewer than four workers was part-time, compared with only 3.7 per cent of the labour force in plants with more than 100 workers. These issues have also been addressed by Scott *et al.* (1989) in their study of management and industrial relations in small firms. They examined 397 firms in four sectors, and discovered that the proportion of full-time employees rises according to the size of the establishment.

It is also worth pointing to sectoral differences in part-time working. Curran *et al.*'s (1993) research on employment and employment relations in small service sector firms examined employment mix (full-time, part-time and self-employed workers), and discovered substantial differences in employment mix between the sectors. They found that the use of full-time employees ranged from nearly 80 per cent of the workforces in computer services to only 37 per cent in the free house, wine bar and restaurant sector, where they suggest that the 'typical' employee is part-time. Curran *et al.* (1993) also discovered that the vast majority (96 per cent) of firms in this sector used part-time labour. The main rationale offered by employers for using part-time workers was to match personnel with workload requirements, either because the job required only a limited number of hours or because the firm faced uneven demand over the course of the working day or week. Curran *et al.* (1993) define this as a form of labour flexibility and go on to argue that in the free house, wine bar and restaurant sector, where employers were particularly in favour of being able to call workers in at busy periods and lay them off in slack periods, this was not a new form of labour flexibility, but merely the continuation of long-standing practices in the industry. When Curran *et al.* (1993) asked part-time workers in their sample the reasons for working part-time, they discovered that the majority were working part-time to fit in with other non-work commitments. The DfEE (1997) notes that many employees find positive advantages in working on a part-time or temporary basis. The research found that some workers felt it allowed work to be balanced with other commitments, such as a family. Further, it found that 27 per cent of employers using flexible working methods adopted them in response to employees' demands. Indeed, the majority (81 per cent) of women working part-time reported that they did not want to work full-time.

The HtF (1996) discovered that, in 1994, the majority of employees in the hospitality industry (65 per cent) worked part-time (fewer than 30 hours per week). It found that in the catering services sector, 70 per cent of employees classified themselves as part-time; in the commercial sectors, 60 per cent. The proportion of part-time workers was highest in pubs' bars and clubs. The HtF research also demonstrated that in the commercial sectors, pubs, bars and clubs had the highest proportion of part-time employees, and suggests that this is a result of the pattern of business in this sector.

Lucas (1995) argues that most part-time work in hotels and catering is regular, because the need for it is continuous, and using Guerrier and Lockwood's terminology, it is core rather than peripheral in terms of organization structure. Thus, Lucas maintains that this constitutes a numerically flexible form of employment, and that there is more numerically flexible employment in hotels and catering than in the economy as a whole. Lucas also suggests that the high proportion of part-timers in the industry is a function of demand for this form of labour that is mirrored by a plentiful supply of labour, mainly women, that is prepared to work on this basis. Lucas proposes that most hotel and catering businesses are subject to widely varying patterns of demand which render the utilization of full-time labour uneconomic. In these circumstances, she argues that part-time employment is used as a control mechanism to manage fluctuating demand. She maintains that employers do not want to pay workers to stand idle and that most part-time labour is also cheaper in direct terms (lower wages and other employment costs), and, therefore, part-time employment offers considerable cost benefits to employers.

It is impossible to discuss part-time employment in the service sector without some comment on the relationship between womens' work and part-time employment. The DfEE (1997) states that part-time employment is predominantly taken by women. In 1994, 81 per cent of part-time employees were female, and 46 per cent of all female employees were part-time, compared to 10 per cent of males. Bagguley (1990) argues that the growth of women's part-time employment is central to any consideration of service sector restructuring and employment change, as it accounts for the vast majority of growth in service sector employment. Employers who face high variations in demand for personal services will seek labour flexibility through part-time employment. (For a full discussion of explanations of the increase of women's part-time employment in the UK see Bagguley, 1990.)

Bagguley (1990) further notes that the tendencies towards task or functional flexibility are greatest in the smaller hotels. He argues that employers have been seeking numerical flexibility for some time, and maintains that those occupations in which part-time working is predominant are largely filled by women. For Bagguley, numerical flexibility is thus irreducibly gendered, since women take part-time work so that they can manage a home as well as a job. He argues that there is a distinct gender division in the form and extent of flexibility, believing that men are more likely to be involved in functional flexibility. One implication of this, he argues, is that part-time employees, mainly women, do not have the opportunity to develop a wide range of skills and experiences to be as functionally flexible as full-time employees, where more men are likely to be found in employment. He proposes that labour flexibility leaves vertical occupational segregation by sex largely untouched, while horizontal segregation may be blurred. Bagguley believes that functional flexibility occurs within a range of occupations for women, which seem to form a sex-typed 'family' of occupations within the industry. These, he argues, are the jobs most likely to be part-time.

Casual and temporary workers

It is difficult, though important, to differentiate between casual and temporary workers. This task is made even more complex when one tries to define casual or temporary work separately. As Curran *et al.* (1993) note, temporary work can take the form of one-off periods of casual work or repeated periods of employment at the same firm. It can be organized informally or through an agency based on formal fixed-term contracts. Kitching (1994) agrees that it is difficult to define temporary work, and illustrates this with the case of a free house owner who may have a pool of workers who can be used as and when demand requires. He stresses that these workers may work regularly and may or may not be considered as temporary by the employer or the employees themselves.

Curran *et al.* (1993) discovered that temporary work accounts for a relatively low proportion of all jobs in the UK. In their work on small firms in the service sector, they found that temporary workers were used by the majority of firms in all four sectors: 70 per cent of employers overall reported the use of temporary workers. They go on to suggest that there was little evidence from employers in their sample that there had been any conscious change towards an increased use of temporary workers. Rather, it was more likely that there had been a continuation of established patterns of employment.

It has been suggested by Kitching (1994) that where changes in the workload are short term, employers will recruit temporary workers. He also proposes that the availability and source of temporary staff will differ according to the culture of particular sectors. In his research on small service sector firms, he discovered that employers in the free house, wine bar and restaurant sector often had access to a pool of labour on which they called to meet periods of peak demand.

Casual employment is a well-established feature of the labour market in industries with a marked seasonal change in demand. The hospitality and tourism industries are no exception. As a result of the nature of this type of employment, no reliable figures for the numbers employed are available. According to Lucas (1995), casual work can be hourly, daily, weekly, monthly or seasonal. In some cases, agencies are used to supply labour on a casual basis. Lucas (1995) suggests that all these types of temporary employment may 'disguise permanence', because some of these workers may have worked for the same employer for a number of years. Lucas (1995) uses data from the WIRS3 to show that fewer employees worked on short-term fixed-term contracts in hotels and catering and private sector services than in all industries and services and all service industries. Kitching (1994) found that such a practice was more likely to be found in workplaces employing 100 employees or more.

Kitching (1994) also discovered that employers in the free house, wine bar and restaurant sector were more likely to report that temporary workers were used because a permanent worker was not required. Wood (1992) argues that there are many advantages in employing casuals. He suggests that they are often available for work at short notice and can therefore help employers to plug gaps caused by fluctuations in the demand for services. Kelliher (1989) and Guerrier and Lockwood (1989) have examined numerical flexibility and its relationship with low-skilled operative grade work in hotels and catering. Kelliher discovered that many employers develop their own pool of temporary employees familiar with organizational practices who can be called on when required. Guerrier and Lockwood (1989) found some departments in hotels in their sample with a heavy reliance on casual staff, especially departments such as banqueting.

There are obviously different views on the heavy reliance of temporary/casual work in the tourism and hospitality industries. Authors such as Ball (1988) do not accept that temporary work in tourism and hospitality is a 'poor relation' because, he argues, it provides valuable temporary work and job experiences for 'voluntary' participants (for example, students) and respite from unemployment for 'involuntary' participants. Lee-Ross (1993), on the other hand, argues that seasonal seaside jobs in hotels would appear to have a low skill content relative to that of other service jobs.

Whatever the attitudes towards the positive or negative impact of the high number of temporary or casual jobs in the tourism and hospitality industries, there is no doubt that employing this type of worker has major implications for the management of employee relations in small firms in these industries.

Hiring casual workers allows a high degree of flexibility on the part of the employer, and Price (1994) goes as far as to argue that this indicates a lack of long-term commitment towards casual employees. This has implications for the way in which these employees and the entire system of employee relations is managed, and has led Mitchell (1988, p. 485) to suggest that, 'while this philosophy prevails, it is unlikely that internal labour market structures encouraging flexibility and high productivity will develop'.

Ethnic minorities

One other important feature in the profile of employment and employee relations in small tourism and hospitality firms is the position of workers from ethnic minorities. Wood (1992) suggests that discussions of ethnic and migrant workers in the literature on hotel and catering work are complicated by a failure to define terms such as 'migrant' and 'ethnic'. He argues that these terms are often used interchangeably, and that indigenous ethnic populations are rarely distinguished from visiting workers. Wood further argues that this lack of precision obscures a complex of racial discrimination and exploitation of ethnic minorities, and suggests that overseas workers often came to the UK because catering work in the UK frequently provided better pay and career opportunities than existed in their own countries. Others, he suggests, came to learn English. Wood (1992) stresses, however, that for whatever reasons the employees came, employers engaged overseas workers because of the difficulties in finding members of the indigenous population prepared to work for the kind of wages on offer. As a result of this, the majority of overseas workers who came to work in the UK hotel and catering industry ended up in the worst paid jobs. Many employers in the industry could not attract the indigenous unemployed into the industry, and had active recruitment strategies to appoint overseas workers (Dronfield and Soto, 1980; Byrne, 1986).

As far as indigenous ethnic minorities in the UK hotel industry are concerned, the most extensive piece of work ever to be undertaken was the research conducted by the Commission for Racial Equality (CRE) in 1991. This was devoted to large hotels and only investigated the recruitment and selection practices of the 20 largest hotels in the UK. The results of the survey were disappointing in terms of the industry's implementation of professional personnel policies and procedures. The CRE found a lack of systematic personnel and recruitment procedures which was detrimental to the recruitment of ethnic minority employees. It is suggested here that although research has yet to be conducted on small tourism and hospitality firms and the employment of ethnic minorities, it is highly unlikely that the picture in small firms would be any more rosy (CRE, 1991).

Research has been conducted on small ethnic restaurants by Worsfold (1996), who realized the difficulties of carrying out research in such a culturally specific context. He identifies the difficulties he experienced, such as small family-run businesses being wary of external investigation. He found that this problem was exacerbated by the researcher being from a different ethnic group, having a different cultural background and not understanding the language being used in the workplace.

Worsfold (1996) also outlines previous research conducted in Chinese and Indian restaurants, and discusses such issues as lack of education and poor knowledge of English, which place severe restrictions on job opportunities in the UK. He cites Chan's (1986) research, which discovered that employment in a Chinese-operated business requiring only limited contact with the indigenous population may be the only job opportunity for many immigrants.

In general, small business research work (i.e. that not specifically in the tourism and hospitality industries) has been done into the employment of ethnic minorities in small businesses. A consistent theme to emerge is the importance of family firms and family labour. Jones *et al.* (1993) studied ethnic businesses and found that in a survey of 403 Asian, Afro-Caribbean and white businesses in 15 locations, 35 per cent of respondent firms used unpaid family labour. Jones *et al.* (1993) suggest that the use of family labour is a traditional and important feature of all small firms.

According to the DfEE (1997), ethnic minorities will form an increasing proportion of the labour force. They have a younger age profile and a higher proportion in the 16 to 24 age group in education than the white population. Over time, ethnic minorities will gradually make up a larger share of the total population, and hence the labour force. It remains to be seen whether these future employees will seek employment in small tourism and hospitality establishments.

EMPLOYEE RELATIONS

Two of the most frequently recurring themes in the literature on employment relations in small firms are the extent to which they are characterized by harmony or conflict and formality or informality.

Harmony and conflict

A much contested issue in small firms research surrounds the notions of 'harmony' and conflict-free patterns of industrial relations. This was a recurring theme in the Bolton Report (1971) and the research conducted by the Acton Society in 1953 and 1957 (Curran *et al.*, 1993). Some of these views were based on the absence of overt conflict in small firms (particularly strikes), the frequent lack of trade unions in these firms and a belief that, where businesses are small, communication between employers and employees is direct and straightforward, eliminating industrial conflict (Henderson and Johnson, 1974, p. 28; Curran, 1991).

This view has been debated extensively, and has been criticized for being naive and simplistic. It is obviously dangerous to assume that just because overt conflict does not exist, employee relations are trouble-free, as actions such as strikes are only one way of expressing conflict and are only appropriate in particular contexts: for example, where a trade union exists. It is also rather unrealistic to believe that just because communication is direct, this will eliminate conflict. Rather, it could be the case that this method of communication is entirely one-way and may help to increase the feeling of dissatisfaction as employees may feel that decisions have already been made and they have not taken part in the decision.

Alternative views have portrayed the small firm as a 'sweatshop', where employment relations are poor and exploitation is high (see, for example, Rainnie, 1989). Curran *et al.* (1986), however, have argued that this simple picture of owner-manager paternalism and harmony, or perceiving the small firm as a sweatshop, is inadequate for providing a proper understanding of what goes on inside enterprises.

Friendly and close personal relationships have been found within small firms, where employees claimed to get on very well or quite well with their supervisors (Curran *et al.*,

1986). This led the authors to suggest that vertical social relations (between shopfloor workers and owner-managers) can be seen as the most distinctive aspect of social relations within the small firm.

In their research, Curran *et al.* (1993) also found that employers believed their relations with employees were satisfactory. Eighty per cent of employers felt their relations with employees to be 'good' or 'excellent'. The free house, wine bar and restaurant sector was slightly more likely (86 per cent) to describe relations in this way. Employees in the sample in this sector maintained that the 'general sociability' found in the sector influenced relations between employer and employees.

In this research, employees tended to see socializing with others – customers, fellow workers and employers – as one of the main rewards of working in this particular sector: 83 per cent of employees in the free house, wine bar and restaurant sector said that they had high levels of satisfaction with social relations in their place of work. In this sector, employees stressed the friendly, relaxed atmosphere of the firm. This 'one big happy family' theme was also a feature of Price's (1993) research on hotels and restaurants, and one of her respondents said: 'We work in a true family atmosphere where everyone helps each other and works as part of a team' (Price, 1993, p. 51).

Close relationships between employees within and outside work is a feature of tourism and hospitality employment, where many employees live in, usually in accommodation provided by the employer (Shamir, 1981). Although, as yet, no one has conducted research specifically into this issue within small tourism and hospitality firms, it is likely that close personal relationships between employees exist in such firms.

Key research in this area (Curran *et al.*, 1993) indicated that the trend that emerged when describing relations with employees as 'good' or 'excellent' was due to the fact that temporary workers kept coming back to work at the firm. One of the sample said:

> the fact that the part-timers, for instance a young lady who has been coming back, she's been working part-time since she was at school, she's now at University, she keeps coming back. The head chef, again, there are other things he could do, career wise, but he has now been with me for five years ... I can only judge it on people wanting to stay.

This loyalty to the firm has also been found in research currently being conducted by the author of this chapter. It appears that where there is a heavy reliance on the local labour market, and more specifically on local families, members of the families pass the job on to younger siblings when they move away from home. In a seasonal location (Scarborough), several hotels employ almost exactly the same people every season, and one hotel has done so for the past eleven years. Friendly social relations in small firms are aided by recruitment methods where some employers deliberately recruit people they already know. This led one employer in the authors current research to say: 'Oh, we only take on people that we know, we never employ strangers, if we need someone I would usually ask someone across the bar if they were interested or would approach someone in the village.' Curran *et al.*'s (1993) research concludes that in their sample of firms there were few overall indications of sweatshops' relations, and suggests that this description has been applied mainly to small firms in older manufacturing industries.

The 'one big happy family' concept is also a recurring theme in the tourism and hospitality industry literature (see, for example, Shamir, 1981; Wheatcroft, 1985; Wood, 1992; Lucas, 1995). This, however, can mask many of the other features of the industry, such as low pay, long hours, low union density and high labour turnover, which in themselves affect the entire pattern of employment relations in tourism and hospitality. However, again, no author has attempted to isolate size as a variable and conduct research into the concept of harmony in work relations specifically in tourism and hospitality. What is clear is that the strength of this notion of 'harmony' in small firms has obvious implications for the levels of formality and informality in the management of employee relations within these firms.

Formality and informality

One theme that has been emphasized in discussions of employment relations in the small firm is the informality of relations between the employers and the employees. A correlation has been found to exist between the size of firm and the level of formality (see, for example, Scott *et al.*, 1989; Curran *et al.*, 1993). The Bolton Report (1971) discovered that relations were friendly, relaxed and close, as, in small firms, people worked in small groups, often alongside the owner. This report also found that work roles were flexible and each worker was treated as an individual. Obviously, these views must be seen in context, and factors such as industry, sector, occupation and skill levels must also be considered.

One suggested reason for informality in the small firm is that it is usual for face-to-face contact to take place between all those involved (Curran *et al.*, 1993). Curran *et al.* cite Gunnigle and Bray (1984), who argue that employers may not feel any need to formalize procedures that deal with issues such as consultation and communication. Another suggestion is that a practical reason is the heavy workload of many owner-managers, which leaves little time for a planned approach to their employees (Henderson and Johnson, 1974). Whatever the reasons for this informality in employment relations, it is a prominent feature in the small firms sector.

Price (1993) found a strong correlation between size and the degree of formality within establishments in her survey of UK hotels and restaurants. She discovered underdeveloped policies in personnel and industrial relations in hotels and restaurants. She argues that:

> Employment practices within the industry are still far too informal and unregulated to conform to what is commonly understood as good practice within the 'Personnel and Industrial Relations' ideal-type laid out in Storey's (1992: 34) classificatory system.

In her research, she found the least amount of formality in small, single-establishment proprietorships, where many owners said they saw little need, given their caring approach to staff, which was often described as treating them 'as part of the family'.

The cornerstone of any employment relationship is the contract of employment. It is also a key area of formalization of the relationship between employer and employee (Curran *et al.*, 1993). The current legal obligation is for an employer to provide an employee with a written statement of the terms and conditions of employment within four weeks of starting work.

When Curran *et al.*'s research was conducted in 1993, the legal requirement was to provide written particulars of the main terms and conditions of employment within 13 weeks of the commencement of employment. Curran *et al.* (1993) found that 65 per cent of small service-sector employers provided one or more of their employees with a written contract of employment or a statement of the main terms and conditions of employment. Scott *et al.*'s (1989) work showed that 73 per cent of their employers provided employees with a written contract or written particulars. In Curran *et al.*'s (1993) research the sector with the lowest number of firms providing employment contracts (27 per cent) was the free house, wine bar and restaurant sector. When employees in Curran *et al.*'s research were asked whether they had a written contract of employment or a written statement of their main terms and conditions, there were substantial differences between sectors, which, they argue, reflects the different characters of the sectors. The free house, wine bar and restaurant sector had the lowest proportion of employees (10 per cent) with a contract of employment or statement of main terms and conditions. In one other sector in their sample (advertising, marketing and design), 76 per cent fell within this category, and the other two sectors had similarly high levels. Curran *et al.* argue that this appears to point to different employment practices between this and the other sectors. This could be owing to many factors, but one of the main reasons is likely to be the heavy reliance on part-time casual and temporary workers. This in itself should not mean that these employees should work without the protection of an employment contract; instead, what is a distinguishing feature of this sector is the view from employers that these types of employees do not 'need' contracts of employment.

In Price's survey in 1992, 74 per cent of respondents issued written contracts. However, when size of establishment was examined, the lowest percentage of respondents issuing contracts was the one to ten employee category. Only 59 per cent of establishments in this category had used written contracts. Firms employing between 31 and 60 employees exhibited the most frequent use of contracts (93 per cent). Importantly, Price notes that the firms in her sample tended to be some of the higher quality and more progressive employers. In the light of this, it is suggested that it is highly likely that the vast majority of small tourism and hospitality employers do not issue contracts of employment to their staff. It is argued here that this is more than just an oversight on the part of the employer. It is suggested that the contract of employment lays the whole foundation of any pattern of employment relations in any firm, irrespective of size. The existence or absence of a contract can illustrate how knowledgeable the employer is about employment relations, how sophisticated the pattern of employment relations can be and how the employer actually manages employees and employment relations within any firm. The initial findings of research currently being conducted by the author on deregulation and employment legislation in small tourism and hospitality firms suggest that, in the vast majority of small firms in the sample, employers stated that they had no written contracts of employment. Furthermore, the main reason they gave for the absence of contracts was that they did not need them because most of their staff were part-time and/or casual. Their comments included: 'Ah well, they are not on formal contracts, but are employed as long as they want to work and as long as we need them. They are not a legal requirement anyway, are they?'

Other small firm employers in this research believed that they did not need contracts because they employed only part-time and casual workers. This argument is legally flawed and will become even less acceptable in future as a result of the present government's approach to the protection of these types of workers. Although there is a high level of informality regarding contracts of employment in the small firms sector, this should change in the future owing to increasing European intervention and changes in the rights of casual and temporary workers.

Another area in which this degree of informality is evident in small firms is in consultation. Curran *et al.* (1993) asked employers whether any arrangements existed for consulting employees about matters that affected them. Over three-quarters of the employers claimed that arrangements of some kind existed. Employers indicated that a whole range of issues were discussed, from the general running of the firm to very specific issues, such as the content of particular work roles or new product opportunities. The sector with the lowest level of formal and informal arrangements for consultation was free houses, wine bars and restaurants. This sector had a 68 per cent level of consultative arrangement, compared with 84 per cent in the highest sector, namely computers services and employment, secretarial and training.

Curran *et al.*'s research found that as the size of the firm increases, the formality of consultation arrangements increases. In the fewer than five employees category, 41 per cent of firms reported no consultation arrangements, and 12 per cent had formal arrangements. In the 20 or more employees category, 78 per cent had formal arrangements.

There is a notion in the small firms literature that written procedures are not a major factor in small firm employment relations, although Curran *et al.* (1993) found a higher incidence than this literature has implied. They found that in a small number of firms in their sample the level of formalization was very similar to what might be found in some larger firms. They suggest several reasons for this (Curran *et al.*, 1993, p. 82), and argue that one reason for variation in levels of formality across the sample is the differences between sectors. The sector with the lowest levels of formality was free houses, wine bars and restaurants. Curran *et al.* argue that this was entirely expected because of the informal character of much employment in the sector, where relations are characterized by casual and temporary employment patterns and very high levels of labour turnover.

Other research (Price, 1993) concludes that employment practices are still very informal in hotels and restaurants, and that the smaller the establishment, the smaller the likelihood that good practice exists. Research that specifically focuses on small firms within tourism and hospitality needs to be conducted in the near future to establish if this is still the case and to examine the impact this has on employment relations.

CONCLUSIONS

As has been illustrated by the literature, in general, any understanding of industrial relations has been heavily oriented towards large-scale settings that tend to be dominated by male (usually full-time) employees (see, for example, Curran *et al.*, 1986). Curran *et al.* suggest that, in this context, industrial relations has focused on collective issues, including trade unions and collective bargaining, and any analysis of conflict has been within the large firm domain.

As many authors have argued forcefully, a small firm is not a microcosm of a large firm, but a fundamentally different phenomenon, requiring different starting points for analysis and different methods of enquiry. As far as industrial relations is concerned, sectors should be handled differently, as should variations in size. Most industrial relations research is being carried out in manufacturing; most small firms research has also been conducted in the manufacturing context.

This is of little value in aiding an understanding of firms in the service sector that have a high proportion of their labour force who are female and work on a part-time or casual basis. To date, there has been no systematic and rigorous research on industrial relations in small tourism and hospitality firms that takes account of employers that rely on a secondary labour market and employees who work within weak internal labour markets guided by poorly developed informal and often unprofessional personnel practices and procedures. It is argued here that these features of small tourism and hospitality firms make their patterns of employment relations different not only from non-tourism and hospitality small firms, but also from large tourism and hospitality firms. As such, sector-specific and size-specific research should be conducted in order to make sense of the pattern of employment relations in small tourism and hospitality firms.

REFERENCES

Atkinson, J. and Meager, N. (1994) 'Running to stand still: the small business in the labour market', in J. Atkinson and D.J. Storey (eds) *Employment, the Small Firm, and the Labour Market*. London: Routledge.

Atkinson, J. and Storey, D.J. (eds) (1993) *Employment, the Small Firm, and the Labour Market*. London: Routledge.

Bagguley, P. (1990) 'Gender and labour flexibility in hotel and catering', *Service Industries Journal*, **10(4)**.

Ball, R.M. (1988) 'Seasonality: a problem for workers in the tourism labour market?', *Service Industries Journal*, **8(4)**, 501–13.

Bolton, J.E. (1971) *Report of the Committee of Enquiry into Small Firms*. London: HMSO.

Byrne, D. (1986) *Waiting for Change?* Low Pay Pamphlet no. 42. London: Low Pay Unit.

Chan, A. (1986) *Employment Prospects of Chinese Youth in Britain: A Research Report*. London: Commission for Racial Equality.

Commission of the European Communities (1989) *Industrial Relations in Small and Medium Sized Enterprises – Final Report*. Berlin: Enterprise Policy.

Commission for Racial Equality (1991) *Working in Hotels*. London: CRE.

Curran, J. (1986) *Bolton Fifteen Years On: A Review and Analysis of Small Business Research in Britain*. London: Small Business Research Trust.

Curran, J. (1991) 'Employment and employment relations in small firms', in J. Stanworth and C. Gray (eds), *Bolton 20 Years On: The Small Firm in the 1990s*. London: Paul Chapman Publishing.

Curran, J., Kitching, J., Abbott, B. and Mills, V. (1993) *Employment and Employment Relations in the Small Service Sector Enterprise – A Report*. London: ESRC Centre for Research on Small Service Sector Enterprises.

Curran, J., Stanworth, J. and Watkins, D. (1986) *The Survival of the Small Firm, Volume 2: Employment, Growth, Technology and Politics*. Aldershot: Gower.

Department for Education and Employment (1997) *Labour Market and Skill Trends 1996/1997*. London: DfEE.

Dex, S. (1985) *The Sexual Division of Labour*. Brighton: Wheatsheaf.

Dronfield, L. and Soto, P. (1980) *Hardship Hotel*. London: Counter Information Services, Anti-report no. 27.

Goldsmith, A., Nickson, D., Sloan, D. and Wood, R.C. (1997) *Human Resource Management for Hospitality Services*. London: International Thomson Business Press.

Guerrier, Y. and Lockwood, A. (1989) 'Flexible working in the hospitality industry: current strategies and future potential', *Contemporary Hospitality Management*, **1(1)**, 11–16.

Gunnigle, P. and Brady, T. (1984) 'The management of industrial relations in the small firm', *Employee Relations*, **6(5)**, 21–5.

Henderson, J. and Johnson, B. (1974) 'Labour relations in the smaller firm', *Personnel Management*, December, 28–31.

Hospitality Training Foundation (1996) *Catering and Hospitality Industry – Key Facts and Figures, Research Report*. London: The Industry Training Organisation.

Hotel, Catering and Institutional Management Association (HCIMA) and Touche Ross Greene Belfield-Smith Division (1992) *Salaries and Benefits in the Hotel and Catering Industry 1991 Survey, Volume 1*. London: Touche Ross Greene Belfield-Smith Division.

Johnson, S. (1989a) *Employment Change in Small Businesses: Expectations and Reality*. Leeds: Policy Research Unit, Leeds Polytechnic.

Johnson, S. (1989b) *Small Firms and the UK Labour Market in the 1990s*. Leeds: Policy Research Unit, Leeds Polytechnic.

Jones, T., McEvoy, D. and Barrett, G. (1993) 'Labour intensive practices in the ethnic minority firm', in J. Atkinson and D.J. Storey (eds) *Employment, the Small Firm, and the Labour Market*. London: Routledge.

Kelliher, C. (1989) 'Flexibility in employment: developments in the hospitality industry', *International Journal of Hospitality Management*, **8(2)**, 157–66.

Kitching, J. (1994) 'Employers' workforce construction policies in the small service enterprise', in J. Atkinson, and D.J. Storey (eds) *Employment: the Small Firm, and the Labour Market*. London: Routledge.

Lee-Ross, D. (1993) 'An investigation of "core job dimensions" amongst seaside hotel workers', International Journal of Hospitality Management, **12(2)**, 121–6.

Lucas, R. (1995) *Managing Employee Relations in the Hotel and Catering Industry*. London: Cassell.

Marchington, M. and Parker, P. (1990) *Changing Patterns of Employee Relations*. Hemel Hempstead: Harvester Wheatsheaf.

Mitchell, P. (1988) 'The structure of labour markets in the hotel and catering industry. What do the employment law cases indicate?', *Service Industries Journal*, **8(4)**, 470–8.

Price, L. (1993) 'The limitations of the law in influencing employment practices in UK hotels and restaurants', *Employee Relations*, **15(2)**, 16–25.

Price, L. (1994) 'Poor personnel practice in the hotel and catering industry: does it matter?', *Human Resource Management Journal*, **4(4)**, 44–62.

Purcell, K. (1993) 'Equal opportunities in the hospitality industry: custom and credentials', *International Journal of Hospitality Management*, **12(2)**, 127–40.

Rainnie, A. (1989) *Industrial Relations in the Small Firm*. London: Routledge and Kegan Paul.

Riley, M. (1996) *Human Resource Management in the Hospitality and Tourism Industry*, 2nd edn. Oxford: Butterworth-Heinemann.

Roberts, I., Sawbridge, D. and Bamber, G. (1992) 'Employee relations in small and medium sized enterprises', in B. Towers (ed.) *A Handbook of Industrial Relations Practice*, 3rd edn. London: Kogan Page, 240–57.

Scott, M., Roberts, I., Holroyd, G. and Sawbridge, D. (1989) 'Management and industrial relations in small firms', *Research Paper no. 70, Department of Employment*.

Shamir, B. (1981) 'The workplace as a community: the case of British hotels', *Industrial Relations Journal*, **12**, 45–56.

Storey, D.J. (1994) *Understanding the Small Business Sector*. London: Routledge.

Storey, D.J. and Johnson, S. (1987) *Job Generation and Labour Market Change*. Basingstoke: Macmillan.

Thomas, R., Friel, M., Jameson, S. and Parsons, D. (1997) *The National Survey of Small Tourism and Hospitality Firms, Annual Report 1996–1997*. Leeds: *Centre for the Study of Small Tourism and Hospitality Firms*, Leeds Metropolitan University.

Wheatcroft, P. (1985) 'Trusthouse Forte behind the image', *Working Woman*.

Wood, R.C. (1992) *Working in Hotels and Catering*. London: Routledge.

Worsfold, P. (1996) 'Working in ethnic restaurants', IAHMS Spring Symposium, Harrogate.

ELEVEN

Using information technology

Alistair Mutch

INTRODUCTION

If one were to take the evidence from the information systems strategy literature at face value, one could be forgiven for thinking that the tourism industry was the most developed user of information technology (IT). This impression might be gathered from the attention paid to the Thomson Holiday reservation system TOPS, which is frequently given as a key example of how organizations can gain competitive advantage from the use of IT (Earl, 1989). Such references are often backed up by others to the SABRE reservation system of American Airlines. One would, of course, be mistaken in such an impression, for such systems, while both vitally important and impressive in their scale, are far from representative of practice in tourism. They represent solutions to problems which are not the same as those faced by, for example, the owners of small tourism attractions. However, the problems of such people are not a prominent feature in either the computing or the tourism literature. The emphasis in the former tends to be on the problems of the larger organization, and quite a large volume is building up suggesting ways in which IT might be used more effectively (Ward, 1995, is a good recent example). In the tourism literature, the major focus is on the airline central reservation systems (CRS) and their wider impacts (Poon, 1993). These systems are not without impact on small enterprises, not least those who operate in international markets. The impact here is an indirect one, in that, without access to the distribution channels offered by the CRS, small enterprises are unable to tap potential business (Buhalis, 1993). To counter such one-sidedness in distribution channels, it could be argued that the public sector has a role to play in building alternative IT-based networks (Archdale, 1993). In a similar vein, by altering the balance of competition in the travel agency sector, the combination of airline CRS and on-line tour operator systems has the potential to push small agents towards computerization (Hitchins, 1991). However, these trends are often discussed at a sector or industry level, without a detailed consideration at the level of the small enterprise. This chapter looks at the implications of IT for small tourism and hospitality enterprises, the differences in the use of IT by large and small enterprises and the lessons which can be derived for smaller enterprises. Considerable advantage can be derived by smaller firms, but there are some important constraints to be taken into consideration. A key focus of the chapter is on distinguishing the importance of information from its supporting technology. Too close a link between the two, it is argued, can blind us to the gains which can be made from, on the one hand, an improved questioning of the information enterprises need to succeed and, on the other, an effective employment of technology.

TOURISM, INFORMATION AND TECHNOLOGY

Superficially, tourism would seem to be an ideal area for the application of information technology. As Poon argues:

> Unlike consumer and industrial goods, the essentially intangible tourism service cannot be physically displayed or inspected at the point of sale. It is normally purchased well in advance of the time and away from the place of consumption. In the marketplace, therefore, tourism is almost completely dependent on representations and descriptions in printed and audio-visual forms. (Poon, 1988, p. 533)

However, such a passage should alert us to the dangers of confusing data with information. As we can see, tourism information can come in many forms, many of which are intangible or difficult to capture in machine readable form. While the capacity of computers to handle different types of information is expanding, they excel in handling quantitative data. Such data, like airline seat availability, are crucially important, but far from being the only type of data we need to run operations successfully. Moreover, this chapter takes the perspective that information is not a 'thing' which can be stored and processed in advance (as can data) but rather, in the words of Boland, 'It is meaning, and can only be achieved through dialogue in a human community. Information is not a commodity. It is a skilled human accomplishment' (Boland, 1987, p. 377). This is not an empty debating point. It places the emphasis on the skill of those using and interpreting information and, as we will see, this could be argued to give those in small enterprises something of an advantage. It also gives a clue as to why, in large organizations, the history of the application of IT has often not been a happy one. There are complex reasons for the failure of often large investments to bring about the expected improvements in productivity, but among these reasons, it has been argued, has been an inability of users to get full value from the information potentially available from the new tools (Strassman, 1985). In fact, when we examine the successful large company systems in detail, we find that even so-called competitive/strategic systems such as American Airlines' SABRE system have a very large 'data processing' component (Wiseman, 1985). This data processing element can be about either the need to process large volumes of data or the need to communicate across distance (or both). Such needs may have a lesser place in the small enterprise, where lines of communication and business volumes are both of a lesser magnitude. However, this is a point which is returned to below; we have first to review some technological trends and see what their implications might be for small enterprises.

The dominant technological trend has been the continuing improvement in the power/cost ratio of all types of computing equipment. Power may be measured in a number of ways – the number of millions of instructions processed per second, the number of pages printed per second, the volume of data stored – but whatever measure we choose, the capacity of computers has been increasing at a steady rate. This improvement has qualitative dimensions as well (it is not just the number of pages a laser printer can produce, for example, but the fact that they can be of camera ready quality, or in colour) and shows no signs of diminishing. At the same time, real costs have been decreasing. In 1990, a major study by the Massachusetts Institute of Technology (MIT) on the development and impact of IT argued that, while capital equipment in six selected areas had shown a productivity increase of nearly one and a half times over a ten-year period, the equivalent for IT was 25 times (Scott Morton, 1991).

One implication of such changes is that technology has moved from being a constraining factor to achieving commodity status. To explain this it is necessary to review, briefly, the development of computing technology. From the first commercial application in the early 1950s to the advent of the personal computer (PC) in the 1980s, computers were expensive pieces of specialized equipment. They required their own specialized environment, were extremely expensive and demanded an army of technical specialists. Part of the role of these specialists was to coax the optimum performance from the equipment. This meant that all the skill and ingenuity was focused on efficient data storage and manipulation; there was no resource left for making the system look attractive or easy to interrogate. These machines were supplied by a very few companies, dominated by IBM. In turn, only the largest of organizations could afford to buy and maintain computers. However, the advent of the PC changed this situation dramatically. Many computers now work on the desktop and can be run by those with fairly limited knowledge of their internal make-up. This is not to argue that some computing applications are not complex, or that specialized staff are not needed in some areas; rather, it is to argue that technical considerations are no longer the dominant factor. With the growth of both a mass market and volume production, prices have tumbled and computers have become a commodity. IBM is now only one (albeit still large and significant) player among a multitude of competing companies.

What this means for small enterprises is that computers and their potential are very much within their reach. It also means that the focus has switched from the hardware to the applications which can be run on it. Ideally, one should now be able to select the application one wants and then acquire the hardware as a secondary consideration. However, one suspects that all too often this is not the route followed, and that too many computers are purchased as a solution looking for a problem. Part of the cause of this may be a failure to look at what information is needed to run an operation and then to look for ways of supporting these needs. In theory, the task of the small business should be easier by the growth in availability of packaged software. An understanding of this point again demands a brief detour into history. Computers require specialized sets of instructions, or programs, in order to run. In the early days of computing, such programs were written within organizations themselves, to satisfy their own needs. However, it rapidly became apparent that many companies had standard needs, particularly in areas such as accounting, and so common applications, called packages, were written and offered for sale. The attraction of these is that someone else has incurred the development cost and that they ought to be usable without the need for particular technical expertise. We examine the truth or otherwise of these claims below, but suffice it to say for the present that the existence of packaged software ought to make life very much easier for the small business.

One further trend which is of some importance to the discussion that follows needs to be introduced. In a brilliant review of the implications of computers for work,

Shoshana Zuboff, an American sociologist, argued that machines have historically been used to automate work (Zuboff, 1988). That is, they have been used to mimic human actions. The benefits to be gained have been through a more regular and certain action and through the combination of machines into new production processes. Thus, the automation involved in a machine tool does not fundamentally alter the task, even if it does fundamentally alter the way that task is organized. However, the coming of computer numeric controlled (CNC) machine tools adds a new dimension, in that as part of the process information is collected. We can automatically capture, for example, when the process stopped and started. This information can then be used for control and monitoring purposes. Zuboff argued that this was a qualitatively different process from automation, and she gave it the somewhat clumsy label 'informatization'. We can see this process at work in the supermarket tills, which collect data on our spending patterns automatically, or in the ability to award frequent flyer rewards. This ability of IT places a great emphasis on our ability to be able to identify and use information effectively.

Let us use some tourism examples to illustrate the potential. Arran Ranchettes is a self-catering establishment on the Scottish island of Arran. Founded in 1969, this consisted of 26 wooden chalets in the grounds of a former country house, now itself a hotel. The self-catering side was run by a husband and wife team who lived on site, and it prospered in the 1970s thanks to its anticipation of the growth in demand for self-catering. Customers, largely from the North East of England and Central Scotland, were reached by advertisements in a variety of newspapers, both local and national. These advertisements all contained a department number intended to measure response rates. A provisional booking was pencilled into a wall chart, to be inked in when a deposit was received. Completed booking forms were stored in date order to await payment of the final balance and then transferred to a shoe box 'archive'.

Two information-handling problems arose from this system. One was a matter of day-to-day running, but one which could have serious consequences. Standard bookings were ideally for a fortnight, thus decreasing the number of change-overs at which chalets would need to be cleaned. They would also be staggered to maintain an even balance of change-over work. However, chalets could be let by the week and a small number were reserved for mid-week change-overs, in recognition of the fact that the ferry was often fully booked at peak weekends. This system led to a complex wall chart, understandable by the owners but potentially misleading for anyone else who attempted to take a telephone booking.

The other problem did not result in such immediate operational or financial consequences, but could have had a considerable impact on the business. This was the inability of the owners, through time pressures, to do anything with the volumes of information that the booking forms potentially represented. Thus, while the forms might have been coded with their source, no formal analysis of this was carried out to ascertain advertising effectiveness. Instead, this was done on the basis of 'gut feeling'. Similarly, much of the business, as is common in tourism, became repeat business, but the full extent of this was never quantified. Nor were the stored forms used as a basis for direct communication with former customers. All these omissions were the result of the physical problems of sorting and processing the data manually.

Let us compare this to Country Holidays (Mutch, 1993). While now part of the Thomson empire, this company, the market leader in UK cottage holiday letting, started in 1979 with just 200 cottages. A computer system was installed in the following year, and enhanced to deal with business volumes which had climbed to around 7000 cottages by the end of the 1980s. Most of the business was transacted by telephone and to cope with the volume a piece of equipment known as an automatic call distribution (ACD) system was installed. This not only allowed better utilization of staff time but also provided the facility to attach a telephone number to each type of media used for advertising. The incoming telephone numbers were automatically recorded by the ACD, so an accurate response rate could be calculated for each type of media. When this was combined with booking data from the database, a cost per booking could be calculated, which allowed for a precise comparison of different media. Thus, it became clear that, while advertisements in, for example, The *Sun* produced a high response rate, they produced few bookings. Owing to the costs of not only placing the advert but also fulfilling brochure requests, this resulted in a high cost per booking. In distinction, advertisements in the *Guardian* produced a lower response, but a greater conversion ratio (Green, 1992). One can see in this example how IT, with its automatic capture of data, can bring considerable business benefits – provided the right questions are asked.

The focus here, then, is on the importance of information. Good data are vital for this, but are not the full picture. What one might argue is that much of the work on information systems has confused the two, and that on closer examination prescriptions relating to *information* have in fact been addressing issues of *data* (Mutch, 1996a). This has been particularly the case in large organizations, where solutions have been dealing with two problems particularly associated with size: data volumes and coordination. While the ability to deal with these successfully can give large organizations a competitive edge, what they often grapple with unsuccessfully is the local nature of much information interpretation. What is meant by this is the often tacit and implicit knowledge that can respond intuitively to changes in the environment. There has been a renewed interest in such knowledge over recent years in a number of unrelated fields, be they a response to free market economics (Wainwright, 1994), a critique of the fallacies of strategic planning (Mintzberg, 1994) or a challenge to artificial intelligence (Winograd and Flores, 1986). What all these writers stress, in their different ways and with different emphases, is the impossibility of codifying all the information necessary to run processes and organizations. This flies in the face of a huge amount of effort spent deriving prescriptions for large organizations. Some of this is deliberately aimed at solving the perceived problems of recording organizational knowledge. Thus a work on information economics can suggest that the value of IT lies in its capacity to endow the organisation: '(1) with greater intelligence to compensate for the lack of workforce competence; (2) with greater intelligence to facilitate competitive edge and change; and (3) to capture competence before it is lost' (Parker and Benson, 1988, p. 34). These claims often prove to be chimeras, but it is often easier to propose tangible IT-based solutions than to adopt softer measures such as workforce training. It is here, with the deployment of tacit knowledge to enhance information, that the small business might have its real edge. This suggests that the focus of IT use ought to be on supporting this process, rather than being solely, or even primarily, about transaction processing.

One implication of this is that small businesses need to question very closely whether IT can actually fill this role. A useful example of how a simple recognition of what is needed, with some attention to manual processes, can bear fruit is that of Butterfly World in Stockton. The concern here was with the effectiveness of the advertising budget, which was being directed at visitors from out of the region. A customer satisfaction survey indicated, however, that most visitors came from the immediate locality. This resulted in a refocusing of advertising, together with a paper-based system to monitor advertising responses (DTI, 1995, pp. 10, 19). This ability to ask the right questions can be displayed through examples of companies which have adopted IT with a degree of success. As the two companies, and much of the material which follows in the chapter, are located in the cottage holiday letting agency sector, some introductory comments about the environment are in order.

CASE STUDY: THE COTTAGE LETTING INDUSTRY

Cottage holidays were one of the success stories of UK tourism in the 1980s. While precise data are difficult to ascertain, the number of cottages available for let has been estimated around 30,000, and the number of adult holiday-makers in 1988 at 3.5 million (Mutch, 1993). This growth was fuelled by the increase in holidays taken by social classes AB, with a particular emphasis on second holidays. A feature of the growth of the sector was the parallel rise of letting agencies. By making reservations easier and by improving quality standards, these agencies were an integral part of the success of the sector, and their numbers grew considerably during the decade. The sector is dominated by one firm, Country Holidays, which had a market share (measured by numbers of cottages handled) of some 30 per cent in 1990. A further three firms had over 1000 cottages on their books, accounting for a further 27 per cent of the market. The rest of the market was shared by at least 80 firms, with the majority of these having fewer than 50 cottages.

Country Holidays is a good example of how IT can help a small business to grow. The company was started by the son of a Yorkshire dairy farmer in 1978. Responding to shifts in the farming industry and demands for self-catering accommodation, Philip Green started with 200 cottages. From the early years of the business, he recognized the potential of IT to help him deal with increases in business volumes, despite his own lack of computer knowledge. His search for solutions began in 1979 and evolved through a number of systems. The use of IT was clearly a key enabler in the company's dramatic expansion to a situation where some 7000 cottages were being claimed in the early 1990s. The systems used were *bespoke* ones: that is, systems designed to meet the specific requirements of Country Holidays. This was in large part owing to the lack of suitable packages in the market. The running of such systems called for the employment of specialist staff. The arrival of these staff saw a sea change in the organization. It was sold to its managers for £14 million in 1989, and a new database was installed to handle the ever-growing volume of business. As noted above, the company was sold to Thomson Holidays in 1994 as part of its diversification into the UK tourism market. It therefore no longer 'qualifies' as a small tourism enterprise, but it shows just what an impact IT can have.

To assess this impact, however, we have to place it in its context. One clear statement was that the use of IT was from the start envisaged as 'a marketing and selling system with administration and accounts bolted on rather than the other way round' (Green, 1991). This points to the success factors we need to explore. One was that this was a growing market which was ripe for the approach being taken. There were letting agencies in existence, but these tended to aim for the higher end of the market. Country Holidays aimed its products squarely at the middle of the market, emphasizing good quality at competitive prices. Its ability to sell holidays efficiently meant that it could extend the traditionally short letting season, thus compensating owners with a greater total revenue despite lower unit prices. It emphasized the necessity for owners to maintain and improve quality standards, using the computer to analyse customer satisfaction surveys and the results to weed out substandard properties. The company ploughed back much of its initial revenues into advertising and the production of attractive promotional material, building high levels of repeat business – which in turn could be serviced by the database. Finally, a strong emphasis was placed on the recruitment of quality staff, who could use the combination of the telephone and the database to sell holidays rather than simply answer queries. The use of IT reinforces these success factors, as well as being an important factor in its own right. However, what seems particularly important is the recognition of the potential of IT within the framework of a determination to use this potential to generate information rather than just process data.

A similar emphasis can be seen in the case of another successful player in the same industry, Classic Cottages. Based in Helston, Cornwall, the company was founded in 1977, and has between 300 and 400 cottages on its books. It has deliberately aimed for the higher bracket and places a high emphasis on marketing. The success of this marketing strategy, aimed in particular at repeat business, is supported by an emphasis on the close analysis of effectiveness: 'We've put a great deal of effort into ensuring that every response to an advertising campaign is traced and analysed' (Tregoning, 1991, C29). Just as in the case of Country Holidays, the company used computers from an early stage to enable this analysis, with an emphasis firmly on the production of management information. Thus, weekly management information is produced, including occupancy percentages and conversion ratios. In a departure from the Country Holidays case, the owner here did have some prior exposure to computers, and much of the development work has been done in-house.

One interesting element in the company's use of IT is the attention paid to taking the base data from the booking systems and manipulating them further in a set of financial models. Constructed with spreadsheets, these used a series of assumptions, based on trend history, to allow the company to forecast future demand and adjust strategies accordingly. While admitting that some elements of the model were complex, the company argues that 'the key to its effectiveness was that, once it had been set up, it allowed a wide variety of possible scenarios to be examined quickly and easily' (Tregoning, 1995). The power of this was demonstrated when the weekly monitoring statistics started to indicate a decline in demand in the early 1990s. Combining this indication with revised forecasts based on the models prompted the company to change its strategy. It abandoned a planned expansion, increased marketing expenditure and reduced overheads, a combination of activities which, it argues, enabled it to weather a potentially damaging recession. Without the use of the information produced by the effective use of IT, the company 'may have survived the recession ... but they are sure that their financial position would have been considerably weaker' (Tregoning, 1995, C56). Again one sees a number of recurring patterns, particularly the powerful influence of the owner, the emphasis on marketing-led strategies and a strong awareness of the information needed to bolster these.

Given the clear role that IT has played in the success of these small tourism enterprises, the question which needs to be asked is: what prevents its more widespread use? It is clear that small enterprises in general continue to be resistant to the use of IT. The Federation of Small Businesses estimated in 1996 that only a third use computers (Gould, 1996). This confirms a continuing resistance seen in a 1993 survey commissioned by the accountancy software firm Sage, which found that 66 per cent of small businesses surveyed (those employing up to 19 staff) had no computer and of these, 80 per cent had no intention of buying one in the next two years (Anon, 1993). While factors such as cost and lack of expertise were cited as factors behind the latter statement, the dominant response, at 67 per cent was 'no benefits to me'. These surveys, of course, cover enterprises from all sectors. Detailed figures are not available for tourism and hospitality as a whole, but research on the cottage holiday sector bears out the general thrust of these surveys, and this is summarized below (Mutch, 1995b).

The research was based on a survey sent to 83 companies, which produced a 54 per cent response rate. The 42 organizations that responded handled 12,597 cottages and employed 270 staff. Seventeen firms, or 40.5 per cent of the sample, indicated that they did not use computers in the core part of their business. Given the comments about non-response outlined above, it is feasible that half the firms in the sector do not use IT, despite its apparent applicability. The profile of these firms was that they were smaller in terms of both staff (average numbers employed four, as against seven for the total sample) and cottages held (299 cottages against 603). Of the 17 firms, four said that they were actively considering the implementation of a computer system, thus reducing the core of non-users to 31 per cent. This is still a reasonably high percentage, although not one which bears out the findings of the Sage survey. What might be the reasons for this resistance?

Respondents were asked to indicate which of the following categories applied to them, although many chose to give fuller answers: cost, no need, lack of suitable applications, lack of expertise, difficult to ascertain need. Five firms indicated that they considered that there was no need and a further two thought it was difficult to ascertain a need. While for some companies this was because they handled few cottages, often as part of a wider business (such as an estate agency), their ranks included an agency handling 500 cottages. These responses indicate a need to consider whether 'need' is determined by purely 'rational' considerations – or what are rational considerations in the context of this sector. This necessitates somewhat of a detour into how agencies operate. The starting point is that an agency can be started at low initial cost. Premises are required, but the business, particularly at inception, can be run from the owner's premises. Other capital costs – principally a telephone line – are low and the major operating cost is advertising. Several owners enter the business because they have been cottage owner/letters themselves. The nature of the business allows them to remain local and small scale, with its key feature being personal relationships with cottage owners. Many make a virtue of their small scale, and their aversion to the use of IT reflects deeply held beliefs: that they wish to stay small scale and that computers will remove the personal touch from the business. Thus they are not only content but defiantly happy to continue their use of 'low-tech' methods such as wall charts. This lies behind the strongly put views of one owner with 86 cottages, that she is 'fighting the use of IT'. She felt that the core of her business was built around her personal contact with owners and the communication of the resultant information to her staff. Introducing an intermediary in the form of a computer would destroy this personal touch. Another agency handling 50 cottages as an adjunct to an estate agency also argued that 'manual is as good as the computer'. The strength with which these view were expressed might indicate that the 'rational' information-handling component of computers conflicts with deeply held beliefs about the nature of business. Clearly, such barriers are unlikely to be overcome unless the image of the computer as the 'awesome thinking machine' is dramatically altered (Martin, 1993).

Others related the lack of need to more structural factors, such as the size of their operation. Thus, one owner of 70 cottages felt that 'I could only justify it by saving half a person or expanding', and another with 175 cottages felt that 'they were at the limits: if business expands then must consider, but at the moment within our scope'. This leads to a consideration of the responses to the statement 'no suitable applications', to which four firms assented. The position of one agency, related to packages rather than bespoke solutions, was made quite clear: 'We obtained consultants' advice about five years ago – and no system showed advantages over the quill pen.' Since that date there will obviously have been changes, and it is these changes which have persuaded the largest non-user (with over 1000 cottages) actively to consider their use. However, there are still small firms which consider that the software industry has failed to meet their needs adequately, and this is a point that will be returned to when we consider the type of software that is in use.

Cost was important to two firms, perhaps reflecting the low margins which have affected the industry, but lack of expertise was considered the key in four cases, as reflected in this comment: 'Although a computer would be very useful for analysis of advertising returns, booking patterns, etc. and we do have a computer available, we seem to manage very well manually and with the word processor and never seem to get the time to get training on the computer!' This might be linked to the feelings of owners as expressed above, but might also be connected with the staff employed. Might it be that as contemporaries of owners, and from often rural areas, they will have had less exposure to computers and correspondingly more doubts about their ability to adapt?

This analysis suggests that some small business will remain resistant to the use of computers no matter how far the price drops and no matter how user-friendly they become. This would relate to both the limited training with which they enter the business and the limited expectations for growth which they may possess. Thus, in a survey of hoteliers in Hampshire it was found that many did not make the most of their business because they had no desire to make it grow (Hankinson, 1989). How far this satisficing behaviour can last in an industry which is seeing pressure on margins and the interest (with the take-over of Country Holidays by Thomson Holidays) of major players remains to be seen. We can draw a number of lessons from a comparison of success and failure in this part of the industry with the broader literature on small business computing. Factors found to impact on small businesses in particular have been a lack of resources in general and of computing expertise in particular, coupled with a lack of prior experience. In small tourism enterprises in Cornwall, Shaw and Williams found low levels of finance and suggested that firms were being 'controlled by relatively inexperienced business people who may have little or no conception of the need to draw up management strategies for their businesses' (Shaw and Williams, 1987, p. 345). This lack of experience carried into the field of information system selection meant that they had no model of a formal selection process to rely upon, and decision-making was often 'dictatorial'. In such cases, the prior attitudes of the owner/manager or staff were likely to have a key impact, particularly given the closeness of working relationships in small enterprises (Lees and Lees, 1987). The importance of the top manager was explored by Martin (1989), who found a range of possible types of involvement. The information awareness of the owner/manager was argued to be a crucial factor in success at Country Holidays. This reflects their tendency towards active involvement in all areas of the business. Lees and Lees (1987) found that prior experience with computing had a favourable impact on satisfaction with the resulting information systems, something which seems to be at least partially borne out with the case of Classic Cottages. One can expect, therefore, that the attitudes and opinions of owners will have a considerable impact on the use or otherwise of computers.

This suggests that an important priority is the raising of an awareness of the importance of information in the management of organizations. The need to add this to the portfolio of skills raises comparisons with an issue which has been prominent in the literature on IT problems facing the large organization, the debate over the 'hybrid' manager. Put simply, proponents would argue that to make the best use of IT to gain business benefit, there is a need for managers who couple both business knowledge and technical knowledge (Earl and Skyrme, 1992). The search for these paragons has proved somewhat elusive, and the debate seems to have moved on to the need for a continuum of skills within a team working environment (Dance, 1994). However, the small business has always had to run with 'hybrids' given the lack of managerial resource. These resource constraints point to the need for IT awareness to permeate training and education in the field. However, one doubts, at the time of writing, the extent to which this happens in practice.

The nature of such training is also important. In a large-scale computing paradigm, considerable emphasis is placed on formal planning mechanisms. These exist at all the stages of a systems life cycle. Thus, there are detailed strategic planning frameworks incorporating methods and tools for identifying opportunities (Ward *et al.*, 1990). Once a system has been decided on, there are elaborate prescriptions for its evaluation and development (Ward, 1995). Many of these procedures are irrelevant or wasteful for the small business. They are necessary in large businesses largely owing to problems of scale and complexity, but even there the rigid use of frameworks has been criticized for stifling innovation and creativity. The work of Lees and Lees (1987) indicated that the area of importance for small businesses was the specification of requirements stage, particularly as most small businesses will be involved in buying their applications in, either as packages or as bespoke systems. Whittaker (1987) found, in a survey of the implementation of IT in hotels, that in over half the cases no form of feasibility study had been carried out and that there was 'a series of *ad hoc* and uncoordinated decisions based on vague intentions'. In this context, the experience of the cottage sector is again instructive.

Of the 25 companies that did use computers, the overwhelming majority (80 per cent) had systems using IBM compatible PCs. Of these machines, nearly half had Intel 80286 processors, suggesting ageing systems. Seventeen systems were capable of being used by more than one person, with numbers of users ranging from two to 50. All these systems were able to show property details, handle bookings and invoice the customer, with most being able to handle owner accounting and produce management information. However, nearly a quarter of systems fell down in the latter area. Only a third of the companies employed specialist staff to support their use of IT, the rest being supported either by self-trained members of staff or externally.

As discussed above, there are three principal methods for developing information systems: self-development, purchase of a package or bespoke development by an external party. The questionnaire sought to establish which methods were used in the sector. Of the 26 companies using computer systems, half were using a bespoke system, nearly a third had developed their own systems and only five were using packaged solutions. This appears a surprisingly low figure for packages, and perhaps suggests that offerings in this sector are not considered to be adequate for their purpose. Indeed, this was the opinion of one large firm which had not yet computerized. Despite having been approached by companies on several occasions, it had always felt that the products on offer lacked functionality. However, it also felt that these shortcomings were being addressed, and that this meant that it would be likely to adopt a computerized system in the near future.

While all respondents exhibited a considerable degree of unanimity over the importance of the computer system to the day-to-day running of business, those using bespoke systems were less convinced of the contribution of their systems to the overall success of the business, leading one to speculate as to whether this reflected a less involved stance with the use of IT. It was noticeable that on ease of operation and facility of obtaining management information, self-developed systems had significantly higher scores. These figures could represent on the one hand the problems of identifying requirements adequately enough either to get a package to fit the situation or to get an external body to interpret them correctly. On the other hand, could it reflect a more hands-on approach to IT, with a clearer idea of information requirements: that is, one that goes beyond a simple automation of existing procedures?

A further issue was the perceived success factors of the business. The responses to questioning on this produced a degree of agreement about the primary importance of the quality of the product on offer, but then there was an interesting divergence between those operating packaged and bespoke systems on the one hand, and those who had developed their own systems. The latter regarded computers as more important in the success of their business. Also noticeable was the lower status accorded to the state of the economy compared to other users. Could this reflect a more proactive approach to the running of the business, and is this sort of approach linked to the successful use of computers? This may, of course, be too tenuous a conclusion, based as it is on a rather slim sample. One returns, however, to the examples of Country Holidays and Classic Cottages. One sees there a strong emphasis on the importance of a clear view of the market and customers, with IT being used as a support mechanism. This clarity of objectives seems an important part of the success of the organizations. The necessity for IT to support and enable the main business objectives is a general theme in the large firm literature, but this symbiosis may be easier to achieve in the smaller enterprise. This, of course, depends on the existence of clarity about the general business strategy, and we again return to the points raised by Shaw and Williams (1987). The argument may be that small tourism and hospitality enterprises need, above all, education in broad managerial skills, through which information awareness should permeate. The danger is that the response to IT involves a focus on hands-on IT skills. While these may be valuable, they tend to take the focus off the more general issues of information and how IT can play a role in providing this. The dangers might be illustrated by an examination of the response to the Internet.

SMALL BUSINESSES AND NETWORK TECHNOLOGY

The MIT study referred to above suggested that the predicted advances in technology coupled with continued real price decrease would have three main business impacts. These were in the increased ability to manipulate and relate data through databases, the improved quality of the interfaces between people and systems and the growth in 'connectivity'. The Internet, of course, existed at the time of writing (having had its origins in the post-war period as a secure defence network), but one suspects the authors could not have envisaged the massive explosion in usage. Public awareness of the Internet is growing and users are put in the tens of millions. This use has been fuelled by the replacement of an obscure and complex character-based interface with one which allows the display of graphics within the familiar Windows or Macintosh interface. Commercial applications are creeping on to the network, with, for example, British Midland offering a free seat reservation and booking system. Small businesses are being urged to take advantage of these opportunities, as a way of competing directly with larger companies. Thus one service provider urges: 'An Internet connection allows you to set up a virtual business, and be far better informed and in touch than you are by any other method of communication. You can be just as efficient, and take on the appearance of a much larger company, by having an effective electronic mail service and a web page' (Gould, 1996, p. 21).

The way in which small hospitality enterprises might take advantage of these opportunities can be seen in the example of Brighton. Here, a number of hotels have a presence on the Web. Some are simply advertising pages connected to a list of accommodation run under the heading of 'Virtual Brighton'. The advantage to be gained here is simply a new advertising channel. Others however, have their own Web site, which allows for a greater degree of interactivity and the possibility of taking bookings. One can see the process in a much more developed form in the shape of the Boston restaurants listing. Here it is possible to input the type and price range of cuisine desired, together with location details. This will not only bring up a list of restaurants, but also allows the browsing of reviews. The potential exists for small tourism and hospitality enterprises to control the transmission of information about themselves and to be part of a dense network of linkages. In this way, they could share the advantages of the large company networks and, in some cases, by-pass existing distribution channels, speaking directly to the customer. However, some words of caution are in order. One is that the setting up of one's own site requires careful consideration. This is not so much about the technical issues, which could be handled by a service provider, but about processes for dealing with new business and, crucially, about market positioning. One has to consider carefully the target market. The demographic profile of Internet users appears to be largely male and in the age range 15 to 35. Tourism enterprises have to ask themselves if this is likely to be their market, and also to consider Internet access channels. While there has been growth in both domestic and business connections, the dominant access channel is via higher education institutions, particularly given that rapid growth in traffic has continued to mean network congestion, with a consequent increase in cost. It may be that the spread of cable, with its potential for delivering high-quality signals directly into a familiar 'interface device', the television, offers a means to alter dramatically the shape of the market. Here too, however, it is necessary to be cautious (White, 1995). A watching eye is called for, but one would suggest that for the majority of small enterprises access will continue to be indirect. Here, it is likely that tourist boards have a large part to play, and a number of regional tourist boards in England already have a presence (Mutch, 1995a).

The emphasis here has been placed on the Internet as a marketing tool, but there is also the issue of its use as a tool for information gathering and transmission. Many are sorely disappointed when they realize that behind the glamorous facade there is often little content. In practice, much more valuable data are often available on the commercial on-line services – but at a price. It is here that the example of some large organizations, such as Zeneca, in using Internet methods for internal communication may be instructive (Moody, 1995). The 'Intranet' is used to allow easy access to material such as procedure manuals. This example could be extended to the sharing of information between small enterprises. One might look to the tourist boards to take a lead here. It might be one way of allowing access, under appropriate conditions, to the vast store of data about, for example, visitor flows. This might enable them to enhance the service they give to members and, at the same time, allow small enterprises to get a 'feel' for the Internet.

CONCLUSIONS

This brief look at the potential offered by the Internet returns us to themes which have cropped up a number of times in this chapter. There is a clear danger in the automatic equation of information with technology. For many small enterprises, technology is inappropriate. A considerable amount of value can be extracted from reorganizing existing manual processes and instituting new ones within the context of an awareness of the information needs of the organization. The first issue is: how well prepared are those who manage small businesses to appreciate the information they need? The argument here might be that one of the key advantages such businesses possess is easy access to tacit knowledge, but that the assumptions which underlie this knowledge need to be surfaced and developed. This might suggest that those responsible for supporting small business through training and development might do well to prioritize this approach, rather than an explicitly IT-based approach, and use examples of information use such as those which figured in the cases above.

The next stage is the recognition that IT can have an important role to play in the provision of this information, but that such a role should always be subordinate to general business objectives. Prescriptions drawn from large business experience can be seen as inappropriate here, deriving as they do from problems of complexity and coordination. In the small business these are replaced by an often excessive reliance on a key individual. The one area in common is that information requirements need clear specification. The fulfilment of these requirements is often going to demand the ceding of a degree of control to those outside the organization. The management of this relationship is likely to be crucial, and this suggests another area for training and development needs.

Much of this training will of necessity be aimed initially at owner-managers, but it will have to emphasize the need to build up the skills resource base of the organization. It appears increasingly likely that with the expansion of higher education many more graduates will end up working for small and medium-sized enterprises. This obviously raises challenges for those organizations in terms of their use of the graduates' capacity, but in terms of IT it appears clear that many of these graduates will of necessity be 'hybrids', given that small organizations will find it difficult to support specialists. This raises questions about the role of information management in higher education curricula in general, and in those aimed at this sector in particular (Mutch, 1996b). One suspects that provision is patchy and under developed, with the emphasis often on skills development. This might suggest the need to review the place of information management.

The suggestion is that for IT to be used effectively in the small business, agencies beyond the ranks of the small business arena itself will need to play an active role. In part this relates to educational institutions, but largely it points firmly at the important role that could be played by tourist boards at both national and regional levels. Whether such a role sits easily with demands on these bodies to be more commercially aware and self-funding is an issue for debate (Hoseason, 1993; Robinson, 1993; Mutch, 1996c).

REFERENCES

Anon (1993) 'Small firms give IT the cold shoulder in Sage survey', *Computing*, 2 September, 8.

Archdale, G. (1993) 'Computer reservation systems and public tourist offices', *Tourism Management*, February, 3–14.

Boland, R. (1987) 'The in-formation of information systems', in Boland, R. and Hirscheim, R. (eds) *Critical Issues in Information Systems Research*. Chichester: Wiley.

Buhalis, D. (1993) 'RICIRMS as a strategic tool for small and medium tourism enterprises', *Tourism Management*, October, 366–78.

Dance, S. (1994) *Infopreneurs*. London: Macmillan.

DTI (Department of Trade and Industry) (1995) *Making Information Work for You. A Briefing for Senior Managers of Small and Medium-sized Companies*. London: DTI.

Earl, M.J. (1989) *Management Strategies for Information Technology*. Hemel Hempstead: Prentice Hall.

Earl, M.J. and Skyrme, D.J. (1992) 'Hybrid managers – what do we know about them?', *Journal of Information Systems*, **2**, 169–87.

Gould, H. (1996) 'Internet welcomes small fish', *Guardian*, 13 February, 21.

Green, P. (1991) Interview with the author.

Green, P. (1992) 'Handling direct response', *Insights*, January, A79–A83.

Hankinson, A. (1989) 'Small hotels in Britain: investment and survival', *Cornell Hotel and Restaurant Administration Quarterly*, **30(3)**, 80–2.

Hitchins, F. (1991) 'The influence of technology on UK travel agents', *EIU Travel and Tourism Analyst*, **3**, 88–105.

Hoseason, J. (1993) 'Undermined by ministers', *TravelGBI*, June, 16.

Lees, J.D. and Lees, D.D. (1987) 'Realities of small business information system implementation', *Journal of Information Systems Management*, January, 6–13.

Martin, C.J. (1989) 'Information management in the smaller business: the role of the top manager', *International Journal of Information Management*, **9**, 187–97.

Martin, D. (1993) 'The myth of the awesome thinking machine', *Communications of the ACM*, **36(4)**, 120–33.

Mintzberg, H. (1994) *The Rise and Fall of Strategic Planning*. Hemel Hempstead: Prentice Hall.

Moody, G. (1995) 'Users for whom the Net is more than just a tool', *Computer Weekly*, 5 October, 64.

Mutch, A. (1993) 'Successful use of information technology in a small tourism enterprise: the case of Country Holidays', *Journal of Strategic Information Systems*, **2(3)**, 264–75.

Mutch, A. (1995a) 'Destination information and the World Wide Web', *Insights*, September, D5–D9.

Mutch, A. (1995b) 'IT and small tourism enterprises: a case study of cottage-letting agencies', *Tourism Management*, **16(7)**, 533–9.

Mutch, A. (1996a) 'No such thing as ... information resource management', *Management Decision*, **34(7)**, 58–62.

Mutch, A. (1996b) 'Information management: a challenge for undergraduate business education', *International Journal of Information Management*, **16(6)**, 445–56.

Mutch, A. (1996c) 'ETNA: a case study in inter-organizational failure', *Tourism*

Management, **17(8)**, 603–10.

Parker, M. and Benson, R. with Trainor, H. (1988) *Information Economics*. Hemel Hempstead: Prentice Hall.

Poon, A. (1988) 'Tourism and information technologies', *Annals of Tourism Research*, **15**, 531–49.

Poon, A. (1993) *Tourism, Technology and Competitive Strategies*. Wallingford: CAB International.

Robinson, K. (1993) 'Commercial members express grave concern over proposed funding cuts for England', *Tourism Enterprise*, June, 12.

Scott Morton, M.S. (ed.) (1991) *The Corporation of the 1990s*. Oxford: Oxford University Press.

Shaw, G. and Williams, A. (1987) 'Firm formation and operating characteristics in the Cornish tourist industry – the case of Looe', *Tourism Management*, December, 344–8.

Strassman, P.A. (1985) *The Information Payoff*. New York: Free Press.

Tregoning, S. (1995) 'Classic Cottages 1990–1994', *Insights*, May, C47–C56.

Tregoning, T. (1991) 'Classic Cottages, Helston, Cornwall, 1987–1990 marketing campaign', *Insights*, May, C29–C35.

Wainwright, H. (1994) *Arguments for a New Left: Answering the Free-market Right*. Oxford: Blackwell.

Ward, J. (1995) *Principles of Information Systems Management*. London: Routledge.

Ward, J., Griffiths, P. and Whitmore, P. (1990) *Strategic Planning for Information Systems*. Chichester: Wiley.

Whittaker, M. (1987) 'Overcoming the barriers to successful implementation of information technology in the UK hotel industry', *International Journal of Hospitality Management*, **6(4)**, 229–35.

White, R. (1995) 'Interactivity: paradigm shift or quantum leap?', *Admap*, October, 22.

Winograd, T. and Flores, F. (1986) *Understanding Computers and Cognition. A New Foundation for Design*. Reading, MA: Addison-Wesley.

Wiseman, C. (1985) *Strategy and Computers*. Homewood, IL: Dow Jones-Irwin.

Zuboff, S. (1988) *In the Age of the Smart Machine*. Oxford: Heinemann.

TWELVE

Strategies for growth

Michele Webster

Although some firms grow, they are the exceptions. The majority of small businesses which survive continue as *small* businesses and have no apparent aspirations to grow. Thus, Gray (1992), in a general review, identifies little empirical evidence of any widespread desire or ability to grow among Britain's small business owners. The tourism and hospitality industries appear to be no different from most other sectors of the economy in this respect (Shaw and Williams, 1994; Thomas *et al.*, 1997).

Growth rates vary, and some commentators have attempted to segment firms into different growth categories. One example is the new venture classification scheme based on growth produced by Hisrich and Peters (1992), whereby firms may be located in one of four categories: lifestyle small firms, marginal small firms, high-growth firms and successful small growing firms. They believe that the growth of a new entrepreneurial venture is a function of both market and management factors. The market factors presented are the nature and size of the target market and the opportunities available (which in turn reflect the existing competitive conditions, the degree of technological advancements and the amount of protection in the form of patents, copyrights and trade secrets). The management factors involve the ability to manage growth and the psychological propensity for growth.

The authors comment that statistics for the USA indicate that most new entrepreneurial firms are lifestyle or marginal small firms. However, it would appear that lifestyle firms are those which are privately held and usually only achieve modest growth owing to the nature of the business (existing primarily to support the owners). Marginal firms might be those which are very small, part-time or temporary, and consequently are unlikely and unable to grow. High growth firms are often those which are created from research and development, and lay the foundations for a new industry. Presumably, because of the innovation which they are exploiting, they have both a high ability to grow and a high propensity to grow, in that rapid growth enables market leadership to be established, with all the concomitant advantages. It is logical that this type of firm is relatively rare, whereas there are likely to be more successful small growing firms which are progressing steadily, if undramatically, and despite being able to grow may not actually be doing so to any great extent.

As has been demonstrated in Chapter 2, various commentators have proposed alternative means of classifying small businesses. In order to avoid repetition, readers are referred to that chapter for a comprehensive discussion of the issue. In order to understand small business growth – and the role of strategic decision-making in that process – this chapter takes Storey's (1994) position as its starting point. His highly regarded review suggests that there are 'three key influences upon the growth rate of a small independent firm: the background and access to resources of the entrepreneur(s), the firm itself, and the strategic decisions taken by the firm once it is trading' (Storey, 1994, p. 113). The influences will be discussed in detail under the headings 'small business owners', 'characteristics of small firms' and 'growth as a strategic option'. They will be related to the tourism and hospitality industries wherever possible.

SMALL BUSINESS OWNERS

In Chapter 2, Dewhurst and Horobin examine the role and characteristics of small business owners in detail. It is therefore only necessary here briefly to identify issues relating to business growth. It is commonly recognized that people become self-employed for various reasons. Hakim (1989) identifies two consistently acknowledged reasons: independence and the possibility of greater financial reward than from employment by others. However, her research showed that 55 per cent of small firms had no ambitions to grow at all, with a further 35 per cent planning slow, steady growth, leaving only 10 per cent of small business owners seeking rapid expansion. This parallels a variety of other studies presented by Storey (1994), which show that a majority of owners do not seek substantial growth. When one considers tourism and hospitality businesses, there are many examples of lifestyle firms: pubs, teashops, cafes, sandwich bars, restaurants and take-aways. For the owners, running a small business represents a lifestyle decision and growth, with all its inherent difficulties and risks, may not be an issue for serious consideration (Williams *et al.*, 1989). There are also examples of marginal small businesses, which are effectively an addition to a main income, such as bed and breakfast in the family home or holiday cottages on a farm. Growth of these businesses, which may only require one person working a few hours a day or a few weeks a year, is unlikely. There is, therefore, evidence that even if market forces may allow for quantitative growth, this may not coincide with the personal interest of the entrepreneur (see also Johannisson, 1990).

Boer *et al.* (1997) summarize the issues most prominent in the literature in relation to the influence of the characteristics of the owner on small business growth. They list six major themes: motivation, education, gender, age, family history and ethnicity. It is interesting that there appears to be no conclusive evidence indicating that any particular aspects of the six characteristics are essential for small business growth. Boer *et al.* (1997) also consider the experience of the owner separately, under the headings management experience, prior self-employment, functional skills, firm size experience, sectoral experience, training and unemployment. Of these, they identify that there may be an association between functional skills in marketing and small growing firms, although they warn that the research evidence is scant. the other aspects of owner's experience are, unfortunately, inconclusive.

Stanworth and Curran (1986) challenge the well-established 'stage' model of growth, whereby small firms are established and grow in a predictable way, as being idealized and unable to explain adequately the real situation in relation to small firm growth.

They propose a social action view of the small firm which focuses on understanding the internal social logic of the small firm as a social grouping. They draw on their own and previously published research evidence to identify that there is 'no one single, stereotyped entrepreneurial role and thus, by implication, no single pattern of growth' (Stanworth and Curran, 1986, p. 86).

However, they suggest three 'latent identities' which occur with some frequency: the 'artisan' identity, the 'classical entrepreneur' identity and the 'manager' identity. The authors are unable to draw clear conclusions about which type is likely to want to grow the business, although each type will have different needs, which outsiders wishing to help small firms grow should be aware of.

Gray (1995) stresses that, as well as responding to the structural realities of the business cycle and the economic situation, individual owners of small and medium-sized enterprises (SMEs) are affected by their self-concepts, which in turn reflect the broader cultural context from which they come. Thus, only some SME owners will be growth-oriented, and they will vary as to the different stages of their business and personal development, to the extent that in some cases modest growth may satisfy them.

CHARACTERISTICS OF SMALL FIRMS

There are many forms of ownership available to entrepreneurs. These are commonly sole trader, partnership or limited company. Storey (1994, pp. 140–1) identifies a clear association between limited company status and fast growth. However, it is not possible to establish a causal relationship, as limited company status may result from a change of status when the owners wanted to grow the business and wanted increased credibility (perhaps to attract financial backers or company clients).

Storey (1994, pp. 138, 142) also reviews nine studies which have examined the extent to which business size is a variable affecting growth. Generally, it seems that smaller businesses (measured in terms of employees) grow more rapidly than larger ones (this was the case in six of the nine studies). Storey argues that this is possibly explained by their need to achieve what he terms a 'minimum efficient scale'. He also suggests that the need for a minimum efficient scale explains why young firms are more likely to grow than older ones, which is an overwhelming conclusion of these studies.

Stage models

The concept of 'stage models' is prominent in the literature about strategic planning, and has been widely discussed in relation to small business growth. There is a view that business progress through a series of developmental stages, each of which has different characteristics and problems. These stages might typically be birth, survival, growth and maturity. Bennett (1989, p. 4) identifies an 'urgent' need for planning in all areas of the business during the growth stage. She acknowledges that the growth process is different for every business, as each business has specific critical success features. In summary, she states that 'the formula for success includes setting objectives, planning and co-ordinating marketing activities, understanding money, setting up systems, and organizing a management team' (Bennett, 1989, p. 6).

Gray (1993) reviews several of these models, which are based on the product life cycle and show a linear progression from start-up to growth to maturity. Gray is particularly keen to discredit this view, which he identifies as being 'riddled with unsupported assumptions' (p. 150). He goes on to comment that early stage models have obvious weaknesses, which lie

> in its fundamental neo-classical economic assumptions which ignore the reality of small business management and the fact that only a tiny minority of small firms ever grow to a size where internal functional divisions and professional top management teams are in any way feasible. Even as a model for entrepreneurial development it appears to be too static and unreal. It is assumed that a management learning process occurs but, by and large, these models do not provide an explanation of why the firm was founded in the first place and what relation there is between the founding motivations and objectives and subsequent developments. (Gray, 1993, p. 150)

Other models, such as that provided by Churchill and Lewis (1983), attempt to link business objectives and organizational structures and styles to different stages of growth. When a firm is formed (stage 1, 'existence'), it is directly managed personally by the owner and typically has a simple organic structure. Then, a more complex structure is developed, with some tasks delegated but supervised by the owners (stage 2, 'survival'). Functional management appears (stage 3, 'success') where the owner is concerned with maintaining profitability and consideration of growth as a personal aim. Stage 4 ('take-off') occurs when growth has been decided on and a more divisional management structure becomes necessary. The final stage (5, 'resource maturity') results from the internal systems and complexity involved when a firm is concerned with maximizing its return on investments.

Later models are variations on the same theme, and Gray is also critical of them, as they are usually based on only two dimensions: size of firm (usually defined by workforce numbers) and relative maturity (usually linked to management structure complexity). He is particularly concerned that management attitudes to growth are absent from the models and prefers the approach used by Greiner (1972), which he feels is more realistic.

Greiner's model of strategic change proposes a linear progression from a small young firm to a large mature firm. The key feature of this approach is the identification of 'crisis points' which have to be resolved before further progress can be made. These are crises of leadership, of autonomy, of control and of red tape. Growth is identified as occurring in five phases: through creativity when the business is young, through direction, through delegation, through coordination and through collaboration as the business reaches maturity.

Gray (1993, p. 152) persuasively argues that the more useful aspects of earlier stage models are:

- start-up (including attempting a management buy-out);
- survival (exhibiting the decision and drive to continue in business);
- take-off (whether or not to go beyond personal control);
- professionalize (introduce a devolved organizational and management structure);
- transformation (shift from being a small firm to a larger enterprise).

He particularly stresses that the owner's business objectives and personal motivations will be very significant in determining whether a business will grow through the five stages. His research shows that it is in the first two stages (start-up and survival) that the vast majority of self-employed people are located. Thus, there are only a minority of small firm owners for whom continued growth is an issue and for whom the important matters of successful delegation and the need to seek external equity finance are relevant.

Barriers to growth

Storey (1994) presents an alternative perspective to growth in small firms, in which 'barriers to growth' are identified. The assumption in this viewpoint is that a proportion of small firms wish to grow but are prevented from doing so by 'barriers': notably (and fundamentally) lack of motivation as well as shortages of finance, of skilled labour and because of government controls. He identifies an overall pattern for fast-growth small businesses, where the key constraints upon growth are related to 'matters of finance, employment and markets' (Storey, 1994, p. 156).

STRUCTURAL FEATURES OF THE TOURISM AND HOSPITALITY INDUSTRIES

As the introduction to this book has shown, the tourism and hospitality industries are heterogeneous and dominated by extremely small enterprises, many of which are lifestyle firms and, therefore, unlikely to grow to any significant extent. However, structural changes in these industries are noteworthy, for they influence the potential for small business growth in some sectors.

Knowles (1996) identifies that, over the past twenty years, franchising has increased within the hospitality industry, especially in the fast food sector. This growth strategy is a way of expanding an established product/service in a relatively low-risk way, and has proved to be very attractive to would-be self-employed people. Hing (1996) examines the marketing, financial, operational and administrative benefits and limitations for food service franchisees. She cites work by Mehndelsohn (1990), who contended that franchised outlets become viable and achieve positive cash flow more quickly than independent businesses, owing to their market recognition and the elimination of unnecessary start-up expenses. This appears to indicate that growth is faster with a franchised concept than for an independent business. She also cites work by Williams (1992) which establishes that accelerated profitability and a proven business concept contribute to a higher survival rate of franchised over independent businesses.

It is interesting to consider the situation in respect of small, independent take-aways, as they provide a particularly relevant insight into small business growth. Ball (1996) describes and analyses the transformation of an entire industry sector:

> with the arrival of the multi-unit fast food chains, particularly those from the United States, the take-away scene has been transformed and the market has experienced dramatic growth. The chains have been the key to this growth and have significantly undermined the position of the traditional take-away operators. Many of the small independents have struggled as the strongly branded and highly competitive chains have relentlessly advanced across the UK to the point where they are now virtually omnipresent. (Ball, 1996, p. 25)

Although franchisees may be classed as self-employed, the business format of franchising as a method of growth has led some franchisors to transform themselves into large corporations; McDonald's is an obvious example.

Another significant structural change in the hotel industry has been the rise of the influence of consortia. Knowles (1996) argues that, despite a trend towards concentration in the market, there are still many small firms, mostly operating single hotels. However, he suggests that since small independent hotels have severe difficulties competing against large hotel chains which invest heavily in branding and marketing, the only way in which smaller operations can compete is by joining a consortium. He quotes figures from Huddersfield University's Hotel and Catering Research Centre, which show that between 1988 and 1992 the number of independent UK hotels and rooms in consortia grew by 20 per cent to 1215 and 32,843 respectively. Obviously, taken alone, this is insufficient evidence to judge his assertions. Clearly, the issue requires further research.

Morrison (1994) examines the current competitive pressures facing small hotel firms and considers them in relation to the theory related to strategic alliances. She particularly focuses on the development of cooperative approaches to small hotel marketing, and identifies four potential marketing strategic alliance partners for the small hotel firm: public sector referral; reservation services; marketing consortia; and others, including airlines, car rental agencies, credit card companies and tour operators. This reinforces the view expressed by Olsen *et al.* (1992, p. 163), who comment that:

> Strategic alliances among all elements of the travel industry will become more prominent as industry firms struggle to maintain market share. Principal growth activity will no longer be through the purchase of hotel assets; it will be through joint ventures and limited partnerships with real-estate investors wherein hotel firms enter into management contracts for specified periods of time.

This brief discussion of developments suggests that structural changes and trends in forms of business organization have a bearing on small business growth within the tourism and hospitality industries. However, further research is required before conclusive judgements can be made regarding their relative importance compared with other variables affecting growth.

GROWTH AS A STRATEGIC OPTION

There is a large body of literature on business strategy, very little of which relates to either small businesses or the hospitality industry. However, despite debates about the value of strategic planning and gaps between the theory and actual practice in firms, there is a general consensus that 'All organizations make strategic decisions and have done so since the dawn of history ... strategic decisions can be taken carefully or negligently, deliberately or haphazardly or systematically' (Argenti, 1974, p. 18).

'Strategy is about the major moves made by a firm' is Hall's (1995) opening statement in his discussion of strategic planning and the small firm. He notes that a formal planning process would include a variety of information-gathering and action-based activities. Argenti (cited in Hall, 1995) presents a blueprint for successful strategic planning, which typically might include:

- set corporate objectives and targets;
- forecast performance in key areas, comparing predictions with targets;
- assess strengths and weaknesses;
- generate alternative strategies;
- decide on the appropriate strategy;
- evaluate the chosen strategy;
- develop action and business plans;
- monitor progress.

It is important to recognize that growth is only one of the strategic options, albeit the one most often associated with successful business management. Robbins and Coultar (1996) discuss the grand strategies framework, which is a popular approach to understanding corporate level strategy. A corporate level strategy seeks to answer the question: 'What business or businesses should we be in?' It is relevant to the head of a business because it is important for the manager of a business to be able to develop and evaluate strategic alternatives and select strategies that best capitalize on its strengths and environmental opportunities.

Growth strategies can broadly be split into two areas (Thompson, 1990): internal (through concentration, market development, product development and innovation) and external (through horizontal integration, vertical integration, concentric diversification and conglomerate diversification). In practical terms, Robbins and Coultar (1996) note that a growth strategy is achieved by increasing the level of the organization's operations, and is often measured by more sales revenues, more employees and more market share. Thus, the major methods of achieving growth are via direct expansion, merging with or acquisition of others, or diversifying.

For tourism and hospitality firms, it is possible – even if only anecdotally – to identify many examples of growth through direct expansion. In recent years, many pubs have developed their catering business through the increasingly sophisticated provision of bar meals, or the addition of restaurants and function rooms. Mergers and acquisitions have long been a feature of the hotel sector, although they are probably more significant to businesses which are not extremely small, as the costs associated are generally large. An example of diversification would be the development of holiday cottages on a working farm.

Robson *et al.* (1992, p. 37) comment that although there is a substantial amount of literature on diversification in large firms, there is very little work on the advantages and disadvantages of diversification for small firms. Their work shows (perhaps unsurprisingly) that most small firms operate in only one business line, and that there is poor growth performance of diversified companies with fewer than 30 employees compared to their non-diversified counterparts. As they comment:

> This provides strong evidence that for very small companies, diversification lessens the likelihood of growth and limits the magnitude of any growth that can be achieved ... One explanation is that until a sound base has been established in a primary line, then expansion on additional fronts creates more difficulties than it compensates for. (Robson *et al.*, 1992, p. 45)

Hanlon and Scott (1994) make some interesting observations about strategy formulation in small firms, and remind readers that the discipline of strategic management has its historical roots in the normative (planning) model of strategy. This view of strategy has been strongly criticized and is particularly inappropriate for small businesses, for, as Hanlon and Scott (1994, p. 20) go on to say, 'while some small businesses do make formal plans, this model is not sufficient to account for the behaviour of most small firms; furthermore, the applicability of rigid planning models to the entrepreneurial context is especially questionable.'

Although debates about the nature of formal strategic planning and the implementation of major strategies (such as retrenchment, stability or growth) are interesting, the key issues for small businesses are to what extent the people managing them are strategically aware of the position of the firm, how opportunities for change affect the firm and how the business can be managed effectively.

Scarborough and Zimmerer (1993) believe that successful small business managers need to understand the process of strategic management. They point to the evidence of many empirical studies which have concluded that the presence of strategic planning is a key determinant of the ultimate survival of small companies. They identify lack of planning and systematic decision-making as key reasons for failure, and propose that developing a strategic plan is critical to the creation and sustenance of a competitive edge for a small business. However, they state unequivocally that it is

> a mistake to attempt to apply big business strategic development techniques to a small business because a small business is not a little big business. Because of their size and their particular characteristics – resource poverty, a flexible managerial style, an informal organisational structure, and an adaptability to change – small businesses need a different approach to strategic management. (Scarborough and Zimmerer, 1993, p. 83)

They recommend that an appropriate strategic management procedure should rely on a relatively short planning horizon (two years or less), be informal and not overly structured, encourage the participation of employees and outside parties to improve the reliability and creativity of the resulting plan, not start with objective setting (which may interfere with the creative processes needed) and focus on strategic thinking, not just planning, by linking long-range goals to day-to-day operations.

This reinforces the need to recognize that small businesses are basically organic in terms of their organizational form (Robbins and Coultar, 1996). The structure is likely to be low in complexity, formalization and centralization. Much of the work on business strategy is designed to overcome some of the shortcomings of mechanistic or bureaucratic organizations where rigid hierarchical relationships, a high degree of formalization and centralized decision authority mean that any management process has to be carefully organized. Hall (1995) is not convinced of the value of strategic planning, and makes some interesting concluding remarks to his chapter on strategic planning and the small firm, in which he comments that 'Formal strategic planning would not appear to be particularly common among small firms but neither is the evidence overwhelmingly persuasive that this is to be regretted' (Hall, 1995, p. 81). However, leaving formal strategic planning to one side, there are some aspects of business strategy which can be considered important to small firms. These are linked to the degree of strategic awareness of the market place which small business owners have.

In the context of small businesses, it is relevant to examine the literature on strategy which considers business-level strategy. Here, the work of Porter (1980, 1985) has been particularly significant. The debate about competitive strategy was profoundly influenced after Michael Porter published *Competitive Strategy* in 1980 and followed it with *Competitive Advantage* in 1985. Porter pointed out that there are only two routes to superior performance: either to become the lowest cost producer in an industry or to differentiate the product/service in ways that are valued by buyers to the extent that they will pay a premium price to get these benefits. These strategies can be applied to either a broad market or a narrow, focused market.

Bowman (1990) provides a very clear summary of each of the options outlined by Porter: the generic strategies of cost leadership, differentiation and focus. Differentiation and focus are particularly relevant to small tourism and hospitality firms. A differentiation strategy requires more than just being different – it is necessary to be unique in ways which the customer values. The business seeks to attract a segment of the market which will not consider other providers as substitutes, and customers who will be loyal. The nurturing of 'locals' by pub landlords is an example of a differentiation strategy: the products on offer (beer, spirits and perhaps food) may not be very different from other providers', but strong efforts might be made to make regular customers welcomed and recognized by staff and to hold events such as quizzes or barbecues to develop a sense of community among regular drinkers. A focus strategy involves the selection of a market segment and meeting its needs better than the broader targeted competitors. An example of a focus strategy might be a small luxury hotel which targets price-insensitive customers wanting short breaks in beautiful surroundings. There is a danger that the target segment may disappear (changing tastes, demographic shifts, new competition coming along).

Porter (1980, 1985) suggests that firms which have not made a choice about being low cost or differentiated run the risk of being 'stuck in the middle' and being poor performers (unless they happen to be in a growth market). Although the research evidence is not available, it is reasonable to suppose that the majority of small hotel/ restaurant businesses have to follow differentiation or focus strategies to be successful. The success of franchized concepts could in part be attributed to a proven marketing concept (Hing, 1996) whereby the strategy is developed and formulated by the franchisor. It is possible to argue that many independent small hospitality and tourism firms are 'stuck in the middle', having no clear strategic direction. They are perhaps family-run and, therefore, in a position to keep their costs low, but unable to be cost leaders; they may attempt to offer too wide a range of products and services to attract a broad market.

The competitive practices of differentiation and focus which appear widespread in the tourism and hospitality industries are logical, and appear to follow the position in other industries. Hendry *et al.* (1995) review the literature on competitive practices for small firms, and conclude that small firms are advised to specialize, operate locally and provide products/services with a high degree of added value. Thus, small firms often adopt a niche strategy (where there are few competitors) and concentrate on a few customers.

CONCLUSIONS

This chapter has shown that it is difficult to understand small firm growth in general and in the tourism and hospitality industries in particular. This is because of the diversity of the small firm sector and because the influences affecting small firm growth are complex. This is compounded by limited research, with very little directed at small tourism or hospitality firms.

The chapter has been structured around the view of Storey (1994), who proposed that there are three components to consider in the growing small firm: the entrepreneur (including initial resources), the firm and the strategy. Small business owners exhibit many different characteristics, but there is strong evidence that the aspirations of small business owners and their desire (or lack of it) to grow are very significant in helping to understand why some businesses grow while others do not. There are several relevant aspects of the characteristics of small firms which this chapter has presented: the many forms of ownership, the limited value of stage models and (briefly) the barriers to business growth. Growth in the hospitality industry has been shown to be pronounced in two areas – franchising and consortia – although further research is required in both of these areas. Strategic alliances have also been mentioned as an increasing trend for businesses when they seek substantial growth.

Several aspects of growth as a strategic option have been reviewed. The formal planning process has been outlined, despite a lack of consensus about whether it is relevant to small firm development, and types of growth strategy have been presented, with some comments about the difficulties of diversification for small firms. There followed a review of business-level strategies and in particular the generic strategies of Porter, whose work on business positioning in relation to the market supports the widely expressed views that finding a market 'niche' is necessary for small business success.

Finally, although Storey's (1994) position – that only where a particular blend of the three matters referred to above is present will small businesses grow – is generally supported here, it is evident that a great deal of research activity is needed which focuses specifically on small tourism and hospitality firms. Only then will it be possible to understand more precisely the nature of that blend and, therefore, the relative importance of each component.

REFERENCES

Argenti, J. (1974) *Systematic Corporate Planning*. Windsor: Nelson.

Ball, S. (1996) 'Wither the small, independent take-away?', *International Journal of Contemporary Hospitality Management*, **8(5)**, 25–30.

Bennett, M. (1989) *Managing Growth*. Harlow: Longman.

Boer, A., Thomas, R. and Webster, M. (1997) *Small Business Management: A Resource Based Approach*. London: Cassell.

Bowman, C. (1990) *The Essence of Strategic Management*. Englewood Cliffs, NJ: Prentice Hall.

Churchill, N. and Lewis, V. (1983) 'The five stages of business growth', *Harvard Business Review*, May/June, 30–50.

Dewhurst, J. and Burns, P. (1991) *Small Business and Entrepreneurship*. London: Macmillan.

Edgar, D.A. and Nisbet, L. (1996) 'Strategy in a small business – a case of sheer chaos!', in Conference proceedings, 1996 IAHMS spring symposium, Issues relating to small businesses in the tourism and hospitality industry, Leeds Metropolitan University, Leeds.

Gibb, A. and Davies, L. (1990) 'In pursuit of frameworks for the development of growth models of the small business', International Small Business Journal, **9(1)**, 15–31.

Gray, C. (1992) 'Growth-orientation and the small firm', in *Small Enterprise*

Development. Policy and Practice in Action. London: Paul Chapman Publishing.

Gray, C. (1993) 'Stages of Growth and Entrepreneurial Career Motivation', in F. Chittenden, M. Robertson and D. Watkins (eds) *Small Firms: Recession and Recovery*. London: Paul Chapman Publishing, ch. 8.

Gray, C. (1995) 'Managing entrepreneurial growth: a question of control?', Paper presented at the 18th ISBA Conference, Paisley, November.

Greiner, L.E. (1972) 'Evolution and revolution as organisations grow', *Harvard Business Review*, July/August, 37–46.

Hakim, C. (1989) 'Identifying fast growth small firms', *Employment Gazette*, **97(1)**, 29–41.

Hall, G. (1995) *Surviving and Prospering in the Small Firm Sector*. London: Routledge.

Hambrick, D.C. and Crozier, L.M. (1985) 'Stumblers and stars in the management of rapid growth', *Journal of Business Venturing*, **1(1)**, 31–46.

Hanlon, D. and Scott, M.G. (1994) 'Strategy formulation in the entrepreneurial small firm', in S. Birley and I.C. Macmillan (eds) *International Entrepreneurship*. London: Routledge.

Harrison, L. and Johnson, K. (1992) *UK Hotel Groups Directory*. Huddersfield: Hotel and Catering Research Centre, Huddersfield University.

Hendry, C., Arthur, M.B. and Jones, A.M. (1995) *Strategy through People. Adaption and Learning in the Small-Medium Enterprise*. London: Routledge.

Hing, N. (1996) 'An empirical analysis of the benefits and limitations for restaurant franchisees', *International Journal of Hospitality Management*, **15(2)**, 177–87.

Hisrich, R.D. and Peters, M.P. (1992) *Entrepreneurship: Starting, Developing, and Managing a New Enterprise*, 2nd edn. Homewood, IL: Irwin.

Hotel and Catering Training Company (1994) *Catering and Hospitality Industry – Key Facts and Figures*. London: HCTC.

Johannisson, B. (1990) 'Economies of overview – guiding the external growth of small firms', *International Small Business Journal*, **9(1)**, 32–45.

Knowles, T. (1996) *Corporate Strategy for Hospitality*. Harlow: Longman.

Lincoln, G. and Kusyj, B. (1996) 'Direct marketing for the small hospitality business', in Conference proceedings, 1996 IAHMS spring symposium, Issues relating to small businesses in the tourism and hospitality industry, Leeds Metropolitan University, Leeds.

Manchester Business School (1995) *Small Business Briefing – Hotel and Catering*. Manchester: Manchester Business School.

Mehndelsohn, M. (1990) *The Franchisee's Guide*. Wilbeforce NSW: Franchisors Association of Australia.

Mintel Marketing Intelligence (1995) *Small Businesses in the UK*. London: Mintel International Group.

Morrison, A.J. (1994) 'Marketing strategic alliances: the small hotel firm', *International Journal of Contemporary Hospitality Management*, **6(3)**, 25–30.

Olsen, M.D., Tse, E. and West, J.J. (1992) *Strategic Management in the Hospitality Industry*. New York: Van Nostrand Reinhold.

Porter, M. (1980) *Competitive Strategy*. New York: Free Press.

Porter, M. (1985) *Competitive Advantage*. New York: Free Press.

Robbins, S.P. and Coultar, M. (1996) *Management* 5th edn. Englewood Cliffs, NJ: Prentice Hall International.

Robson, G., Gallagher, C. and Daly, M. (1992) 'Diversification strategy and practice in small firms', *International Small Business Journal*, **11(2)**, 37–53.

Scarborough, N.M. and Zimmerer, T. (1993) *Entrepreneurship and New Venture Formation*. Englewood Cliffs, NJ: Prentice Hall.

Shaw, G. and Williams, A.M. (1994) *Critical Issues in Tourism: A Geographical Perspective*. Oxford: Blackwell.

Slattery, P. (1992) 'Unaffiliated hotels in the UK', *EIU Travel and Tourism Analyst*, **1**, 90–102.

Stanworth, J. and Curran, J. (1986) 'Growth and the small firm', in J. Curran *et al.* (eds) *The Survival of the Small Firm*. Aldershot: Gower.

Storey, D.J. (1994) *Understanding the Small Business Sector*. London: Routledge.

Thomas, R., Friel, M., Jameson, S. and Parsons, D. (1997) *The National Survey of Small Tourism and Hospitality Firms: Annual Report 1996–97*. Leeds: Centre for the Study of Small Tourism and Hospitality Firms, Leeds Metropolitan University.

Thompson, J.L. (1990) *Strategic Management, Awareness and Change*. London: Chapman and Hall.

Williams, A.J. (1992) 'Data on franchised firms and their owner/managers in Australia (1973–1990)', in Franchising Task Force, *Franchising – Australia and Abroad: Supplement to the Franchising Task Force Final Report*. Queanbeyan, NSW: Better Printing Services.

Williams, A.M., Shaw, G. and Greenwood, J. (1989) 'From tourist to tourism entrepreneur, from consumption to production: evidence from Cornwall, England', *Environment and Planning A*, **21**, 1639–53.

NAME INDEX

SUBJECT INDEX